The Earth Garden WATER BOOK

EARTH GARDEN BOOKS
Trentham, Victoria

EARTH GARDEN BOOKS
PO Box 2
Trentham,
Victoria, 3458,
AUSTRALIA.
Phone (03) 5424 1819 Fax (03) 5424 1743.
Email: <info@earthgarden.com.au>.
World Wide Web site: <www.earthgarden.com.au>

A.C.N. 086 043 567
A.B.N. 69 086 043 567

ISBN 0 9586397 2 8

This book is printed on plantation-grown paper in the interests of preserving our planet's precious resources.

Project and Editorial Co-ordinator: Linda Wheeler, with assistance from Karen Sandow.

Graphic design by Tony Fuery.

Copy edited by Peter Parsons.

Managing Editor: Alan T Gray.

Distributed by NDD Distribution Pty Ltd, and Brumby Gemcraft Books, Kilsyth, Melbourne.

Printed by Griffin Press, Adelaide.

CONTENTS

INTRODUCTION

HOW ironic that only five years ago many councils throughout Australia refused permits for rainwater tanks in urban areas — in a country as dry as ours. How thinking has changed throughout Australia in this time: now most councils or state governments will pay you a rebate to install a rainwater tank.

The tide has changed in favour of water conservation as councils and politicians have realised that we can't go on destroying rivers and building massive new dams every time we get a bit low on town water.

The politicians and bureaucrats are finally starting to realise what many ordinary Australians have known for years: it doesn't make sense to flush all our water down the drain — in many places flushing it into our storm water systems and therefore our bays and oceans — when we could be trapping and using the rain that falls from the sky.

Most Australians now want to do the right thing with water conservation. Most of us want to find sensible and sustainable ways to reuse and recycle our water. That includes not just the mains water that comes from the tap but the rainwater that falls on our roofs.

Canny rainwater collection devices that come freely installed with every home (called roofs) are a wondrous tool for tapping an untaxed and semi-regular resource.

Of course, rainfall has not been so regular in many parts of Australia in the past five years or so, so there's even more reason to harness the ideas and devices in this book.

We are presenting here a small selection of the many clever and varied water saving devices available in Australia today. Take a walk through your local hardware shop and you'll probably be staggered by the range of devices available. New ideas and products are popping up all the time, but this book, we hope, will present you with much more than just the latest water-saving products.

There are many contributions in the book from water-conscious Australians: people sharing their successful ideas and designs for minimising their water use.

From how to build you own rainwater tank, composting toilet or reed bed, through to installing a commercial or homemade greywater system or simple $20 diverter, we hope you find the ideas in the book useful and practical.

Alan

Alan T Gray
Editor
Earth Garden magazine.

1 Collect

A $200 household water tank

An innovative bushie once gave Colin a recipe to concrete up old rusted water tanks, so he gave it a go. Here, Colin explains how you can save a small fortune by repairing and reusing, rather than forking out for a new tank.

BY COLIN WESTWOOD, *MURWILLUMBAH, NEW SOUTH WALES*

ANYONE who has tasted rainwater from a concrete tank will know that this is the purest, sweetest and most pleasant way to experience nature's elixir of life. The big problem with concrete storage tanks, though, is the initial expense and the difficulty of getting such a large and heavy object into its permanent position.

In 1973 the shack I'd just built was in a remote spot on the forest edge and there was very little in the way of spare cash. However, I had lots of spare energy and an old 800-gallon (3600-litre) rusted water tank to play with. An innovative bushie had given me a recipe to concrete up old rusted tanks, so I gave it a go. The result was so effective that to this day, that tank is full of crystal clear water!

Since then I have concreted several old rusted tanks successfully and recently worked with some friends on a farm near Macksville (just south of Coffs Harbour) on a 2,000-gallon (9,000-litre) rusted-out storage tank. This is the largest one I have ever attempted to concrete and I'm pleased to say that the project was a success. Bearing in mind that rusty water tanks are usually available free, you may like to give it a go yourself. The total cost will be less than $200 if you provide your own labour.

STARTING

Choose a site carefully, as you would for a concrete tank. A compacted level base is the first ingredient. My first effort was a raised base built of cemented river rocks with an infill of beer bottles and sandy gravel, capped with a veneer of cement. The mistake was in building this over some freshly-bulldozed fill which eventually settled, and so to this day it looks like the leaning tower of Pisa. Our recent 9,000-litre effort was simply a level earthen pad which was compacted around the outer edge of the tank with the blunt end of a crowbar.

Tools, materials, and the 2000-gallon (9000-litre) rusted-out water tank that John and his team repaired at a community near Macksville.

The gate valve on the 19 mm (3/4 inch) poly pipe outlet.

John's first repair effort from 1973, still full of water.

If you can fit yourself or a volunteer into the tank without having to cut a hole larger than the inlet or strainer, it will be easier to keep mozzies out when the job's completed. You may get a narrow ladder into the tank for easy access, or make a step of blocks or logs to get yourself in and out while concreting. It is important to wire-brush the inside of the tank wall thoroughly so that your cement will stick to the wall. Make sure to use a good respirator – ideally a twin cartridge version – if you don't want to end up gasping for air. Wear goggles for eye protection too because the fine rust particles may hurt your eyes. The amount of rust and dust shovelled out of our tank filled around two builders' wheelbarrows. This was spread around the garden and orchard.

Materials

For a 9,000-litre tank, you will need:

- a box trailer load of fine sand, preferably the kind used in brick mortar
- 6 bags of type GP Portland Cement or equivalent
- 8 litres of "Silasec Bondall" or "Sealwall Breakwater 700" or equivalent
- heavy duty rubber gloves
- a steel concrete finishing float
- a cement mixer or a large board, shovel and a very strong back
- buckets that will fit into the tank opening
- as many volunteers as you can muster
- plenty of water
- a gate valve and 19 mm (3/4 inch) poly pipe for the tank outlet.

Try to avoid using chicken wire inside the tank. Although this would make the actual concreting job easier, it will eventually lead to the demise of the concrete. As the wire goes rusty, you end up with "concrete cancer". The corroding wire actually causes the concrete to crack. If you should have any huge holes that need patching up, I suggest you try using plastic mesh or some other non-corrosive substance to bridge the gap.

The first coat

Choose a cool, cloudy day or begin the first coat of concrete at dawn because it will become stiflingly hot as the cement "goes off" while you work. Mix three parts of sand to one part of cement. Add around 250 ml of waterproofing compound to the water you now mix with the dry ingredients. To fine-tune the mix, gradually add water until there is a fine texture with no lumpiness. Ideally you'll have one person on the mixer and one or two people in the tank and someone spare to supervise and administer cool refreshments. Those inside the tank should refrain from eating lentils and beans the previous night.

Fit the gate valve and length of 19 mm poly pipe through the outlet hole and stuff a piece of rag into the pipe to keep out cement while you are working. The sides are concreted first. Start at the base of the tank, filling the corrugations of each row completely before working your way up the tank. Place plenty of cement around the poly pipe outlet, leaving enough pipe inside the tank to bend up well above the finished floor level when concreted later. Make sure to wear those rubber gloves or your fingers will be red raw in minutes! Force the cement into the corrugations leaving a rough finish for the final coat to adhere to. This is the hardest part of the job. It may help to throw handfuls of the mixture into the corrugations as you get to the top of the tank.

Cement in an overflow pipe of some sort if there is not one still in place, because you will need to keep any overflow water away from the base of the tank. More than half the ingredients will be used in filling the corrugations. This will need to be left overnight to set and for you to recover sufficiently to continue. A light spray of water onto the inside of the tank after it has set sufficiently is beneficial.

Early next morning (having once again refrained from beans 'n' lentils), spray the inside of the tank and commence the final coat of concrete. This time you will need to work up and down the inside of the tank using the steel finishing float. Start from the base and work your way up holding the float vertical and apply the cement with an upward motion off the base of the steel float. Don't work the cement too much or you will have problems. If you get too hot inside the tank, it is okay to hose down the exterior surface on day two. The first day's concreting will keep the water away from the freshly-spread second coating. Once again you will find it easier to throw a small fistful of cement around the top few corrugations and smooth it as best you can with the steel float.

Pouring the floor

If you have enough energy left after all of this effort, you may choose to carry on and pour the floor on the same day. This part of the operation is quick and easy. It is the same mixture you used on the walls. Pour at least three centimetres over the floor of the tank, smoothing this up to join the wall and remembering to leave a space below the entry point unconcreted so you can get out easily. I used a kerosene drum tied to a rope, to step on and get out of the tank. Haul the kero drum out with the rope, then pour in the last bucket or two of cement, onto the floor and smooth over with a broom. You've earned yourself a cuppa and a lengthy break!

When a few hours have passed you will be able to lightly spray the inside of the tank with water, to help with the curing process. The following day it will be good to put a few centimetres of water into the tank, which will keep it all damp and slowly curing. In another three or four days you may fill the tank if you have water. Don't be concerned if there is leakage at this stage. Over a few weeks any small leaks will seal themselves off with calcium deposits. Any major leakage may require a slurry of the same mixture reapplied to the inside, but I have never found this necessary.

If you use your newly-concreted tank for drinking water, it would be wise to empty and refill the tank at least twice to eliminate the alkaline substances and flavour of the cement. Some old tanks may come without a top cover, which will make the concreting a much more pleasant job, but will make it difficult to eliminate mosquito larvae. This may be simply remedied by adding a large piece of shadecloth tied around the top of the completed tank. Or you may like to add some fish. It could be native Pacific Blue Eyes, your pet goldfish or any freshwater, eating fish. The added bonus here, apart from the odd feed if you're a carnivore, is that if the fish are able to live in the water, then it is most likely to be fairly safe for you to drink.

First flush diverter

These days rainwater tends to be highly contaminated with everything from passing jet fumes, to aerial spray drift, acid rain and bird, possum 'n' bat shit on your roof. My rainwater tank has a simple system whereby the water is directed into the stormwater system unless I otherwise take action.

A simple "T" piece with a screw cap end redirects the rainwater into my tank after a good few centimetres of rain have washed the smoke and toxins from the atmosphere and my roof. When the tank is full, the rain is directed back into the stormwater system and a black plastic bin lid fits snugly over the tank inlet, to exclude light and toxins. With this system you need a separate tank for drinking water, but it's worthwhile when you taste the result, for no finer water will you ever drink!

The *Cryptosporidium* and *Giardia* in the Sydney water supply a couple of years ago came as no surprise to me. Around 60 per cent of the Sydney catchment area is unfenced and available to grazing stock; cattle excrete in excess of 50 kilograms of poo per cow per day. Cattle are major hosts and carriers of *Cryptosporidium parvum*, so it takes no great genius to figure that the drinking water will be at risk!

If you live in a country town, your reticulated water catchment may be completely unfenced and is likely to contain a cocktail of fertilisers, herbicides, detergents, pesticides and parasites all of which escape through the filtration and chlorination process to some extent.

For further information on what our town water or improperly managed tank water is likely to contain, get hold of a book called *The Water You Drink. How Safe Is It?* by John Archer. Another eye opener is the classic *Silent Spring* by Rachel Carson. This was first published in 1962, but is as valid today as the day it was written.

Well, happy concreting to any energetic Earth Gardeners willing to try the above recipe. This rainwater makes the most superb home-brewed beer that you will find and the most excellent brew of coffee too! Cheers, bottoms up and good health to you.

Farm dams: doing the sums

How big should your dam be? Where should you site it and not site it? What other issues should you bear in mind? Here are some of the answers.

CALCULATING CATCHMENT YIELD

Before you start to build a dam you need to calculate how much water you can harvest from your site from run-off. Catchment yield is made up of surface run-off and base flow (from deep and shallow ground water). Steep, well-defined drainage patterns have higher run-off than flat areas, and a catchment with a northerly (sun-facing) catchment will dry out faster than one with a south-facing catchment.

If your annual rainfall is 650 mm or higher then your "storage period" is 12 months. The storage period is the time during which there may be no run-off into your dam. If your annual average rainfall is 450 to 650 mm then your storage period is 18 months, and if your rainfall is 250 to 450 mm then your storage period is 24 months.

The accepted formula for calculating run-off yield (in megalitres) is:
Run-off yield (megalitres) = average annual rainfall (mm) X catchment area (hectares) X yield% (5–8% for shallow sand or loam, 7.5–15% for sandy to elastic clay, 10–15% for clay pans) X 0.01 (conversion to megalitres).

So, on a property with an annual average rainfall of 650 mm, with a 5 hectare catchment of loam soil, the run-off yield will be:
650 mm X 5 ha X 0.05 (5% yield) X 0.01 = 1.625 ML.

An 80 per cent reliability is often used for stock or irrigation dams, so in eight out of ten years it can be expected that the run-off yield will be around 1.625 megalitres for this example.

CHOOSING A DAM SITE

From a cost point of view, a dam should be sited where the largest storage volume can be obtained for the least amount of earthworks. Large areas of shallow water should be avoided because this maximises evaporation losses. Dam sites should also be well away from drainage from sewerage lines, houses, dairies, or any other building that emits effluent. Before a dam is constructed across a depression or gully you should check that it is not a legally documented waterway and that it does not have an existing easement. The land title or local council records should show this. If so you'll probably need a licence or permit from the local or state government authority. In some cases a separate licence may be required to take and use the dam water.

ECOLOGICAL ISSUES

Some areas may appear suitable as dam sites, but a dam may have a major adverse effect on downstream ecology if it prevents run-off from flowing downstream to support river ecosystems. In-stream dams should be a thing of the past in Australia – unless they are re-designed to allow fish to migrate up and down stream. Dedicated rock-lined fishways, built next to dam walls for winter overflow, are a good way to help reverse the destructive environmental effects of existing in-stream dams. To improve the biodiversity of a completed dam, fence the area to keep out livestock, plant trees and shrubs for windbreaks to minimise the erosion from wave action (but not on the banks: this can cause seepage), and stock the dam with suitable fish.

Dam sites should be well away from drainage from sewerage lines, houses, dairies, or any other building that emits effluent.

Many tanks but what works best?

Containers to hold water have been part of the Australian landscape since forever. Chris Martin gives a run-down on the water tanks he's encountered and what has worked.

BY CHRIS MARTIN, *KERNEYS SPRING, QUEENSLAND*

NEXT TO SHELTER, fire and potable water, probably the most important item for living is a container for that water. If one goes back far enough, say 40,000 years, some Australian Aborigines used rock holes with sheet rock lids. They cut grooves in the rock to concentrate the flow.

Humans then progressed through many means of holding this precious (next to wine) liquid from skins through clay-lined rock cisterns to wooden barrels. Some barrels, still to be found below European castles, are big enough to hold more than 50,000 litres.

Within a few years of white people taking this land a new form of liquid storage began arriving in the holds of sailing ships. Square riveted steel tanks with cast iron lids were loaded on board in England.

Child labour was then used to pack pottery and crockery into the tanks, through a small hole in the lid that only a child could fit through, and the load was cocooned in straw. On arrival in Australia the reverse was applied until the tanks were unloaded and distributed far and wide in this thirsty land. A testament to the stamina of their construction is that a few can still be seen rusting away on country farms.

In the late 1800s the French invented the galvanising process and an Englishman invented the process that produces corrugated iron. John Lysaght bought the process as he saw the huge potential for these two inventions and with his workers migrated to Australia.

Thus began one of Australia's most lauded icons, the corrugated iron tank. The product widely known as 'Custom Orb' actually comes in two types: the blue stencilled, more rigid, is for general roofing and red stencilled for bending into bull-nosed verandahs and for water tanks.

Enough of the history lesson! What tank is best for my needs and how much do they cost? The general rule of thumb is that, the bigger the tank, within reason, the less cost per litre to store it. Over the years a number of articles have been written for EG on making your own concrete tank and safety in relation to fire.

This time I want to concentrate on off-the-shelf products: their uses, comparison costs, and risk of possible contamination.

On our property we have had four different types of tanks.

PLAIN GALVANISED IRON

Now used for rain water only and after 17 years there is no sign of rusting. Cost per litre is one of the most expensive due to their generally smaller size. Somehow people always trust this type of tank. We did buy a plain 10,000-litre tank initially for storing dam water but it rusted out in only five years. So have any ground water tested to check its corrosion ability. We intended to cement this tank inside but it blew off the top of our hill in a winter gale and ended up 150 metres downhill in the orchard.

We had another gale the following night which blew it over the boundary fence, across the road, over another boundary fence and a further 200 metres into the neighbour's place. As it was on the way to the local tip we considered letting it find its own way but felt there may have been a problem with public safety.

AQUAPLATE

This is a type of corrugated iron tank that has been factory coated internally with a plastic polymer. It is suitable for most types of water and we use it for storing bore water, our emergency supply in time of drought, which is heavy in iron and other minerals. It was about 35 per cent dearer than an ordinary tank when we bought it about six years ago and has shown no sign of rusting.

PLASTIC MEMBRANE STEEL TANK

This is like a deep swimming pool. It has a 50,000-litre capacity, it's six metres in diameter and it's 1.8 metres high. We purchased this for our main garden and orchard supply and it sits on top of a hill that is not accessible by large trucks so we could not build a concrete tank on this site. Erection is simple but care needs to be taken to ensure the plastic membrane is adequately protected from punctures by taping over all protruding bolts and ensuring there is at least 10centimetres of sand over a 20-centimetre crushed dust base.

The liner has a ten-year warranty, but only if a lid is fitted to the tank, as it has a water level that ebbs with use and is obviously affected by sunlight. The tank cost around $2000 in 1993 and the roof was an additional $1000 from the supplier. We felt this was a bit steep so we made our own from similar material for about $400. Please be careful when erecting this type of tank in

If plain galvanised iron tanks are used for rain water only, they can give many years of trouble-free service.

summer. The reflected heat from the bright new galvanized iron and the enclosed area gave Rhonda, David and I a bad case of sunburn and dehydration. When the liner finally goes we will probably do a concreting job. If you don't consider the replacement cost of the liner this is the cheapest per litre cost of any tank.

Reinforced Concrete Tank

We have had our 60,000-litre unit for close to 17 years; in fact it was the first thing built on Mullionkale – it even predated the first part of the house. We have had no major trouble with cracking, although there are a few sites with white seepage. We think a reliable contractor, a properly compacted and stable base and the fact that this tank is only for rainwater has saved us some of the rusting reinforcement problems experienced by others. When longevity is considered this is the cheapest per litre.

We have had no personal experience with the following tanks but feel that they should be mentioned.

Fibreglass Tanks

These seem to have become redundant since the introduction of poly tanks but they are worth mentioning in case someone buys a second-hand one. They were banned in some USA states, allegedly because of the risk of cancer.

I discussed this briefly with the National Health and Medical Research Council in Canberra about the time we wanted a new large tank. They weren't able to advise positively one way or the other, so we opted for the membrane tank.

Poly Tanks

These are made from food grade polymer, seem to be reliable and are around the middle as far as costs are concerned. While not indestructible they seem to "give" more than other types.

Other tanks

Other tank types include squatter and ring tanks. These may still be available from Southern Cross, more commonly known for their windmill manufacture, and have been used in inaccessible or distant sites where trucking in other types of tanks, because of their bulk, was not an option.

We have not emptied and cleaned out our concrete tank in the 17 years since its construction. It occasionally gets a brown tinge from roof litter but we have been puzzled by not having any problem with this phenomenon. We have a windmill attached to this tank pumping up a hill to a small header tank for household use.

This tank overflows down to the fire tank attached to the house and in turn flows back to the concrete tank. We think that the process aerates the water like a flow-form system which is used to revitalise and purify degraded water.

PS: Thanks to Fred Hillier of Moonbi for some of the historical background.

Make your own tank stand

Earth Garden's owner-building guru, Bob Rich, outlines simple plans to make your own six-metre-high tank stand.

BY BOB RICH, *MOORA-MOORA CO-OPERATIVE, VICTORIA*

WATER is heavy: one litre weighs one kilogram. This means that a full 1000-gallon (4500-litre) tank weighs 4.5 tonnes. If at all possible, I prefer to keep weights like that firmly on the ground. At my place, this has always been easy, because I live in a hilly area. So, when I was asked to give advice on water tank stands, I talked to my mate David. He comes from Warracknabeal – flat country. Dave confirmed my ideas and gave me a few pointers. Of course, there are several factors to consider:

- the volume of the tank
- its height (the same volume can be held in a squat or a tall tank)
- the height of the platform.

For irrigation or stock feeding, the tank needs to be off the ground no more than two metres. Even less may be sufficient. However, to supply water for a house, the usual height is six metres. You don't want four and a half tonnes to fall on your house from a height of six metres so I'll describe a general setup for this height. If the stand is lower, you can dispense with cross bracing, but otherwise you still need to build SOLID.

Figure 1 is a schematic drawing (see page 13). You will need to adapt it to your own situation. So, if you mis-designed it, don't blame me or Dave! Posts can be 100 x 100 mm or the round equivalent (125 mm diameter). Timber should have Class A durability, for example, treated pine, plantation-grown cypress, or a recycled power pole cut lengthwise into quarters.

Set the posts in the ground to a depth equal to one fifth of the above-ground height. For a six-metre-high

For irrigation or stock feeding, the tank needs to be no more than two metres off the ground.

Figure 1. Side view of tank stand.

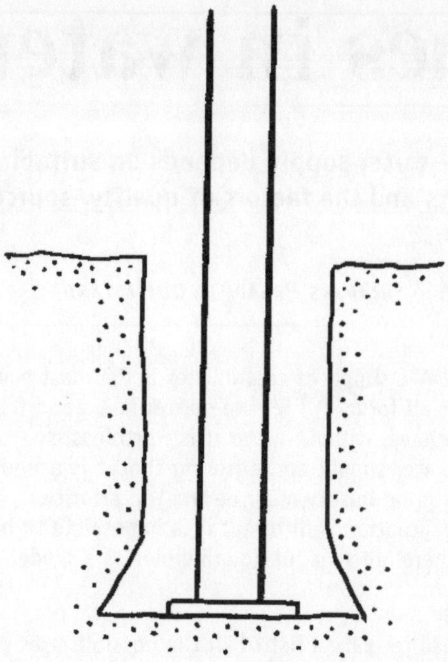

Figure 2. A typical post hole profile.

stand, this is 1.2 metres. Spacing between the posts depends on the size of the beams at the top, and the Light Timber Framing Code can help you decide. Posts at 900 mm centres and 250 x 50 mm hardwood beams would be fairly typical.

One way of producing a strong platform is to make the deck from 75 x 38 mm hardwood, nailed on with about 100 mm gaps between them. Cover this with corrugated iron, nailed through the bottom of the corrugations (not as on a roof). This will reduce rusting in the bottom of the tank, act as horizontal bracing and protect the timber structure underneath. For permanence, I would use galvanised bolts to secure all joints in the structure, even where a diagonal brace crosses a post. Nails eventually rust out.

A full tank may be heavy, but an empty one has another problem: it is flighty. The wind can be strong on the plains. A standard way of tying down a tank is to tie a circle of fencing wire into one of the lower corrugations. Make it tight enough so it won't slip down. Then tie fencing wire to it at regular intervals, fixing these to the structure underneath.

Figure 2 (above) shows a typical post. In stable, firm ground the hole can be 225 mm diameter, reamed out to 300 mm at the bottom, but this may be difficult to do in a deep hole. The foot plate can be a flat piece of stone or a piece of durable timber.

Set the post up in the hole, brace it exactly vertical, then fill the hole with concrete. Once this has set, you can trim all the posts to the same height. Diagonal bracing and the top beams are set into the post and fixed with a single bolt through the centre. Two bolts can actually be weaker, particularly with pine, because the timber moves with changes in moisture content and an off-centre bolt will set up stresses. Nail the platform and the corrugated iron cover with galvanised nails. And let me know in 20 years' time if your platform is still there.

Issues in water supply planning

An effective water supply depends on suitable planning. John discusses determining your requirements and the factors of quality, sources, tanks and piping.

BY JOHN SHAW, *FISHERMANS PARADISE, QUEENSLAND*

AN ADEQUATE supply of clean water is the most basic need for all forms of life. No matter how good the land we have, without water it is worthless, so planning the water supply, and ensuring that it is adequate, reliable and of good quality must be the top priority.

As every situation is different it is impossible to be specific, but there are some basic principles as a guide.

REQUIREMENTS

It is a good idea to make a list of all the possible uses you will have for water. These might be house, garden, livestock or irrigation. Measure or calculate the anticipated water use for each. Much information can be gained from plumbers, appliance and pump suppliers and some local councils about the water needs of households.

WATER QUALITY

You obviously need pure, clean water for your family and your livestock to drink, and for kitchen, washing and bathing. For flushing the toilet and watering the garden a lesser quality can be acceptable. Rain water is usually, but not always, the purest water you can get, but it won't be pure for long if you have possums or turkeys on your roof, or your gutters and tanks are full of gunk. Underground water can be clean and sweet, but should be tested for its suitability for what you want to do with it, as should water from rivers and dams. If you have a sufficient supply of clean, potable water from one source to cater for all your needs, that is fine, but if clean water is scarce, you may need to have two water systems, one for potable water and another of lesser quality for garden or other uses.

SUPPLY AVAILABILITY

Having determined how much water we need, we should now have a look at all possible sources of supply. These can be rain, spring, stream, river, dam, well or bore. Let's look at all of those and consider the pros and cons of each.

RAINWATER

The problem with rain is that it is not constant, so you have to be able to store it when it falls, in sufficient quantity to tide you over the dry times. When calculating the storage capacity you will need, bear in mind that one millimetre of rain falling on one square metre of roof will give you one litre of water. So if you multiply the area of your roof in square metres by the average annual rainfall in millimetres, you will arrive at a theoretical amount of water (in litres) that will fall on your roof in a year. But some years the rainfall will be considerably less and some years considerably more. So you need as much storage capacity as you can afford, to store plenty when it is available and to tide you over the bad times when it's not.

Having got the rain water in to the tank, you then have the problem of getting it out again. If you have electricity, you can use a pressure pump to give you mains pressure in the house. But then, if the power fails, so does the water. This can be critical in a fire situation as power poles tend to get burned down, so you don't have water to fight the fire with. My preference is to pump the water from the collection tanks to a header tank, either on high ground or on a high tank stand, so you can gravity feed to the house. Use either a windmill or a solar-powered pump, so there is no running cost and the power source is reliable. The solar pump is probably best because it can be set up to turn itself off when the tank is full. That is one reason why I would never build a house on the top of a hill, because it is much easier to put your water tank at ground level, on high ground, than it is to build a tank stand.

On the subject of tanks, I have a preference for the plastic ones. They seem to be indestructible, they are light and easy to install, come in a number of sizes and colours and are relocatable.

GROUND WATER

Or more correctly, underground water. This means a bore or a well. Either of these can be very expensive and there is no guarantee of success. Ask advice from neighbours, water authorities, drilling contractors and water diviners. If you want lots of water for irrigation, you will probably have to drill deep to a major aquifer, but for a more modest supply, a comparatively shallow well may suffice. My inclination is to try the cheaper option first. It is vital to have groundwater tested for its suitability for whatever you are going to do with it.

DAMS, STREAMS AND RIVERS

These can be a good source of water, but you will probably need a permit from the state rural water authority. Water quality may vary with the time of year and water flow.

PIPING

Quite obviously, the larger the diameter of the pipe, the more water will flow through it. Many water supply systems have been limited because too small a pipe was used. A pumping specialist can calculate the size of pipe you need, taking into account the head (pressure) required or available, the volume required and the distance to be pumped. And remember that you may wish to add on to the system later on, so put in large enough pipes to cater for this.

To summarise:

- use the cleanest water available,
- keep it clean,
- use the most reliable method of pumping,
- gravity-feed for domestic and stock water,
- ensure pipe size is large enough to give a good flow,
- seek advice from a number of sources; and
- obtain any necessary permits.

In a nutshell, water is the most precious commodity in the world. I would rather live in a tent, with plenty of water than live in a fine house without it. It is better to spend money on a good water supply than to try to save money and end up with a water supply that fails when you most need it. If you have any doubts about your knowledge on water supply systems, seek advice from a number of experts, find out the reasons for their particular advice, and then make up your own mind.

Above right: gravity feed your house supply and stock water from a high tank.

Right: you can dig a shallow well and install the liners with a backhoe.

Build your own diaphragm water pump

This simple but effective pump is capable of lifting water over ten metres. And what's more, it's inexpensive.

BY ANDREW AIDULIS, *KILKIVAN, QUEENSLAND*

HERE IS A simple diaphragm pump that can be made out of recycled materials. It will pump up to six or more litres a stroke depending on what size tyre it is made from.

The pump consists of an old car tyre – I have used a 14 x 195 x 75, but any tyre with reasonably pliable sidewalls will suffice. Two pieces of three-quarter-inch or thicker waterproof plywood, or a round from the end of a tree, or a piece of at least 1.4-inch steel can be used as end plates. Two pieces of at least 75 mm x 45 mm x 2 metres timber for a platform and some smaller pieces for a frame and bracing will be needed. One other long length for a pump handle is also required; the length can be made to suit your own purpose. You will need two 25 mm (the bigger the better) poly one-way valves and elbows, or, if you want, and are handy, you can make your own out of whatever you have on hand.

You will need at least 20 stainless steel, brass or galvanised screws long enough to go through the tyre rim and into the timber. Ordinary steel screws could be used but won't last as long. Some sealing compound like Silastic, or any other thick waterproof glue, is advisable but not absolutely necessary if you take care in placing the screws and use more of them. You will need some long bolts to go through the timber for pivots, or pieces of steel or thick wooden dowel if you don't have steel on hand. A small tap is also handy to prime all the air out of the pump, but is not absolutely necessary as it is basically self-priming. But the pump will work better on deep lifts if all the air is removed.

The pump is made by cutting two discs out of the plywood or steel. These should be cut about 20 mm bigger in diameter than the inner edge of the tyre bead. Place one disc on top of the two long pieces (at least two metres) of 75 mm x 45 mm timber on their edges and space the timbers so they are parallel and about 300 mm apart without overlapping the edge of the disc. Mark the position of the timber on the disc for future reference.

On the same disc make two holes between the timber marks as far away from each other as possible but at least 30 mm from the edge of the disc. These holes should be made so the poly valves can be inserted. A piece of threaded pipe might be needed for this with two threaded collars to hold and seal it.

Secure the valves so that they are opposite in flow direction to each other. An elbow can be screwed on later. Push the first disc with its valves through the tyre rim so it drops inside the tyre (two people might be needed for this). Pre-drill ten evenly-spaced holes around the tyre bead about 5 mm in from the edge. These holes should be drilled with a slightly larger drill than the screws you are going to use, as rubber shrinks back into place a little after drilling. Now, using a block of wood or a besser block for support, flip the tyre so the disc is on the top and the tyre is hanging from it by the lip. Get someone to lift the tyre while you put a bead of Silastic around the inside of the rim.

Next, put the tyre down evenly on the disc so it seals all the way around. Put in all the screws till the rubber just starts to compress. Don't over tighten them as this could pull the bead out of shape. Drill four holes through the disc in the centre of the timber marks you made before, about 200 mm apart. Also drill through the long timbers leaving about 300 mm of the timbers sticking out past the tyre for carry handles. Some short spacers, maybe 30-mm thick, might be needed between the disc and the larger timbers to take up the gap. Put washers on the bolts and some Silastic and bolt the pump to the timbers.

Drill a hole in the centre of the second disc and place a long bolt through it with a large washer on either side. Put some glue under the washers. This bolt can be bent at right angles if you want for the first hinge. Alternatively, a block of strong timber about 80 mm long with a 20 mm slot cut half way down the middle and a hole drilled through the two pieces left sticking up can be screwed on as a hinge. A small tap can be fitted at this time, if you have one, or even a piece of pipe with a blank end cap.

Turn the assembly over. Push the second disc into the tyre with the long end of the bolt and the thread and tap or wooden hinge facing up. Glue and screw this in place on the tyre bead using the bolt or block of wood to hold it in place as a handle.

A frame is now made near the edge of the tyre about knee to waist height depending on your stature. This frame is used as a pivot, so it should be braced back onto the lower frame for strength. A long strong bolt or piece of steel or pipe is now put through this frame and through a piece of the same-sized timber for a handle. The handle should be made so it goes past the centre of the disc by about 50 mm. A platform of timber, a piece of ply or small board, is nailed or screwed on the lower frame to stand on. A short piece of strong timber is cut to go between the end of the handle and the platform so that in the resting position the end of the handle is a comfortable height above the platform.

Now all you need to do is connect some pipe to the valve that flows towards the pump and put it in your water supply, preferably with a non-return valve on the end. But for low lifts this isn't necessary. The other valve end can go to your tank or storage. Grasp the handle with both feet on the platform and start pumping.

Filling the pump and draw pipe with water first through the tap on the top will help if you are lifting over two metres in height from the water supply. A foot valve should also be put on the end of the inlet pipe; this can be the same type as you used for the pump. You should be able to lift water from as deep as ten metres if you are heavy enough, and push it up to your own height depending on your strength. It could also double as an exercise machine!

Tips

TAPS
Stop leaks

Check for worn tap washers. A dripping tap might not appear to be wasting much water, but it quickly adds up.

Repair leaking pipes. A single leak over a long period can waste thousands of litres.

Don't let water run while carrying out tasks such as rinsing dishes, washing fruit and vegetables or washing your hands. A tap running strongly can use 15 litres or more a minute. People who regularly keep the tap running while cleaning their teeth may use about 11,000 litres a year in the process. You could save this water by using a tumbler.

PS: A tyre with a strong stiff tread should be used for high suction lift as a softer one will suck in a bit and waste some of your energy. An old exercise bike or similar could be mounted as well so you can pedal instead. Happy pumping!

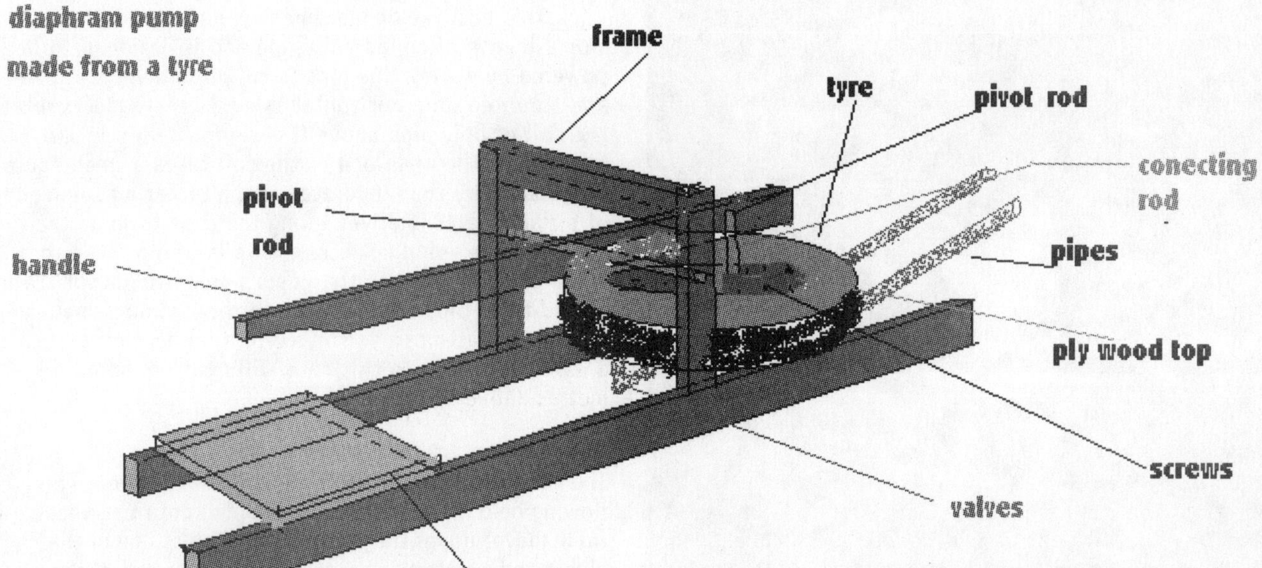

This concept design may appeal to DIY water savers.

Silent water wheel delivers constant supply

Low-impact lifestyler extraordinaire, John Hermans, devised and built a water wheel for Earth Garden's writer and forest campaigner, Jill Redwood. Jill can now refill her water tank from the Brodribb River near her farmhouse in Victoria's East Gippsland. Her water wheel is silent, pumps about a litre a minute, goes 24 hours a day, has only one small moving part, and works on an ancient principle. Here John describes how to build one.

BY JOHN HERMANS, *GIPPSLAND, VICTORIA.*

AS I HAVE no political lobbying or media skills my way of helping the environment campaign is to help those committed to saving forests. My skills lie in the areas of inventing and building. Jill had a 5-hp fire-fighting pump she used to refill her concrete water tank every fortnight or so. I first devised an alternative pump using a set of water wheels, which, via chains and cogs that gave a 4:1 step up, drove a small piston pump.

A happy Jill Redwood with her free energy waterwheel.

The petrol pump was temperamental and noisy. This improved model was temperamental and oily. It did work quite well but was prone to occasional mechanical failure and there was the possibility of it leaking oil into the pristine Brodribb River. So I got to work on an idea I had seen illustrated as a kids' toy. As Jill lives on the upper reaches of the Brodribb River, the small flow in the river was not enough to operate a hydraulic ram pump. The spiral water wheel has the advantage of being environmentally friendly, almost maintenance-free, made of basic cheap materials and is relatively easy to make for anyone with a welder.

This positive displacement pump is made from a single length of coiled poly pipe and is designed to be powered by water. The pipe is coiled in a vertical plane and mounted on a horizontal axle. As the paddles rotate the coil of poly pipe above the water, the lower part is immersed. The open end of the coil takes a small "gulp" of water every time it rotates. An alternating sequence of air and water is driven along the pipe towards the centre of the spiral. Successive coils of pipe lead to a cumulative increase in the pump's pressure output. When a land-fixed pipe is connected to the last and smallest coil, then water can be shifted to a higher point, such as a dam or a tank. In this case, Jill's tank is about 16 metres above the river.

PADDLES AND COILS

The set of undershot paddle wheels (powered from water flowing below, not from water dropping onto the wheels from above) drives the whole show. This is one of the oldest and simplest forms of motor, driving one of the oldest and simplest forms of pump. The whole unit consists of only one small rotating part, called a rotating joiner, or,

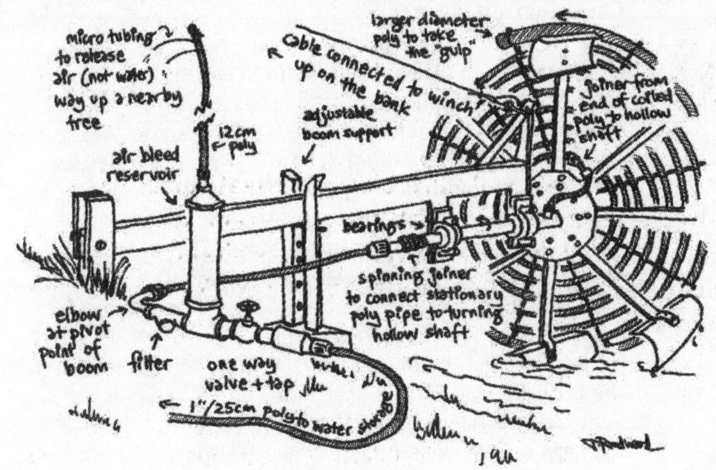

The spiral water wheel replaced a noisy and temperamental petrol pump.

John Hermans with the spiral water wheel he designed and built for Jill Redwood.

in plumber's terms, a spinning nipple.

When assembling the coils on the spokes of the frame, I had no idea how many coils and at what diameter was needed to pump the water to the 16-metre head. The water wheel ended up about two metres in diameter. As the water wheel and the spiral both needed to dip into the water, the coil had to be the same diameter as the paddles.

Three-quarter-inch (19 mm) poly pipe can be coiled down to about 500 mm in diameter before it starts to kink. If the coils are kept close together, around 40 coils can be made. I decided to make two lots of coils consisting of 20 coils each, so there were two openings to take a "gulp". In theory this should have pumped twice the volume of water as a single coil rotating at the same speed. However, this proved to be too heavy for the flow of the stream to move, so I had to remove one coil of pipe. As Jill's place is three hours drive away, there was much guesswork involved in my workshop and redesigning on site.

The final coil design saw 50 metres of three-quarter-inch (19 mm) poly pipe coiled into 20 loops from two metres to half a metre diameter. The pumping rate at this site is about one litre a minute but varies from season to season.

Figuring it out

My theory, then, is that to successfully pump water, the coiled pipe needs to be about three times as long as the height it is being pumped to. That's a 3:1 ratio. I assumed that the size of the pipe is less important than the total length. Larger loops are more effective at forcing water up than small loops but consume more length. Fewer larger loops may be just as effective as many smaller loops.

The water exiting the smallest coil in the centre is piped into the hollow shaft of the water wheel's axle. The end of this then joins a stationary water pipe near the bank, in this case connected to a boom arm (described below). To join the rotating shaft to the fixed poly pipe, a joiner is needed that can spin constantly. Unless the connection is perfectly in line, these watertight rotating joiners can wear out quickly.

To avoid flood damage to this water wheel pump, I mounted the axle and bearings onto a three-metre boom of 100 mm RHS that pivots at the end anchored to the bank. Along this boom, a height adjustable support is set into the bank. A steel cable is attached to the water wheel that is operated by a winch fixed even higher up the bank (see illustration). Not only does this allow it to be cranked out of the water if a flood is imminent and hoisted safely above flood height, but it also allows the water wheel to be lowered or raised to match the high and low flows of the river.

Tips

REDUCE THE PRESSURE

High water pressure increases flow rates from showers, taps, leaks and drips. If you have extremely high water pressure, a registered plumber can fit a pressure reduction valve at your property boundary.

Reducing your water pressure will also reduce water hammer.

INSTALL WATER-SAVING SHOWERS

About 17 per cent of household water is used showering. Install an efficient shower head. Take shorter showers.

DON'T DOUBLE RINSE

Use the "Rinse and Hold" setting on your dishwasher instead of rinsing plates under the tap.

SAVE UP TO 35 PER CENT IN THE LAUNDRY

Washing machines can use between 90 and 200 litres of water a load! Be sure to choose carefully the one that suits you best and match the load setting on the washing machine with the amount of laundry to be washed.

CONSTRUCTION POINTERS

Here are a few more pointers to help with constructing the coil section. To attach the poly pipe to the angle iron spokes, use one-millimetre stainless steel wire (you can order it from engineering suppliers). The end of the three-quarter-inch poly pipe that scoops up the water should be increased in diameter for the last loop. I used one-inch (25 mm) for half a loop and then one-and-a-quarter-inch (32 mm) poly pipe for the last half a loop. This allows for greater volume to be scooped up at each rotation.

As both water and air are pumped up the delivery line together, it is best to send the pumped water directly to the storage tank or dam. If the inlet and outlet line to the tank are the same, a special air bleed line close to the pump will be needed, as Jill discovered when trying to use the taps on the same line or to have a shower!

A one-way valve should also be set in the line to stop water draining back out when the wheel is not pumping. A filter isn't a bad idea either. You can also fix a fly wire guard to the inlet end of the coil that prevents debris from entering the system.

One modification that had to be made over the last couple of years has been a more robust and reinforced hollow shaft. The constant flexing and movement of the water wheel, especially with faster flows, stresses metal and any weak spots are soon discovered. The water wheel was sited on a slight bend in the river where it was narrow and the water had a higher velocity.

Variables that allow this design to pump effectively are:

- river flow
- size of paddles
- number of paddles
- diameter of the wheel
- diameter and number of the coils
- submergence of the coils
- inlet pipe diameter
- height of storage tank or dam

This spiral pump was a direct replacement of a small standard piston pump and has proved to be just as efficient at pumping a set volume each day.

Overall, it's a beautiful piece of alternative technology. And Jill says it also doubles as relaxation therapy: after a torrid session dealing with planet wreckers, sitting by the river watching it quietly turn puts some equilibrium back into the soul.

We built a dam on sand

Are the rainy seasons less abundant than they used to be? Or is it just that the garden has grown? Whatever, nothing solves a water problem like a dam.

BY **JOSE ROBINSON, *WILD CATTLE ISLAND, QUEENSLAND***

Jose fills in the trench around the dam.

AS OUR DRY seasons seem to be becoming longer and drier, we've mulled over the most economical way of storing extra water, mainly for garden use.

We live on a tiny sand island away from the luxury of mainland piped water supply, in a dry belt of 800 to 900 mm of rain annually, and water is always at a premium.

When we first moved to the island many years ago, the rainy season seemed to be more abundant. Or was it just that I didn't have such an extensive garden?

Desalination could be a solution if we received our power from the grid. But we have to rely on the sun and wind for our energy system. Although we have the ocean all around us, desalinating salt water is too energy expensive and inefficient to be able to operate a system with our 18 solar panels and wind generator. So this year we decided to take the plunge and build a dam with a liner.

For obvious reasons it had to be a fairly small dam, but we felt a small dam would be better than no dam.

To do the excavating ourselves, we only had an old Fergie tractor and bucket, but we figured it would be up to the job if we were! After all it was only sand we were moving. We measured and marked out our boundary using a string line and hammered the pegs in. I dug out copious amounts of turf to be used elsewhere on the property, and then the real work began.

After several sessions of tractor work, we began to get bogged each time we tried to go deeper. The work looked like becoming dangerous. We were almost half way to the desired depth when we had to sit down and have a big think about the danger of using the tractor. We borrowed a back blade

One completed dam, half-filled with water.

from a friend. It moved the sand faster but it was still dangerous.

We have a few weekend holiday houses on the island, and as luck would have it, some of the house owners decided to throw in together for the expense of getting a backhoe down to the island to do some levelling. So we joined in and were able to hire the backhoe for an hour, which finished off our excavating.

We checked the cost of commercial fabricated liners and got quotes from two companies with several hundred dollars difference in price – and quality. Ultra-violet rays can be a big problem with liners and their durability. The liner we got was guaranteed for three years, and made from Canvacon 5000.

This is a type of woven poly fabric. It is said to give incredible resistance to puncturing and tearing. They promised delivery within a week, and we collected the liner just five days later. We didn't want to waste any more time with the promise of the last of the season's rain. The liner came in a flat rectangular piece, so we had to pleat the corners to get a snug fit. This we did with the help of our trusty brick weights. These prevented the liner from taking off like a giant sail in the breeze. I had sewn dozens of bags made from old curtains to enclose the bricks, in case some sharp edges punctured the precious liner.

To secure the perimeter we dug a trench all around, approximately 45 centimetres deep, and the width of the spade. We buried the edges of the liner and finally placed a layer of builders' black plastic completely over the side walls. This was to protect the liner from the ultra-violet rays. The floor of the dam liner we covered with a thin layer of sand.

By now all chance of rain seemed very remote and reluctantly we became resigned to having a dry dam for months to come. Several of our friends, upon inspecting our work muttered "You'll not get any water in that until next wet season". But what ho! Our luck was in. A few days later, Cyclone Justin began hovering off the north

Queensland coast. He was a most unusual cyclone. He moved down then up, then in and out. Being so late in the season, we thought it would be a fizzer. He travelled quite fast down near us dropping masses of rain mainly north of us, completely ruining many of the banana plantation crops.

We got our fair share, and soon our new dam was about one-third full. We busied ourselves and acquired some waterlilies planted in pots to float on the surface. The pots were inserted in cut-outs of polystyrene circular floating supports. Naturally waterlilies won't grow on a plastic-lined dam bottom, so we had to be innovative and make these float. A couple of silver perch were then introduced to keep down mosquitoes.

We have toads that have to be seen to be believed. We weren't wanting to provide them with a free breeding area, so up went a bird-wire fence surrounding the dam. This fence worked very well, and apart from the few that went swimming before the fence was secured, we've had no toads since. We scooped out those few and sent them packing.

To save any excess storm-water that may overflow from our water tank, we have set up an underground poly pipe system to direct the overflow into the dam.

The next project has been to set up a water pumping station from the dam to the vegetable gardens. We purchased a 12 volt Johnson 12 mm (1/2") pump with a maximum draw of three amps. It has a constant rating which means it can run indefinitely. We built an adjustable stand for one 40-watt solar panel. This panel can be adjusted for the summer or winter sun. We also installed a maximiser that allows the pump to operate from the solar panel without going through a battery. The maximiser also converts the excess voltage from the solar panel (over 12 volts) into usable amperage.

We are still ironing out the practicalities of the best size of poly pipe to carry the water to the garden area – a distance up a small rise of about 50 metres. There is plenty of power and water force through a 12 mm poly pipe and the energy for it is free from the sun. We're currently experimenting with a larger size poly pipe for an even bigger flow of water to the garden system. Everything is working very well and we are happy with our new dam. When full the dam will be about 14 metres by 8 metres by 2.5 metres.

Materials:

Hire of backhoe to complete excavation
1 roll builders' black plastic
1 roll bird wire by 900 mm
Dam liner from V.P. Industries, Brisbane
Posts for fence (scrap on hand)
Nails to secure wire (on hand)
12 volt Johnson 12 mm pump
Maximiser (on special)
1 by 40 watt solar panel (from our existing solar system)

Tips

NEED A DRINK?
Keep a jug of water in the fridge instead of waiting for the cold water to come through the tap.

TURN OFF WHILE BRUSHING
Wet your brush and fill a glass for rinsing. Or just turn off the tap while brushing. People who regularly keep the tap running while cleaning their teeth may use about 11,000 litres a year in the process. You could save this water by using a tumbler.

Water-powered pumps: from water-wheels to hydraulic rams

The attraction of using water to power pumps has been obvious as long as water has been lifted. Here John discusses methods and their pros and cons.

BY JOHN SHAW, *FISHERMANS PARADISE, QUEENSLAND*

THE IDEA of using the power of moving water has been around for a very long time. In fact the water-powered pump is among the first inventions. Early water pumps employed a large paddle wheel set up just below the bank of a river so that the lower part of the wheel was rotated by the current. Fastened to the rim of the wheel were small buckets which each picked up a little water as the wheel turned, and as the full buckets came up over the top, the water fell out into a flume which carried it to fields for irrigation.

Those primitive pumps illustrate a common feature of all water-powered pumps. They use a comparatively large volume of moving water to provide the power to raise a much lesser volume of water to where it is wanted. When you think about it, that is a pretty environmentally-friendly kind of pump, because it doesn't gulp large quantities of water but only sips a small amount, leaving plenty for other users downstream.

A development of the water-wheel pump, to raise water to greater heights, is to fix the buckets to a belt that passes round the water wheel and then up and over a pulley mounted at the desired height. A cheap variation of this is to use a fluffy rope, which passes round the water-wheel and up over a small pulley at the desired height. As the rope passes over the pulley, some of the water that has adhered to the rope will be flung off by centrifugal force to be led away by a flume. In practical terms, the water-wheel-type pump is very limited in its application. It is the kind of thing that an enthusiast, with the right conditions, might build. I see no reason why a water-wheel could not be made to drive a piston or diaphragm pump by means of a crank or a cam. Water-wheel pumps do work, but tend to be large and cumbersome, not very efficient, prone to flood damage and do not raise water to more than a few metres in height.

In the nineteenth century, and possibly before, it was realised that water running down a pipe contains a large amount of kinetic energy. This led to the development of the kind of pump known as the hydraulic ram.

The hydraulic ram works by running water down a pipe and through a chamber fitted with a large-diameter stop valve and a delivery valve. As the speed of the water increases, it eventually reaches a point at which it will cause the stop valve to slam shut. Thus there is created a massive temporary increase in pressure within the chamber, which causes the delivery valve to open and release some of the water to a delivery pipe.

Because the movement of water down the inlet pipe is now stopped, there is no kinetic energy and therefore a decrease in pressure within the chamber. The stop valve then opens (either by its own weight or by a spring) allowing the cycle to restart. Because the action of this pump is quite violent, with massive changes in pressure, it has to be very robust in construction and there is a need for an air chamber on the delivery side to smooth out the variations in pressure in the delivery pipe.

The great advantage of the hydraulic ram over the water wheel pump is that it can pump water long distances and to great heights. The actual performance is different in each installation, and depends on the height of the intake above the pump and the length of the intake pipe. Disadvantages of the hydraulic ram are that, because it relies on a water hammer effect to provide the energy, it must be very robust in construction and must be securely fastened to a massive foundation. Also, the intake pipe must be straight and rigid. Traditionally, ram pumps were made of cast iron and were very heavy. An interesting development is the Turon Pump, which is made of stainless steel and has a polycarbonate stop valve. There is an anchor sleeve welded on to each side through which star pickets can be driven into the ground to provide an anchorage. The air chamber is similar to the pressure regulator used on domestic pressure pumps, and thus the pump is light weight but durable. However, I suspect it would be wise to install it well out of reach of floods if there is any danger of it being struck by rolling rocks or floating logs in a flood.

A development of the hydraulic ram pump is the Glockemann Pump, which uses a diaphragm in the chamber

A Glockemann hydraulic ram pump.

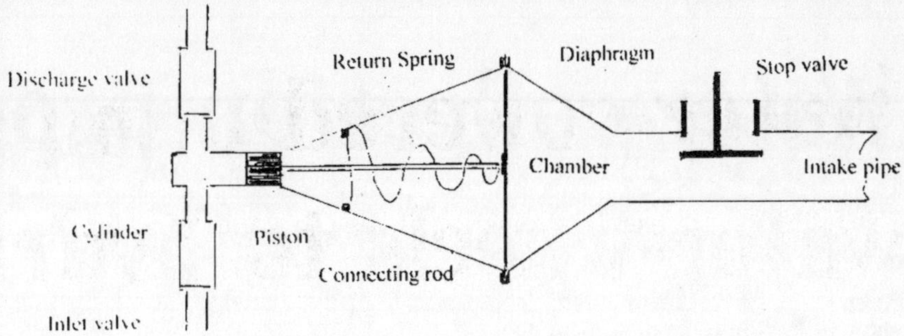

Schematic view of a diaphragm/piston-type water-powered pump.

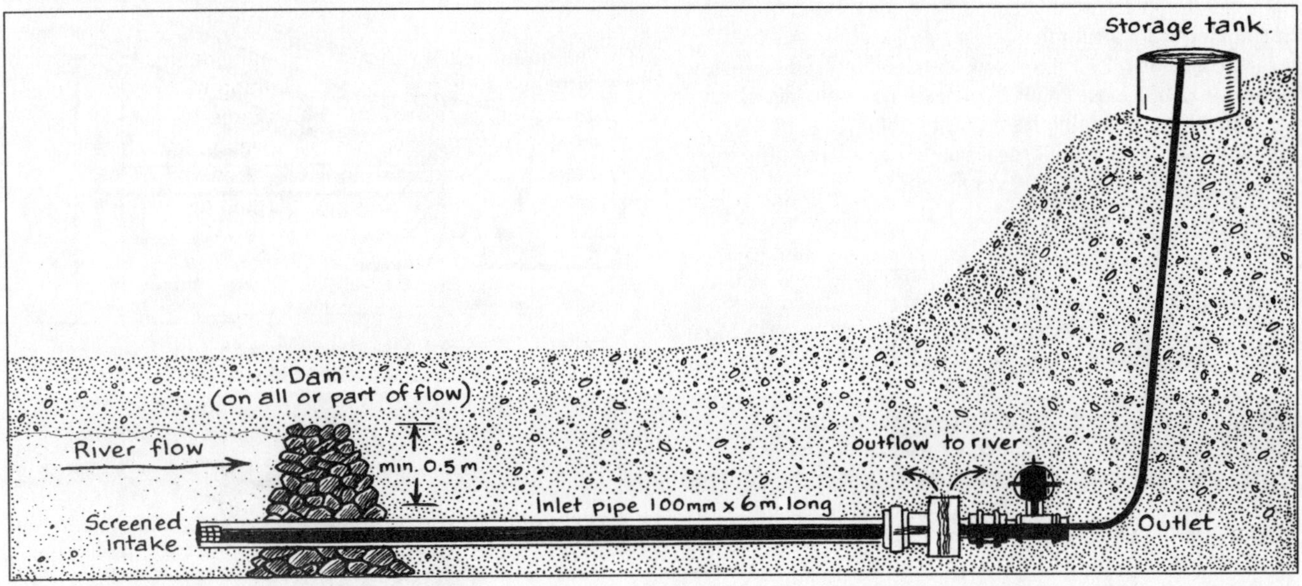

A schematic view of a typical installation.

connected to a piston in a cylinder. Thus, the water coming down the inlet pipe causes the stop valve to shut, as in the ram pump. The resulting increase in pressure in the chamber causes the diaphragm to bulge outwards forcing the piston forward in the cylinder, pushing water through the delivery valve and up the delivery pipe. When the pressure in the chamber subsides, a spring returns the diaphragm to its original position, the piston withdraws from the cylinder, bringing in a fresh charge of water through the inlet valve, the stop valve opens and the whole cycle starts again. This type of pump has a few more parts than the hydraulic ram and is therefore a little more complex, but it has the great advantage of being gentler in its action. This eliminates the need for a mechanism of massive construction; there is less need for the pump to be well anchored and the intake pipe does not need to be straight or rigid.

Generally, you would need an inlet head of at least 500 mm to operate a water-powered pump to deliver water against a delivery head of 30 metres. Performance will be different in each situation, but pump manufacturers can advise for particular installations.

When installing a ram or a diaphragm and piston pump, it is essential to ensure that the inlet is provided with an efficient strainer so that sand, stones and other debris does not enter the pump and block the mechanism.

Any water-driven pump has the obvious advantage of having no fuel cost, but it does rely on the continuous flow of water to drive it. In the right conditions it provides a cheap and reliable means of pumping water for domestic or stock watering purposes.

CONTACT NUMBERS

Glockemann Pumps (02) 9708 0900,
or email info@gpe-waterpumps.com.
Turon Pumps,
26 Hunter St, Parramatta, NSW, 2150
(02) 9893 7586

Water collection products

The following are merely a selection of the thousands of water-saving products available in Australia today.

IT IS IRONIC that up until about seven years ago councils and state governments throughout Australia refused to grant permits for householders who wished to install rainwater tanks in urban areas. These days the turn around in thinking from authorities from every state in Australia means that not only are householders encouraged to install water tanks but most councils or state governments offer valuable rebates ranging from $50 to $500 for approved installations. Phone your local council or water authority for a rebate application and conditions.

RAINSAVER

Rainsaver is an ingenious rainwater storage system that replaces all gutter and stormwater systems. It provides a simple and attractive alternative to flushing away precious water. The standard Rainsaver stores around 1500 litres of rainwater on an average 160-square-metre house. The system supplies gravity-fed potable water to the toilet and external garden taps. A connection to the mains water supply allows Rainsaver to automatically top up the system during extended dry spells, ensuring a continuous water supply. During periods of extreme rainfall, a series of overflow holes strategically placed around the house gently discharge the excess rainwater to ensure it flows away from the house and infiltrates the yard area. Using Rainsaver to supply toilets and external water needs can cut demand from town water by up to 30 per cent. This will not only save money but will cut the consumption of town water and reduce CO_2 emissions created by pumping the water large distances to simply flush toilets. Rainsaver is manufactured from galvanised steel with a 200-micron polymer food grade lining. Rainsaver can be easily installed on most new or existing buildings and is available in a variety of colours and sizes. Rainsaver allows the householder to use up to 80 per cent of the rainwater falling on the roof in an average rainfall year, thus removing a substantial amount of water from the stormwater system.

Rainsaver will last up to three times longer than Colorbond steel gutters, and save around 70,000 litres a year when connected to toilets and garden hose cocks. Rainsaver gutters contain water, not leaf litter, thus eliminating bushfire hazards from within the guttering. In danger areas, a curtain of water can be provided around the house. In cyclonic areas, the Rainsaver will fill during a rainstorm which normally precedes the wind storm. The weight of the filled Rainsaver assists in holding the roof down.

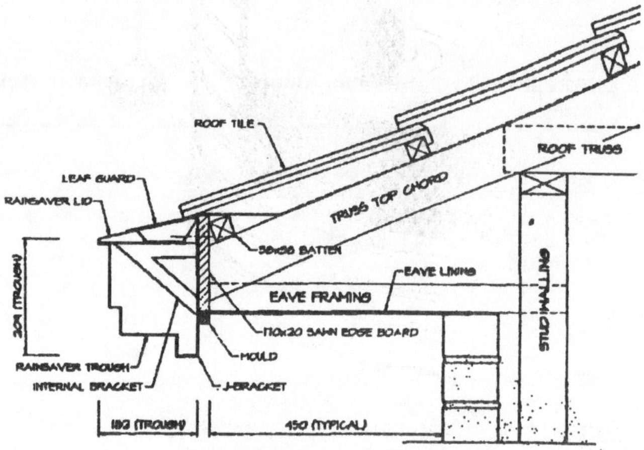

CONSTRUCTION DETAIL

SECTION SHOWING PLUMBING

For further information contact: Rainsaver Pty Ltd, PO Box 1031, Meadowbank, NSW, 2114. Phone or fax: (02) 9874 3996. Toll free Australia wide, phone 1800 700 003, or visit the website: <www.rainsaver.com.au>.

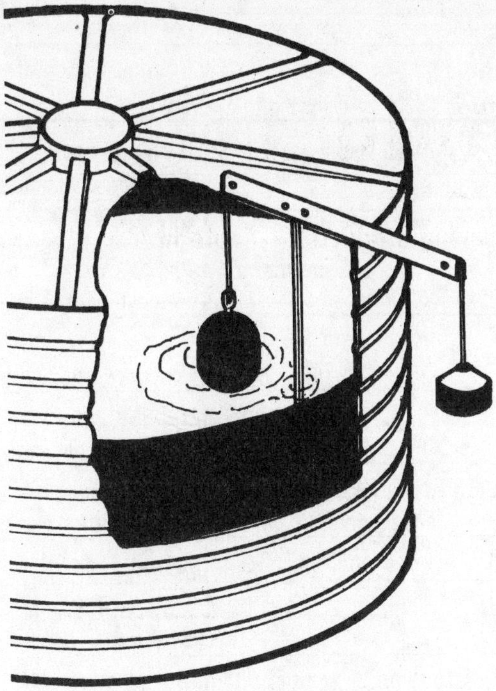

LEVETATOR WATER TANK LEVEL INDICATOR

The Levetator works on the tried and true float–weight–pulley system, but with a difference: it reads correctly. The indicator shows you the actual water level exactly, at all times. The weighted float and indicator are balanced by counterpoise. A rising water level lifts the float, sinking the counterpoise, which pulls the indicator up. When the water level falls, the heavy float pulls the counterpoise up, dropping the indicator, which matches the float, always at the true water level. The unit fits all above-ground tanks of any material and any diameter, up to any height. The Levetator is easy to install: just screw it to the roof of your tank, making two holes for the nylon cords, shortening them as required to match the tank height. It is guaranteed for five years, and is available from Yaktek Industries, 1 Oswald St, Maldon, Victoria, 3463; phone (03) 5475 1116, fax (03) 5475 1126.

FIRST FLUSH WATER DIVERTER

The FFWD has been designed to fit to the outside of most tanks to keep the rainwater clean and still allow free access to the manhole. The advantages of this model are:

- large 60-litre capacity
- available in all tank colours
- easily attached through the roof of the tank
- collects the first 60 litres of sedimented run-off, keeping it from entering the main tank
- keeps manhole access free
- can be fitted to existing tanks
- catchment tank can be easily cleaned.

DIPSTIK

This alternative water level indicator, protruding above the tank roof, is based on a floating pole. It is ideal for "cup and saucer" tanks. High above the tank the indicator can be seen from far away, in every direction, night or day.

On top, out of harm's way, stock can't reach the Dipstik. Birds cannot perch on the aluminium indicator cap.

LIQUIDATOR

Operating on the same principle as the Levetator, the Liquidator uses an external guide tube. The indicator slides up and down on the outside of the tube and the counterweight is contained inside it. Only the float is in contact with the liquid. This indicator is the choice for tanks containing liquids other than water.

Whether water or chemical, the Liquidator gives a true reading. Graduations can be marked on or beside the guide tube for accurate measurement.

It is ideal for water storage tanks for fire protection on industrial sites. Stainless steel wire is available as an optional alternative to polyester cord.

The above three products are available from Polymaster, 161 Karinie Street, Swan Hill, Vic. 3585, Freecall 1800 062 064.

WATER TANKS

Even if you have town water, a rainwater tank makes a lot of sense. Cities are full of natural rain catching devices – called roofs – which are not used, while water authorities dam more rivers, build more storage dams, and try to control the stormwater that flows into the bays of our coastal cities. If suburban roofs caught rainwater it could be used on gardens: simply install a rainwater tank, attach a "Leeaky Hose" to the open valve of your tank, and run it to your garden beds. This simple measure would drop *E. coli* counts in our waterways, and possibly end increasing water demand.

The good news is that some water companies and councils are starting to offer ratepayers water tanks. For instance, Yarra Water in Melbourne supply a 4500-litre (1000 gallon) tank for $1157, sited on a sand bed. This is not cheap, though, compared to an ARI Plastank supplied by Going Solar in North Melbourne for $690. Of course, the Going Solar unit is a DIY tank, where you make your own base and organise your own pumping or flow out system.

CATCHMENT AREA

To calculate the catchment area of your roof, use the following formula:

Roof Area (m^2) X Annual Rainfall (mm) = Catchment (Litres)

So, a 140-square-metre house in Sydney (1226 mm/year) could catch:

140 X 1226 mm = 171,640 litres

Note: 1 mm of rain on 1 m^2 of roof area = 1 litre of catchment water.

SELECTED AUSTRALIAN TANKMAKERS

COMPANY	FIRST FLUSH DIVERTER OPTIONAL?	LARGEST TANK SIZE L (gall)	URBAN TANKS?	AGENTS?	CONTACT
Team Poly	Yes	27000 (6000)	Yes	Most states	(08) 8326 2256; www.teampoly.com.au
ARI Plastank		45,400 (10000)	Yes	Most states	1300 138 265
Bushman Tanks		47,950 (10,548)	Yes	All mainland states	1800 008 888; www.bushmantanks.com
Tankworld	Yes, "Leaf Eater" diverter	45,500 (10,000)	Yes	NSW, Vic, SA,Tas	1800 68 69 70; www.tankworld.com.au
Tankmasta	No, 10 micron filter/leaf strainer	45,000 (10,000)	Yes	NSW, Qld, Vic	1800 658 265; www.linpac.com.au
Pioneer	Yes, Rainsafe & manual kit	54,000+	No, smallest 2,000L	All states	1800 999 599; www.pioneertanks.com.au
Polymaster		31,700 (7,000)	Yes	Vic, SA, NSW	1800 062 064
Kathro	Stainless steel urban drinking water tank with in-built filters				1800 635 995 (03) 9328 4123
City Rainwater	Specialises in city rainwater tanks in Sydney region: St Marys (02) 9623 2414, Ingleburn (02) 9618 3842, Dee Why (02) 9971 9090				

POLY VS CORRUGATED IRON

Most people have traditionally bought "gal" or concrete water tanks – they usually come with a long warranty. We were surprised to discover that far fewer greenhouse gases are emitted in the construction of a polyethylene tank than a galvanised iron tank. According to one of Australia's largest polyethylene tank makers, Team Poly, "to manufacture a corrugated iron tank (from iron ore through to a finished product) the cost is 1200 times more CO2 dumped into the atmosphere than to manufacture an equivalent-sized, Team Poly tank".

Metal tanks are light, can be used above or below ground, and can be custom-made, usually corrugated or coated steel.

Polyethylene tanks are durable, UV-resistant, light and available in many sizes and colours. They are suitable for above and below ground installation.

Concrete tanks are durable, long lasting and usually built on-site. They can be used below and above ground and have light-resistant qualities (preventing algal growth) and keep the water cool. They occasionally crack.

Fibreglass tanks tolerate extreme temperatures, resist rust and chemical corrosion and are more suitable for above ground installations. They are lightweight and available in a large range of colours and sizes.

Roof tanks, an eaves guttering system, are designed to collect and store rainwater. Collected water is used to flush toilets, fill washing machines, water gardens and wash cars.

There are many tank makers throughout Australia; a small selection of tank makers who have agents in most states is listed above.

Remember: if you're moving to the bush, check how much water tank capacity your council requires and how much you'll actually use – the two figures can vary wildly. Use the volume guide below.

WATER VOLUME GUIDE

The toilet – a dual flush uses three litres for a single flush and six litres for a full flush. A single unit uses nine to eleven litres a flush.

The shower – a water-saving shower rose uses about eight litres a minute. Older style shower roses use about 12 litres a minute.

The bath – a bath uses between 50 and 150 litres of water a fill.

Dishwashing by hand – it takes between 15 and 18 litres of water to fill a kitchen sink.

Automatic dishwashers – modern dishwashers use around 15 litres for a fast cycle and 20 litres for a normal cycle.

Clothes washing machine – a modern, front-loading machine uses 50 litres on a normal cycle; a top loader uses 120 to 150 litres on a normal cycle.

General use – such as hand washing, brushing teeth, cooking and household cleaning – approximately 18 litres a person a day.

Watering the garden – a garden sprinkler uses 1,000 litres of water an hour.

Dripping taps or leaking toilets – three drops a second is around 68 litres a day.

Above and right: Space Smart Water Tanks can store water in home walls, as fences and under floors.

OTHER STORAGE SYSTEMS

Space Smart Water Tanks have produced an innovative rainwater storage product available in Australia that is suitable for both urban and country dwellers alike.

These tanks can store water in home walls, as fences, under floors – or even disguised as a garden shed (see photos above).

The Freewater Modular System is a slimline rainwater tank measuring just 190 mm wide – less than the width of this page. Freewater can be installed as a self-standing system (as a fence for example) or can be attached to an existing wall or structure. You can add as many modules as you like to expand your water storage. Modules can be installed and connected in almost any configuration – mounted along walls, connected around corners, linked under windows – and you get to keep access along your side passage! Freewater modules are being incorporated into the walls of a new sustainable house, providing both water storage and superior insulation benefits.

Each Freewater module stores approximately 230 litres of rainwater and is manufactured from food grade UV-resistant polyethylene. Module dimensions are 1800 mm high, 800 mm long and 190 mm wide. The modules can be installed by the home handyperson or by the company. Depending on where you choose to locate your tap outlet, the modular nature of the Freewater system also provides a beneficial filtering effect, improving the quality of your stored rainwater. The Freewater Modular System is an Australian designed, patented and manufactured product. Contact Space Smart Water Tanks, ph: (02) 8230 2380 (Sydney), or visit the website at <www.rainwater.com.au>.

The Rain Reviva resembles a large water sac.

The Waterwall modular system is a rainwater storage solution for urban households.

RAIN REVIVA

Another Australian invention is the Rain Reviva – which has been purpose-designed for under-floor installations. The Rain Reviva resembles a large water sac – with standard sizes measuring 1600 mm wide, 4000 mm long and 900 mm high – holding over 3500 litres of water (see photo above). The sac is manufactured from fuse-welded, food grade, flexible and puncture-resistant polymembrane, and is held in place with a purpose-built galvanised steel frame. The Rain Reviva can be custom built to fit almost any space. Additionally, the sacs can be linked together using standard irrigation fittings to provide unlimited storage capacity and configuration. As the Rain Reviva comes in kit form, it can also be used as a permanent or temporary water storage solution for the farm as it is easily transportable. For instance, a Rain Reviva can be easily placed on the back of a ute and the water used for fire fighting, stock watering or plant irrigation.

The Rain Reviva can be installed by the home handyperson or by the professional install team, depending on your locality. For further information, ph: (03) 9735 1111, web: <www.rainreviva.com.au>.

The Waterwall modular system is a rainwater storage solution for urban households. A slim line tank design, each unit is only 330 mm deep and yet holds 1200 litres of water. Any number of tanks can be connected together, which increases storage capacity. The interconnected tanks can be used as a fence, as a dividing wall in a garden, or be fitted in a narrow sideway. Screens can be used to disguise the tanks if preferred.

The modules, each measuring 2400 mm x 1800 mm x 330 mm, are manufactured from tank grade polyethylene, and are easy to install.

Modules comprise the tank with wall fixing brackets, freestanding frame and joiner kit to link tanks, all sold separately.

Rainwater is diverted into the first tank through a 200 mm hole in the top with an inlet strainer installed; every other tank in a linked system has a 60 mm screened breather cap which seals the tank while allowing air to escape as it fills with water. Hoses link the tanks at the bottom allowing water to flow from one tank to the next. There are eight 20 mm outlets around the bottom of each module, which can be used for a tap, a hose or an external pump.

Rainwater is diverted into the first tank through a 200 mm hole in the top with an inlet strainer installed.

Waterwall Solutions Pty Ltd, Ph. (03) 9689 3055, web: <ww.waterwall.com.au>.

URBAN WATER TANKS

The benefits of installing an urban rainwater tank are many. They include savings on your water bills, easier garden maintenance, natural clear water, reduction of stormwater run-off and other environmental benefits such as a reduced need for dams and a lesser likelihood of flooding.

Most councils these days approve and encourage the use of urban tanks, and many offer rebates on the purchase

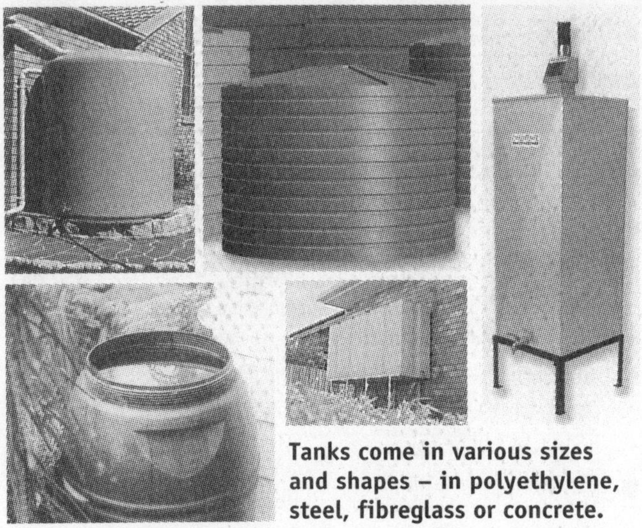

Tanks come in various sizes and shapes – in polyethylene, steel, fibreglass or concrete.

and professional installation by a licensed plumber. Tanks over a certain size, or length, and in-ground tanks usually require planning approval. For information on rebates and regulations, contact your local council.

Tanks come in various sizes and shapes and can be polyethylene, steel, fibreglass or concrete. They can be round with conical lids, slimline rectangular, or ovoid shapes with flat tops that can tuck under a roofline. Round or square, corrugated, smooth or ridged, with or without tank stands, taps and pumps, urban tanks come in most colours.

Installing a water tank

In-ground siting

Prepare the hole. Ensure that the surrounding soil left in the walls of the hole is solid, leaving a six to eight inch (15–20 cm) gap to allow positioning of the tank. It is important that tanks be buried into the ground to only half the tank wall height. If there is major water seepage into the hole from the surrounding soil the site will not be suitable.

A base of two or three inches (50–75 mm) of sand or crusher dust must be put in the hole and compacted.

The tank is lowered into the hole squarely by a crane. The crane hire is the owner's expense.

The tank is then filled with water above ground height, then backfilled with bedding sand.

Fixed inlets must be supported and have flexible hose fitted. A flexible hose length should be placed between the gate valve and other plumbing. This absorbs shock and protects the tank and fittings.

On a slab or pad

Prepare a reinforced concrete pad that is level and greater than the diameter of the tank. Alternatively, an earth pad topped with up to five inches of sand should be provided. The pad should extend 12 inches past the walls of the tank, and have a timber or similar edging to prevent erosion.

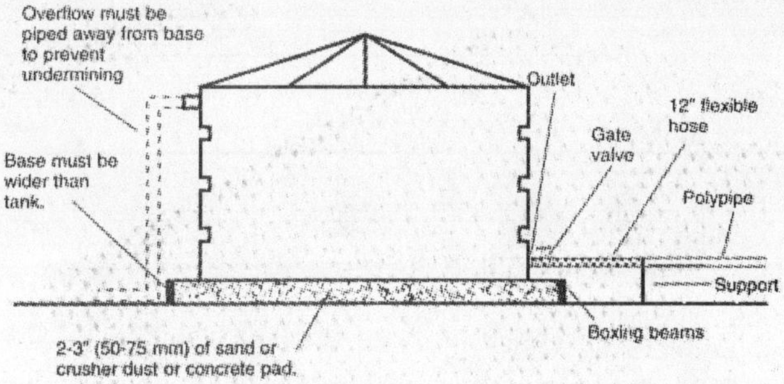

The tank should be rolled into position or moved by crane if access is poor. The tank should then be tied down.

On tank stand

The stand should be made of hardwood decking with gaps no greater than five centimetres. The decking should be supported by bearers strong enough to prevent the decking from sagging when the tank is full.

The tank is then lifted in place by a crane and tied down to the stand; an empty tank could blow away. Overflows should be directed away from the tank base to avoid undermining the stand.

Plumbing requirements may vary according to the type and size of tank and how it is installed. Tank suppliers will advise on the correct plumbing.

CHECKLIST WHEN USING TANK WATER

- **Use safe, lead-free roof paint.**
- **Do not collect water from asbestos roofs.**
- **Regularly check your tank and ensure the lid is secured to prevent insects, rodents, animals and children getting in.**
- **Periodically clean your tank and gutters to ensure they are clear of debris, leaves and dirt.**
- **Ensure light will not penetrate your tank to prevent growth of algae.**
- **Consider installing primary screening and first flush diverters to improve your rainwater quality.**

PUMPS

Many sizes are available: some are for small home and irrigation pressure systems; or dam to tank, aquaculture and hydroponics applications. Others are suitable for large two-storey home and farm irrigation systems, or for commercial water supply and drainage uses.
Pumps may also be equipped with fire fighting attachments and sprinkler systems.

CARE OF PUMPS

- use and maintain the correct foot valve for the application
- periodically check pump for unusual noises to detect any wearing of the bearings
- check filter regularly to ensure no back pressure
- check mechanical seal regularly
- check tank air pressure every six months
- maintain its prime
- don't choke the pump

DAVEY RAINBANK

Australian pump and household pressure system manufacturer, Davey Products, has developed RainBank, a unique advanced control system for rainwater harvesting. RainBank automatically switches the water source from the domestic mains to the rainwater supply stored in the tank whenever a toilet button is pushed or a similar use is required. The controller automatically selects rainwater first and then mains water only as a back up should there be no rainwater stored. The RainBank is normally mounted on top of the pump but it has the flexibility of remote mounting onto a wall or nearby location. Contact: ph 1300 367 866, or web <www.davey.com.au>.

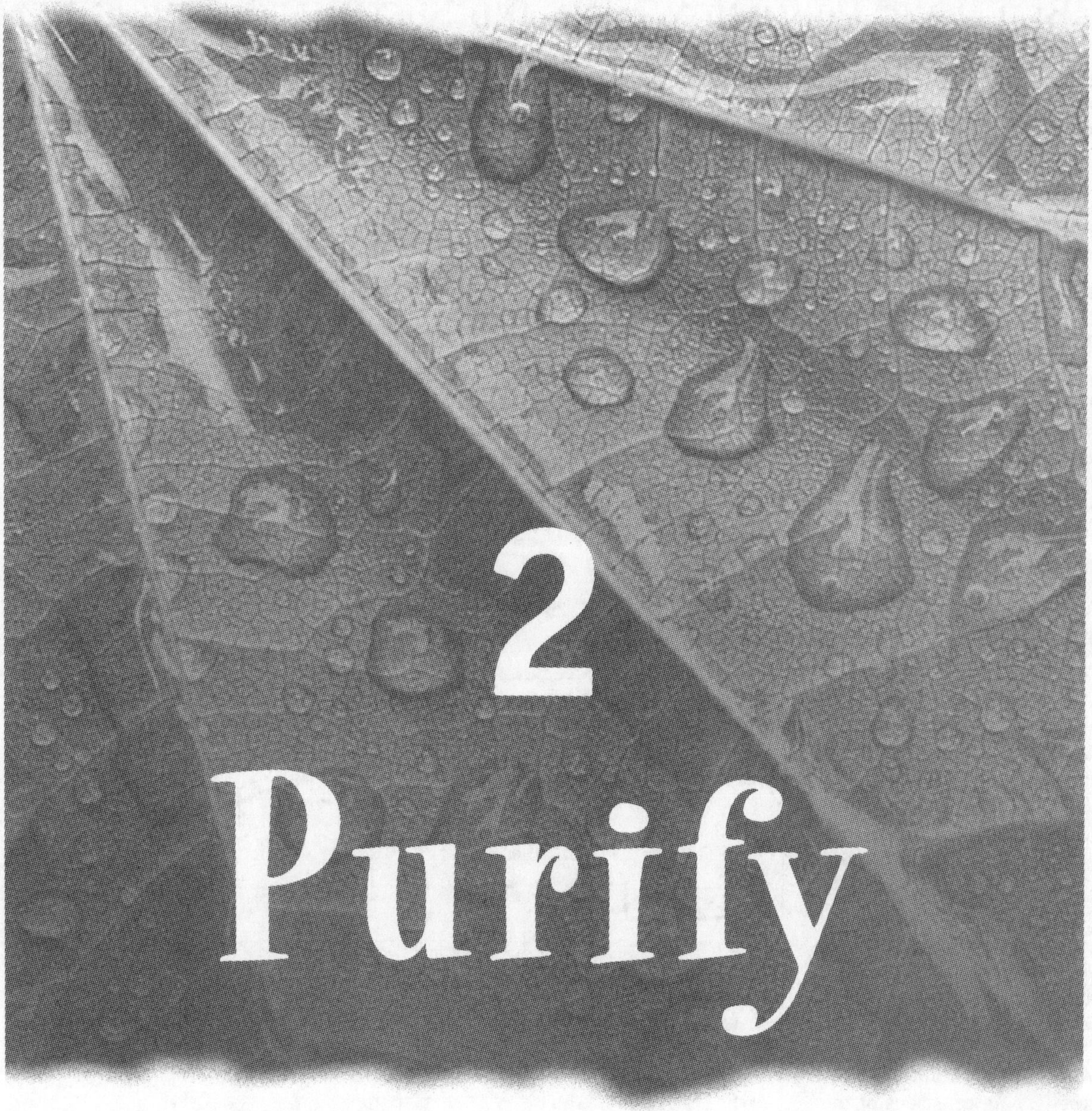

2 Purify

Natural purification in the city

THE BEELARONG COMMUNITY FARM AND SUSTAINABLE LIVING CENTRE

The innovative use of natural water purification processes has made this urban farm a showpiece of sustainability.

THE FARM

The Beelarong Community Farm is in the centre of Brisbane where people can enjoy their leisure in a farm setting. Established in 1997 and run by volunteers, the farm is on a two-hectare site that was supplied by Brisbane City Council. The farm was designed by engineer Keith Burnett and ecologist Wayne Wadsworth, and development was assisted by grants from the EPA, Brisbane City Council, and the Office of Sustainable Energy.

INDEPENDENT LIVING

Not connected to the grid or the sewer it serves as a model of sustainable and independent living for urban dwellers. Visitors can see the entire system from the collection of rainwater to the use of this water for irrigation. Electricity for lighting, to power the pumps and for area lighting comes from a solar system. The farm has a flushable composting toilet, and the effluent is treated using biological means before going to a transpiration area. From there it is recycled via gardens. Greywater is also recycled for irrigation using biological means.

SUSTAINABLE WATER USE

City dwellers are conscious of the need to use water sustainably. The farm serves as a clear demonstration that waste water such as greywater from washing, or effluent from toilets, can be recycled if treated properly. It is also a demonstration of how to turn an effluent problem into an oxygen generation opportunity.

Water is harvested from the roof into a rainwater tank, and after use is recycled for irrigation.

A GARDEN INSIDE THE HOUSE

The farm has a unique concept whereby the greywater of the house is cleaned in the house using biological methods. This treated water becomes part of the biological architecture of the house when it is used to irrigate a garden built onto the verandah.

A grease trap removes fat and grease. Copying nature, water plants grow in an aquatic filter. As the greywater flows past, micro-organisms on plant roots attack

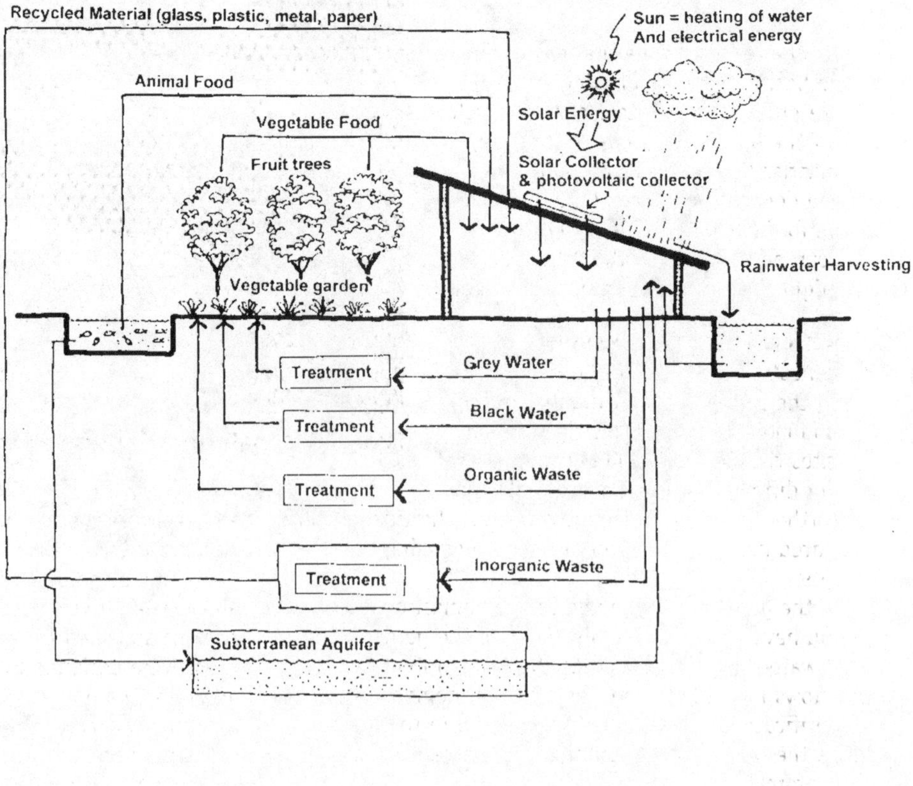

The home as part of the cycle of sustainability.

pathogenic bacteria and pollutants.

Copying nature still, the water passes through a filter of rocks and sand. Micro-organisms living on the rocks attack more pollutants. Wetland plants such as reeds growing in the sand supply gases and compounds to the micro-environment, and aid in the decomposition of toxic organic compounds.

The reeds are cut and returned to the soil as compost. On a larger scale, such a system can be used to treat water from enterprises like farms and caravan parks. Here experimentation is required to select the plants appropriate to the toxic compounds present.

RECYCLING THE WATER

The water that is recovered from this system can be reused, for example, to flush toilets, or for irrigation. At this farm the recovered water is used for irrigation. As shown on the drawing the filtered water passes into an adjacent garden to irrigate food plants.

RECYCLING GREYWATER IN AN INTERNAL GARDEN

Based on the belief that natural processes have the best chance of purifying waste water, water is directed into a garden which is part of the house. This is a rock marsh, which purifies the water. It also contains herbs and decorative plants. (The water is now safe for irrigation.) The raised bed garden can be accessed, without bending, day or night, in the rain or in hot sunshine.

TIDAL ACTION OF THE ROCK MARSH

Daytime heat causes moisture to rise, watering the plant roots. At night, the soil cools, and moisture falls. This tidal action oxygenates the soil daily and encourages the growth of different types of micro-organisms, which further assist the purifying process. The tidal marsh thus created has a high potential for decomposing pollutants.

As the garden is connected to the domestic system, when you have a shower you also irrigate the garden with purified water. Any residual water from this integrated garden flows into a fishpond. As a further demonstration of water purification, a submerged solar pump in the fishpond transfers the water, which contains fish waste, to a set of four flow forms.

As well as being beautiful landscape objects, flow forms also replicate the flow pattern observed in nature, which, in streams, is responsible for rejuvenating polluted water.

This blend of artistic and scientific perception came about when it was noted that the movement pattern in streams appeared to rejuvenate and purify the water. Flow forms were designed to produce this rhythmic circular motion in water, with side-to-side figure-of-eight movement, and a double pulsing action akin to the beating of human hearts in their blood-energising task. Flow forms also exhibit a lung function in oxygenating the water plus a metabolic function in mixing additives.

Flow forms, nature's cleansers, are used to purify water.

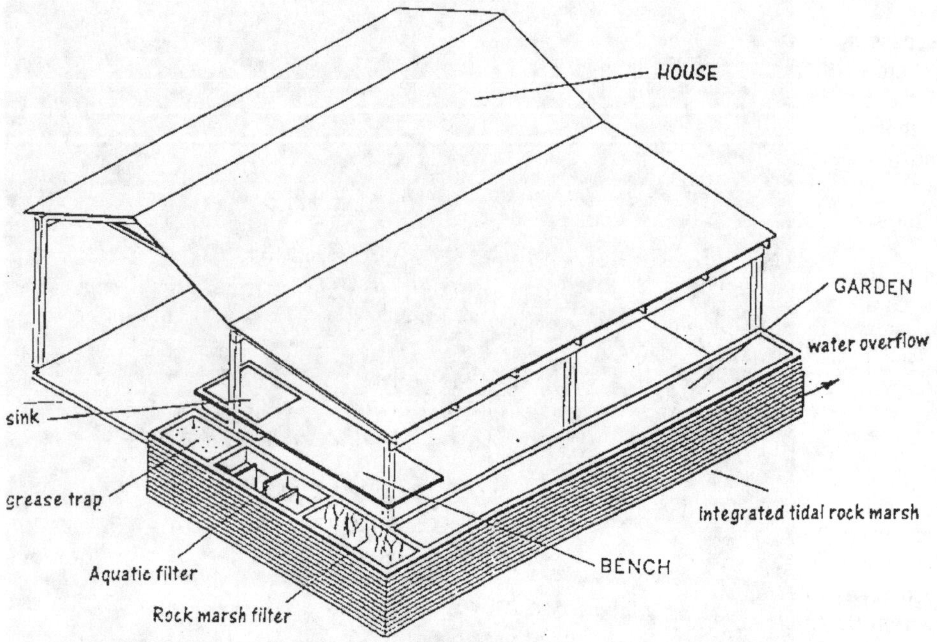

The greywater recycling system at Beelerong.

As well as oxygenating the water, for some reason flow forms improve water quality so that plants irrigated with this water are healthier.

Flow forms are widely used in agriculture to prepare fertiliser and biodynamic preparations, and to purify effluent from dairy farms and piggeries. Because of the purifying effect of the flow forms, this system is used to purify greywater and black water and is also used in swimming pools.

Waste from toilets is widely regarded as a nuisance that must be disposed of as quickly as possible, preferably by transferring it to some else's domain. This is acceptable socially but is diametrically opposed to our concept of sustainability. Normally nutrients in the form of organic matter are consumed and are consequently lost, permanently and irretrievably.

Dry compost toilets have some appeal except that again the nutrients are largely lost.

Normal flushing toilets are costly, owing to the environmental costs of dumping the waste in some remote locality. The water used is lost, often dumped in the sea or a river. With a renewed interest in ecology and man's relationship with the environment, waste-water treatment needs to be re-examined in terms of how it fits into this relationship.

RETURNING UNUSED NUTRIENTS TO THE SOIL

A more sustainable and quite ancient concept is to return the unused nutrients to the land from which they came and to recycle them. To this end, Beelarong Farm installed a Dowmus flushing compost toilet in 2000.

One of the first in Brisbane, it is not connected to the sewer system and recycles 100 per cent of the waste.

It is based on the principle that all organic wastes (including kitchen scraps) are not liabilities but valuable resources. In the warm, moist environment of the bio-reactor, special worms (tiger worms and composting worms) convert the solids into worm castings on a filter bed while liquids pass through the filter. Further flushing dissolves the worm castings, which also go into a trickle bed below.

The addition of biodynamic preparations to the effluent converts it into a highly effective fertiliser.

Bacteria act quickly and compost this liquid, which then passes into a below-ground activated sand filter. A solar pump transfers the emerging cleaned and odourless effluent into a constructed wetland.

Depending on the location and regulations, the treated effluent could also be used for irrigation of trees or lawns, or can be recycled to flush the toilet. Thus the flushing toilet can operate with its own effluent, or use greywater.

RECYCLING WASTE WATER IN THE CITY WITH A CONSTRUCTED WETLAND

From our renewed interest in man's relationship with the environment emerges the need for waste disposal which can integrate society more closely with the natural world, with minimum environmental impact.

The water disposal system at Beelarong copies nature in the form of a constructed wetland, a small area that absorbs the treated effluent. This area was first planted out to native paperbark trees but because of the clay nature of the soil, this quickly became a soggy mess with runoff into the nearby creek.

A species of vetiver grass developed by the Department of Natural Resources was planted and proved successful in absorbing the effluent, drying out the soil, and preventing surfacing. In seven months the grass grew two metres high with roots three metres straight down, and the problems were eliminated. The long blades of the grass transpired the water into the atmosphere. In addition, nutrients such as nitrogen, phosphorus and potassium in the treated effluent were captured and stored in the leaves.

The grass containing the nutrients is slashed and composted, thus returning the nutrients to the soil and completing the cycle of sustainability. Tests showed that the grass absorbed 99.2 per cent of the nitrogen, and similar levels of phosphorous and *E. coli*.

Pollutants, including heavy metals, remain stored in the plant structure, mostly in the roots, preventing possible run-off to the environment.

Swale system

The farm uses a permaculture device of long level ditches, called swales, to capture surface run-off. Water sits in them and slowly penetrates into the soil carrying with it organic nutrients washed in by the rain. Piling up the soil on the downhill side increases the holding capacity of the swales. The water moves slowly downhill at about 10 metres a year, at the same time raising the organic content of the soil. In a short time barren land is converted into moist, rich organic soil.

With almost no evaporation, this is the cheapest and most effective method of storing water. It is also located where it is needed, near the root zone. Any problems with mosquitoes are short-term. As the soil absorbs more organic matter the absorption rate accelerates and soon the water disappears in hours, preventing mosquito infestation.

Disability raised-bed garden

Outside the house another raised-bed garden has been built for older people to access without bending. Disabled people in wheelchairs can tend this garden in the shelter of a shade cloth roof. To make life easier, the plants in this garden are watered automatically using the Brisbane-developed "wetpot" system. Tubes to a water tank connect porous ceramic pots and, as the soil dries out, water oozes through the pots and irrigates the garden. The tank lasts about 14 days and can be filled with a hose. Plants are never over-watered as water will not flow until the soil is dry.

On the farm, nutrients are grown in the form of comfrey, which is used to make liquid manure and supply the needs of the plants. This liquid manure is added to the wetpot tank so that plants get an even flow of nutrients.

Permaculture principles are used throughout. No chemical fertilisers, insecticides, or pesticides are used. Instead, Biodynamics transformed the soil in the first two years into a rich loam full of earthworms requiring little else to grow a wonderful display of food. For a small cost Biodynamics can convert fairly barren soil into rich loam.

No runoff is allowed on the farm. Ditches carry rainwater run-off from gutters in the nearby street and from any flat surface on the farm into the swale system, and weed barriers of lemon grass and comfrey prevent the spread of weeds. Community gardens have been set up so that people can tend their own garden and grow fresh vegetables and flowers.

Tips

KEEPING IT CLEAN

Don't throw cigarette butts or any litter onto the road. Anything that floats will end up in rivers or on beaches.

When building or renovating, make sure sand and other materials are kept away from stormwater drains and gutters.

Wash your car on the lawn, not in the street where detergents can go down stormwater drains.

Use a broom to clean driveways and footpaths and put the dirt in the compost or your own back yard. Don't hose it into the gutter.

Do not wash, sweep or deposit dog or other animal droppings into the gutter or stormwater system. Put them into a rubbish bin.

When you are gardening, use leaves and lawn clippings for compost. Don't hose or sweep into the gutter.

Fix oil and radiator leaks on your car so that these substances don't wash into our waterways.

At the lower end of the farm is a creek frontage, and a tidal lagoon contains a wetland area with a stand of mangroves.

Visitors tend community gardens to grow their own herbs and vegetables, and regular courses are held on permaculture, solar cooking, no-dig gardening, camp cooking, use of herbs, and portable gardening.

Picnic facilities are available for visitors in this delightful setting.

See the Beelarong website on <www.beelarongfarm.org.au>.

Clean water from your roof

Inventor Kevin Sims has devised a cheap and effective new method for making tank water free of contaminants.

BY MARTIN HIRSCH, *POMONA, QUEENSLAND*

AS TOWN water supplies become more expensive, an increasing number of householders have turned to rainwater tanks, either as a standby measure or to supply drinking water. In rural areas, residents use tank water for all needs, conserving it when rains are scarce.

Many city dwellers have rainwater tanks by choice, wanting to avoid reticulated water additives such as chlorine or fluoride. But every rainwater consumer has one common concern and that is how to keep the supply free of contaminants.

Pollutants are widespread and can enter the water supply at different points, the most common being dust from the roads, animal droppings and tree litter which all settle on the roof before being washed into the system. The less visible pollutants include spray drift, paint and metal particles from older roofs, and organisms breeding in depressions and recesses of guttering, pipes and "ground-to-head" feeder pipes where large quantities of water accumulate, sometimes for months.

To ensure a water supply that is as clean as possible, Noosa hinterland inventor and honorary ranger, Kevin Sims, has experimented with a host of diversion systems and has finally come up with a device that is well worth purchasing the parts for and either installing them yourself or getting a qualified plumber to connect them in less than a couple of hours.

The system, which Kevin termed "Flushamatic", is certain to remove the bulk of all contaminants from roof-collected water. Even if all components are bought new, the maximum outlay would amount to $50, but using some second-hand parts, like a tap in reasonable condition, can cut your costs in half.

Most hardware stores or plumbing supplies merchants will stock the following (all 90 mm diameter): a length of stormwater pipe, three elbows, a coupler which is threaded at one end, a screw-on cap, a T-piece with inspection cover opposite the "T", a one-inch ball valve tap, a length of non-stretch nylon or steel line and one pulley.

At 57 years of age, Kevin has found many ways to help the planet. Flushamatic evolved very gradually from a brainstorm about four years ago when he became frustrated at having to empty the sediment at the bottom of water tanks. Sounds familiar, does it not? That black sludge at the bottom, where does it come from?

"I was also concerned about the aerial spraying and industrial pollutants. The council-supplied reticulated water did not come up to my expectations," Kevin said. He did look at commercially produced filtration systems too. "But they were too expensive for me".

Foremost in his mind was the desire to catch as many pollutants as possible before they enter the tank.

"The idea has been all along that when you get the first rains, it washes the roof clean, enters the diverter section and automatically runs away," Kevin explained. Kevin's Flushamatic, for which he has no commercial goals, works well in all but the most extreme conditions such as heavily clogged guttering.

The way he described the installation, it sounded like child's play, although I would expect some first-time DIY's to struggle with one or another part. Having seen the system in full flow, it seems $50 well spent, considering that at the end of it one has quality drinking water.

So here it is: you will need two hessian bags (potato sacks are fine), a length of nylon or steel line, which is connected over a pulley (see Figure 1). When the bags are dry and light, the tap is in the "on" position. Once the rain arrives, the bags get progressively heavier and their combined weight pulls the tap shut.

To assemble the diverter system, follow Figure 2. Once you get to the end cap, drill a hole for the tap and secure well, ideally with a 25 mm (one inch) nut on the other side against a washer. Kevin recommended proper pipe adhesive for a tight seal at all joints.

Any clogging can be prevented by installing an optional mesh-filter into the down-pipe of the T-piece nearest the top of the tank. However, Kevin's best advice was to service the tap end regularly, making sure it operates smoothly and there are no obstructions in the tap itself. (A frog caught at one time in his system defeated the engineering ideals but these incidents are rare).

To get the necessary leverage on the tap, the handle has to be extended with a flat, 40 cm piece of steel.

You need to drill holes at short intervals to help you set the appropriate point at which the tap shuts off completely, thus allowing all water to then empty into the tank. In clean environments early shut-off can be set by connecting the string to the extreme end of the handle, whereas in polluted areas more water needs to be "wasted" to wash the roof clean by attaching the line closer to the tap itself.

It is with this section of the device that you need to exercise some trial and error but, after two sessions, protected by raincoat or umbrella, your system should give you trouble-free operation.

Very few people in this area have spoken of lack of rainwater lately and many have filled their tanks many times over. But seasons change. Rainwater – all water – is precious, and sensible use is better than picking up the telephone to order some in.

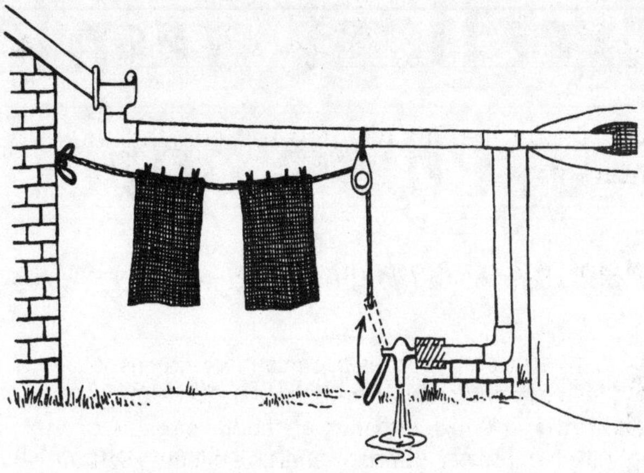

Figure 1: as the hessian sacks get heavier with rain, they shut the tap.

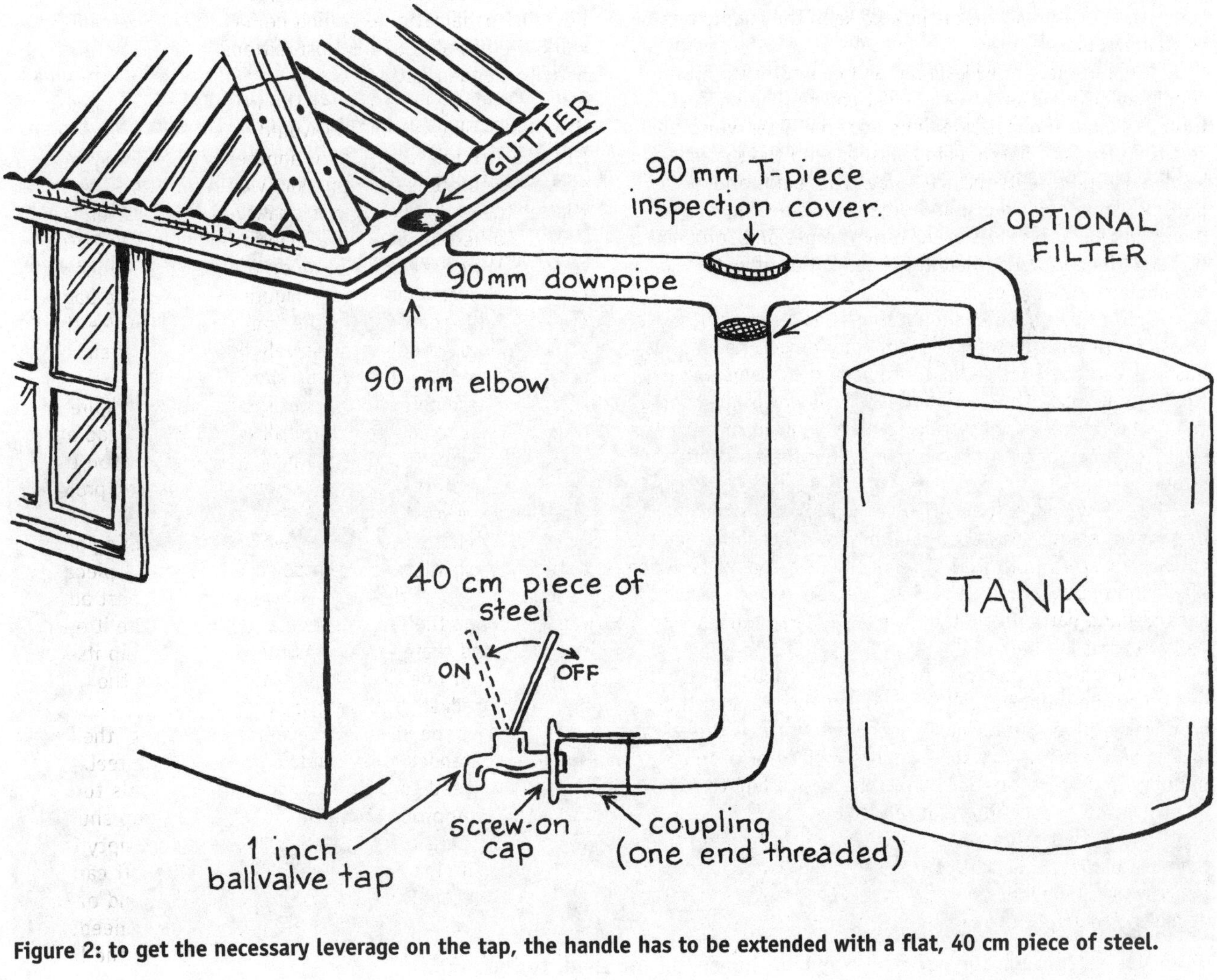

Figure 2: to get the necessary leverage on the tap, the handle has to be extended with a flat, 40 cm piece of steel.

Excellent drinking water from a useless bore

Pam and Herman tell of their relatively inexpensive solution to the problem they had with their salty bore.

BY PAM *AND* HERMAN ODIJK, *CABOOLTURE, QUEENSLAND*

WE ARE NOW drinking the water from our bore, which was once classified as useless. Our water supply now tests 98 per cent pure and costs only 0.0032 cents a litre to produce! And all thanks to our state-of-the-art reverse osmosis water purification plant.

The salt content of our original bore supply was 4,100 TDS – two-thirds that of sea water! As well it had unacceptably high levels of other elements. For example, the magnesium content was 680 mgL while the desirable upper limit is 120 mgL. The chloride reading was 2,840 mgL compared to a desirable upper limit of 350 mgL; hardness ($CaCO_3$) was determined at 4850 mgL while the desirable upper limit is 300 mgL. No wonder that the comment made at the university laboratory at the time of testing was that our water sample was the "worst ever seen in this area."

INVESTIGATING THE TECHNOLOGY

When the worst drought this century saw to it that our dams and tanks were empty and the freshwater well began to dry out, we decided to investigate water purification technology. Our only remaining good supply was our "useless" bore. We thought it was better to see if a seemingly reliable water supply could be purified, rather than spend money searching, perhaps in vain, for another underground supply which in turn might be similarly useless. After all, we only had 14 acres on which to look and most of that was established orchard!

Desalination of saline or brackish water for domestic and industrial use is currently employed in some sixty locations throughout Australia, in plants whose capacities range up to 2,000 m3/d and use any of three methods – RO (reverse osmosis), MSF (multiple stage flash) and VTE (vertical tube evaporation). Desalination of brackish water

Water passes through the purification plant, housed in the shed, to the tank.

promises to become an even more attractive proposition, particularly for large-scale urban settlements, with the development of the CSIRO Sirotherm process.

Apart from desalination, we also needed to remove the extraordinarily high magnesium content. Magnesium is removed from water by ion exchange, which can be done in two ways. Water can be softened by passing it through a column filled with small porous beads that have positively- and negatively-charged sodium ions bound to their internal and external surfaces. As water flows through, a reaction takes place whereby the sodium ions replace the magnesium and calcium ions, and the magnesium and calcium is "exchanged" for the sodium. The alternative ion-exchange process is called mixed-bed ion exchange. This does not add sodium. Instead, the beads are charged with hydrogen and hydrogen ions, resulting in very clean water indeed.

WHAT IS REVERSE OSMOSIS?

RO has well passed its fiftieth birthday. The process was developed by the Indian scientist Sourirajan at the University of California in the early 1950s. It was considered to be such a breakthrough in the desalination of seawater that over $30 million was spent on research and development by the US Department of the Interior. Today the RO process is used wherever there is a need to separate efficiently and economically almost any dissolved substance from water for any purpose at all. The process finds diverse uses from kidney dialysis to metal recovery and pollution control.

It is a simple process and works by forcing water, under pressure, through a special synthetic material called a semipermeable membrane. The membrane attracts water molecules and repels dissolved impurities – even those smaller than the water molecules themselves. The RO membrane is also the ultimate mechanical filter capable of straining out virtually all particle matter, turbidity, micro-organisms, asbestos, even single molecules of heavier organic compounds. The pores of the filter are in the order of 0.0005 microns, making it smaller than that which can be seen by the best optical microscope.

The efficiency of RO systems depend on both the pressure and temperature of the water being used and, typically, it produces water at a slow rate. However, the RO membrane passes oxygen so well that the final result does not even have the flat taste of boiled or distilled water.

PURE WATER WITHIN THREE WEEKS

Having decided on an RO system, we sent the laboratory analysis of our water sample to the Brisbane firm who manufactures and installs these plants. Each water purification plant is built to suit a specific water supply, and is not interchangeable, which means it remains a fixture on your property and you can't take it with you when you leave. It will not suit any other bore or supply. The cost of the plant depends on the amount of water that is needed, and the quality of the water to be treated – in our case, removing the magnesium was the most expensive component. Having the salt removed is relatively inexpensive. The firm we chose was able to give us a quote within a matter of days.

Three weeks later, which barely gave us time to prepare everything, the technician was on his way to install, start up, and test the plant personally. We were also given full instructions on plant operation and emergency procedures should the occasion arise.

Tips

KEEPING IT CLEAN (cont'd)

Use house cleaning products which are low in phosphorus. High phosphorus levels in streams are another major cause of blue-green algal blooms.

Your toilet is not a garbage bin. Do not dispose of tissues, cotton buds, tampons, sanitary napkins, or other undesirable objects in the toilet.

Place used cooking oils in a jar or carton and put it in the garbage bin. Household cooking oils poured into the sink can clog pipes, and can pollute our waterways.

Take used motor oil to a service station that advertises collection for recycling. Your local council can tell you where motor oil can be disposed of. A single litre of motor oil down the drain can pollute 9500 litres of water.

Never pour leftover paints or solvents down the sink or drain. Place used solvents in a tin or jar and stuff with newspaper before resealing. Ask your local council about arrangement for collection of all hazardous waste.

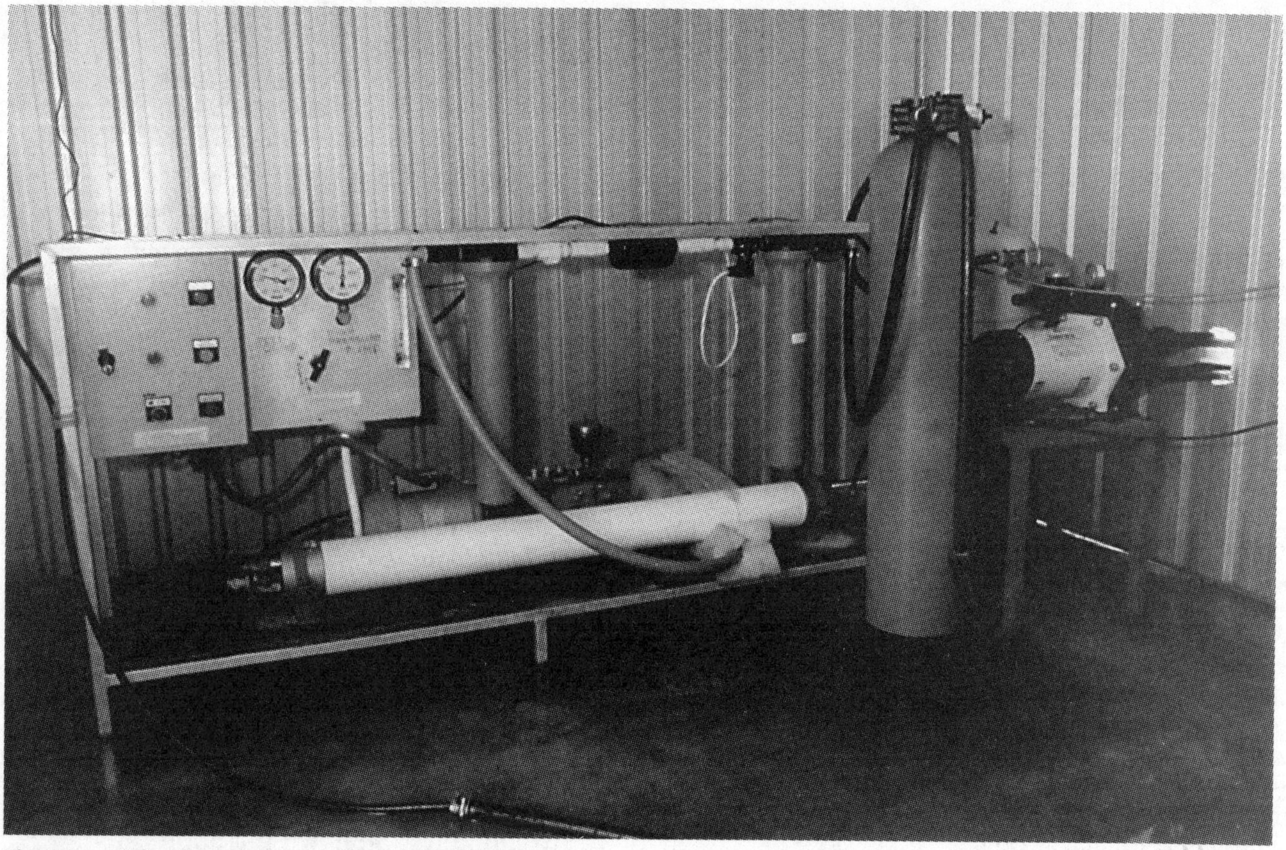

The RO purification plant with pumps and filters.

EFFICIENCY AND NOISE

Our water purification plant (removing both salt and magnesium) produces 7,200 litres (1,600 gallons) a day of almost (98 per cent) pure water from a bore 20 metres (60 feet) deep, delivering a 2,275 litre (500 gallon) an hour flow (of unusable water) via an electric pump. Since we have been actively using the bore flow, this has slightly increased. To accommodate our purification plant, we had a large concrete slab set down on which we placed a (second-hand) prefabricated shed.

This shed houses the plant and the electric pump which pumps water from the bore to the plant. We recently interposed a silver nitrate impregnated charcoal filter between the pressure vessel and the RO plant so the filters in the plant itself need to be changed less often. This filter can be cleaned by back washing.

The pure water passes from the plant to a 22,000-litre (5,000 gallon) concrete tank adjacent to the shed, from where it is pumped, via a smaller electric pump, either to the orchard irrigation tank or direct to the house tanks. The plant need only run when water is required.

We use electric pumps as they are far more economical than petrol driven ones and considerably quieter. Any noise from the plant itself can be muffled by using three or four old mattresses around the walls of the shed.

MATERIALS

Our plant required the following materials and equipment:

Concrete tank, 5,000 gallons (includes delivery and installation)

Levelling of site and laying 12ft x 24ft concrete slab

Prefabricated shed (second-hand)

Water purification plant (desalination & removal of magnesium)

Pressure tank

Electrician's charges for power point on pole, underground cable and installations inside shed (power points, etc)

Tips

KEEPING IT CLEAN (cont'd)

Don't over-use garden fertilisers or chemicals and don't use them near drains or watercourses. Especially avoid using them during windy conditions or when rain is forecast.

When you are walking your dog, make sure that you carry a plastic bag or a "pooper-scooper" to pick up your dog's droppings.

Don't wash equipment, tools or paintbrushes where the wastewater will run into stormwater drains.

Make sure swimming pools are backwashed into the sewer, not the stormwater drain.

Plant native plants that use less water and don't drop as many leaves that pollute waterways.

If you own a farm, fence waterways to prevent livestock from polluting water and eroding banks and creek beds.

Get involved with community groups to share ideas about increasing water quality and reducing pollution.

Use less fertilisers and pesticides on lawns and gardens. These can seep into groundwater or get washed into your local waterways. Nutrients from fertilisers are a major cause of blue-green algae, while high levels of pesticides in our waterways can result in the death of fish and other marine life.

Protect the banks of streams and rivers and the vegetation growing on them. Don't allow vehicles or animals to disturb and degrade them. Always leave a buffer of vegetation to act as filter for soil, nutrients and other pollutants.

Silver nitrate impregnated charcoal filter
(The pumps we already owned and used on the property)

Our cost per litre worked out at 0.0032 cents including costs of electricity and membrane cleaning materials.

GAINS

With our water supply problems solved, we also gained five extra bonuses.

First, with such high water quality, fertiliser efficiency is increased. We use organic fertiliser that is water soluble and is dispersed via our drip irrigation system. The frequency and rate of application is now reduced, resulting in a substantial cost saving. Everything has undergone extraordinary growth since this purer water has been used.

Second, the freshwater well, which, along with rainwater tanks, previously supplied the house, is now able to be given over to irrigating another part of the property which previously had to rely solely on rainfall. The quality of the water in the freshwater well, being naturally sand filtered is very sweet and drinkable, but inferior to the water produced by the RO plant.

Third, because of its use in primary production, (we grow macadamias, pecans, mangoes, paw paws and asparagus) the purchase attracts a tax depreciation over three years.

Fourth, the value of the property has substantially increased as it now has a permanent pure water supply instead of a seasonal one.

Fifth, as the water is so pure, we would be able to bottle and retail it if we wanted an extra sideline income.

Flushing gutters to maintain water quality

How do you clean out the gutters collecting rainwater for your tank without flushing the leaves and dirt into the tank? Read on . . .

BY JOHN CAREY, *PORT WILLUNGA, SOUTH AUSTRALIA*

HAVING lived in houses built for other people all our lives, we decided to design our own home that would be environmentally-friendly, efficient and economical. The house was evaluated by Adelaide University last year and given a five star rating.

Being on a narrow 15 metre-wide block we decided to install a 22,000-litre (5000 gallon) underground concrete tank to store rainwater for the house water supply. We used the mains supply for the garden.

We have used rainwater exclusively at several locations during our life, and thought that in this case we would take care to maintain water quality. We decided that gutters should be cleaned out and washed quarterly, and to install a double filtration system in the kitchen for fresh drinking water.

The problem arose as to how gutters could be cleaned regularly without letting roof dirt into the underground tank. We were unable to find any standard system that would meet our requirements, as all the collection pipes are below ground level and there are eight downpipes feeding water into the collecting system.

We installed a simple "T" arrangement on each downpipe. The "T" is installed at a level so a wheelbarrow can be put under it. A screw cap is fitted under normal conditions. When the gutters are being cleaned the screw cap is removed and a sealed wooden disc is inserted to seat on the bottom section of pipe and to stop any flow into the collection pipe system. Any leaves and dirt are collected in the barrow.

The system works well and when we made a check and cleaned out the tank after three years there was little sediment in the bottom of the tank.

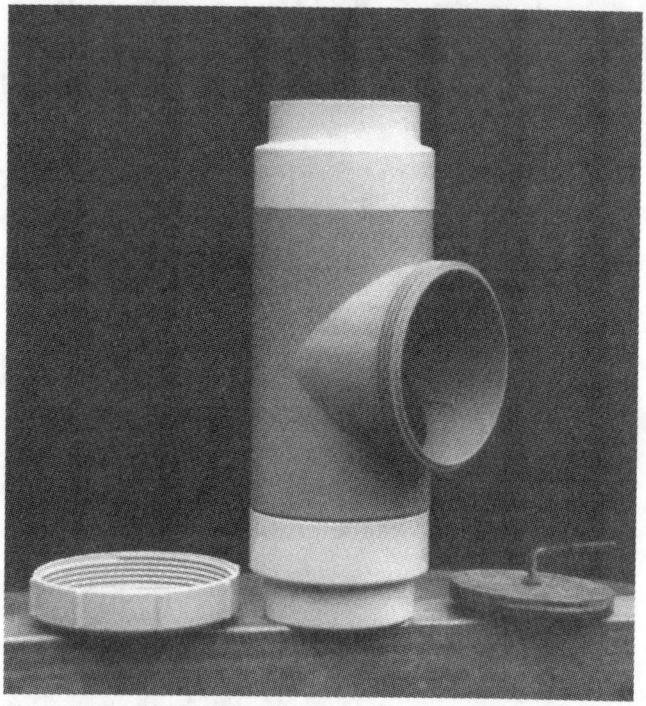

The components of the system.

The flushing system in operation.

Purify products

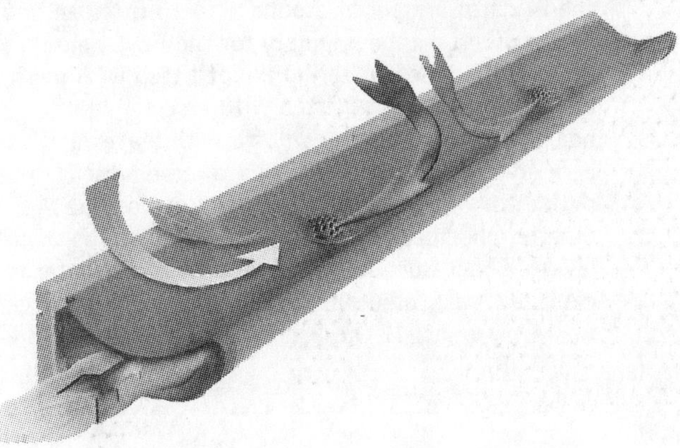

POLLUTION-FREE RAINWATER

EnviroFLO Rainwater Systems eliminate up to 99 per cent of debris and pollutants from rainwater. It is billed as "the world's first complete rainwater system", and includes a self-cleaning gutter that eliminates debris and plant growth build-up and pest accumulation. In the well-known book *The Sustainable House* environmentalist Michael Mobbs chose EnviroFLO Guttering (formerly known as Smartflo) over all other systems. He reported that it excluded almost all bird droppings, leaves and heavy metals from drinking water. This is because EnviroFLO guttering is a self-cleaning, fully enclosed or covered gutter. Michael points out that traditional U-shaped Australian guttering is open to the weather and therefore is an ideal trap to capture and store bird droppings, leaves and heavy metals. EnviroFLO Guttering is designed and made in Australia from ColorBond. For more details phone 1800 642 339, or visit the website: <www.enviroflo.com.au>.

SAFERAIN

Most people on rainwater realise that every time it rains, unwanted materials such as dust, salt, soot and bird droppings get washed into the tank. These pollutants are washed in by the first portion of normal rain or by light rain and heavy dew. If your feeder pipes are above ground then by fitting either a vertical or horizontal SafeRain these pollutants will automatically be diverted away from your drinking water. If your feeder pipes are below ground, stagnant water lying in underground pipes can putrefy due to condensation and light rain washing dust and other pollutants from the roof down into the lowest point in the system. When rain starts the tainted water is the first to move, followed by the sludge. As the rainfall increases water moves faster through the pipe(s) pushing the sludge through to your tank. A SafeRain Reverse-Flow unit will dump this initial water away from the tank until the pre-set flow rate point is reached. A flow rate between 10 and 20 litres a minute is sufficient. The unit shuts and the clean water is diverted to the tank. SafeRain will reset after rain ceases. The straight-through design of SafeRain ensures no back pressure problems in heavy rainfall. Remember, if the stagnant water that lies in your underground pipes enters your tank it can foul the water making it completely undrinkable.

The vertical diversion valve is installed at the "L" shape in the tank feeding downpipe. It has an internal stainless steel leaf screen, is easy to install, will shut and reset automatically. Contact SafeRain at PO Box 298, Blackburn, Vic., 3130. Ph: (03) 9894 3302, email: <saferain@hotmail.com>.

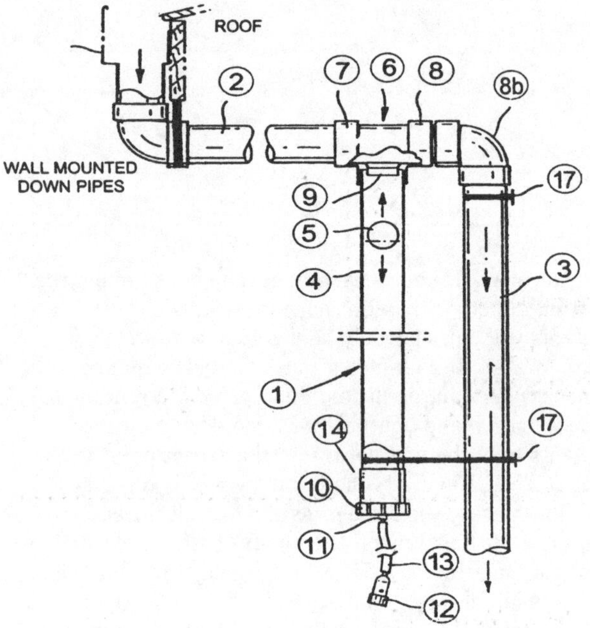

1. Diverter Chamber
2. Infeed from the roof
3. To the tank
4. Diverter Chamber
5. Sealing Ball
6. Tee Junction
7. Chamber Inlet
8. Chamber Outlet
8b. Elbow
9. Ball Seat
10. Screw Cap
11. Drip Outlet
12. Drip Irrigator
13. Irrigator Hose
14. Socket
15. Primary Screen
16. Stainless Steel Filter Screen
17. Pipe/Wall Bracket

LEAF BEATER SYSTEMS

Leaf Beater (left) is another water diverter, or first flush device, which diverts contaminated water to the garden. As a rule of thumb, one litre of water diverted for every ten square metres of roof area will get rid of the most contaminated water. The more water diverted the better the quality of water. When it rains, water slowly builds up in the roof guttering system before it exits the downpipe. At this time the water is saturated with all the nasties and as it exits the downpipe it flows into the diverter tube. As the water rises in the tube so does a ball until it seals off on the seat. This captures the polluted water in the diverter tube preventing it from entering the tank. Fresh water is then automatically diverted to the tank.

The diverter chamber empties itself through the irrigator dripper at around 1 to 10 litres an hour so the diverter tube is empty for the next time it rains. If the roof guttering is not fitted with mesh, or if the outlet is not fitted with a screened rain head, the water diverter will fill with leaves and debris very quickly. It will have to be emptied periodically by unscrewing the end cap on the diverter chamber. In some states of Australia it is law that first flush devices be fitted where water is captured and stored in tanks. Manufactured by Leaf Beater Systems, 12 Old Pacific Highway, Oxonford, Qld, 4210.

NVIRO PIT

This device (right) is designed to prevent stormwater pollution in surface water drainage systems. The pit has a collection basket that is easily removed for cleaning.

Rein Plastics, 14 Williamson Road, Ingleburn, NSW 2565. Ph: (02) 9605 9999.

TANKSACK STRAINER/FILTER

The Tanksack is an "in tank" water filter. The shape of the Tanksack filter bag encourages solids that are filtered out of the water to fill the bag from the bottom, thus preventing premature blocking. The shape also allows the maximum possible flow rate as the water level in the tank rises, and permits the bag to be turned inside out for easy cleaning.

The Tanksack can remove virtually all visible solids and particulates from the water, so the water has a crystal clear sparkling appearance. The rubbish the Tanksack catches is the rubbish you and your family would be drinking if you did not have a Tanksack. The Tanksack unit fits into the top of the tank in place of the standard strainer. The Tanksack is available from Tankworld, 135 Karinie Street, Swan Hill, Vic, 3585.

AQUA-PURE SHOWER FILTER

This filter is designed to reduce chlorine, odours and dirt from shower water and comes with a water saver control that limits water flow. Replaceable filter cartridges last between six and twelve months under normal use. The filter can be installed at the wall or shower rose.

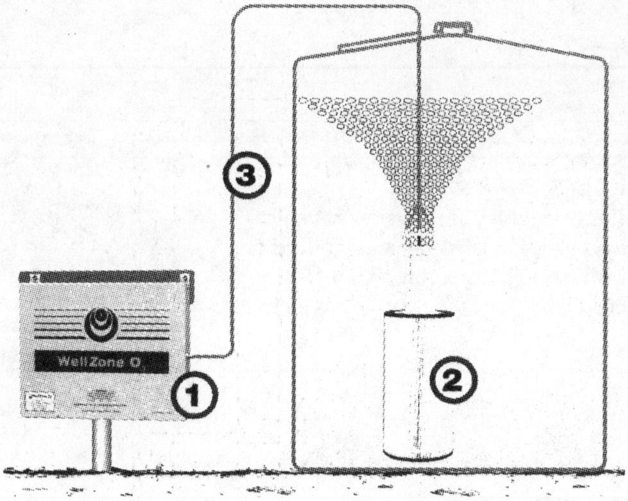

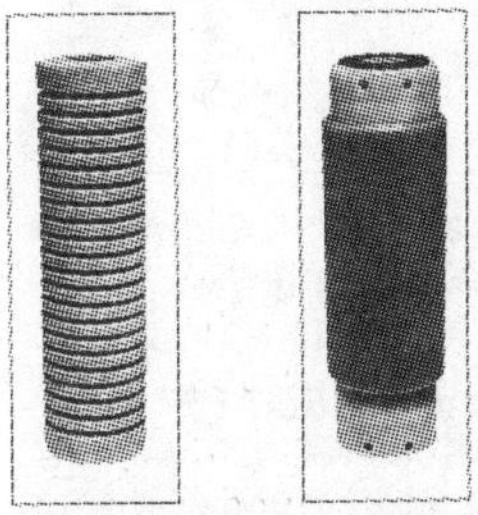

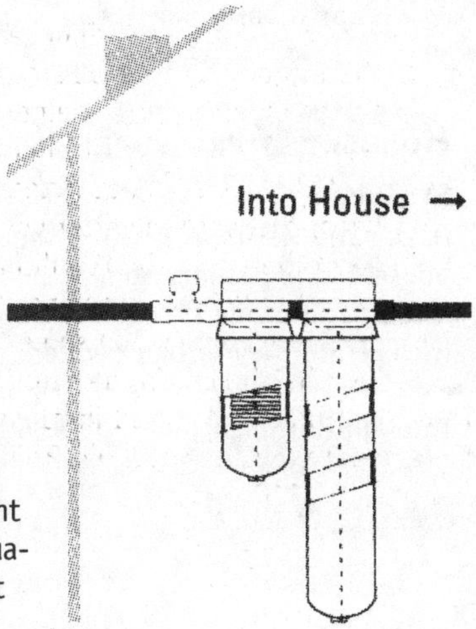

AQUA-PURE FILTERS

Graded density replacement cartridges used in the Aqua-Pure system. Left to right above: dirt and rust cartridge, taste and odour cartridge.

The system is installed on the main water prior to entering the house. Ph: (02) 9671 3700, (03) 9329 9997, (07) 3865 1955, (08) 9478 4488.

THE WELLZONE 03

This system (above) is designed to purify and treat water continuously in a holding tank or reservoir. The system consists of an electrical ozone generator and a filter module with an ozone diffuser submerged in the tank water. Pressurised ozone and air is produced by pumping air through a high-intensity ultraviolet light chamber, which is then fed to the diffuser through an ozone feed tube. The system continuously purifies, filters and circulates the entire water content of the holding tank at a rate of over 2500 litres an hour. Ozone technology is used to purify and condition the water, destroy contaminants, reduce scale build-up and neutralise pH.

PURE-TEC FILTERS.

Another in-line filter system, with units to fit under sink or hand basin or onto tanks. Available through Polymaster. Ph: 1800 062 064.

HEDGEHOG GUTTER PROTECTION SYSTEM

Produced in one-metre lengths and is made of polypropylene bristles containing an ultraviolet inhibitor for long life. Water flows through the bristles even when there are leaves on them. Ph 1800 288 747, web: <www.thehedgehog.com.au>

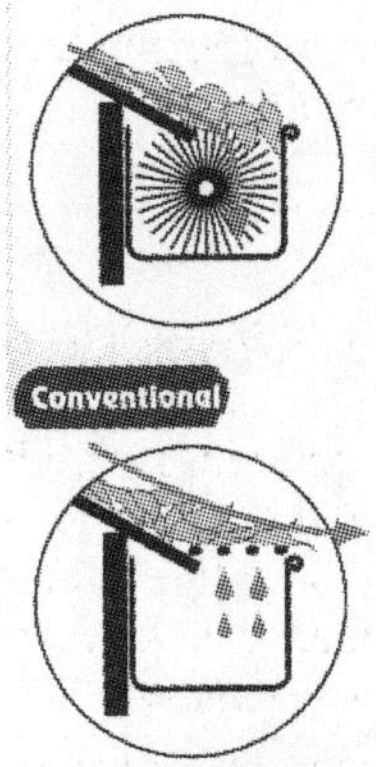

BLUE MOUNTAIN MESH

Gutter mesh systems designed to prevent leaves entering the guttering. Further information: ph 1800 067 744 or web: <www.rainharvesting.com.au>

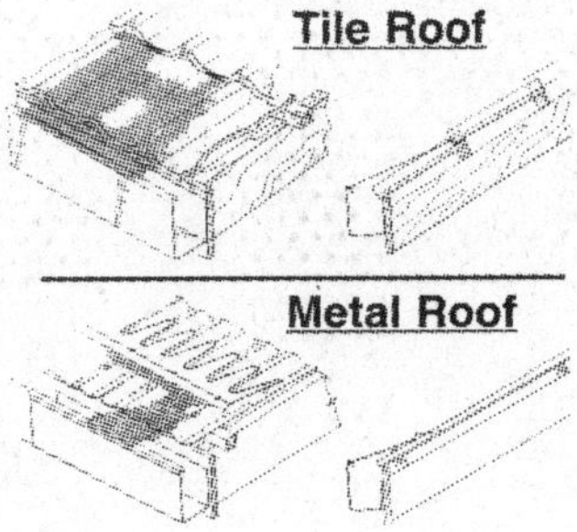

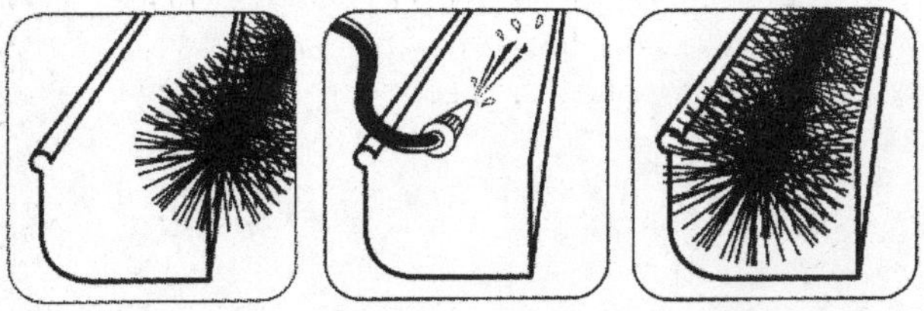

POLYMASTER FFWD

This first flush water diverter fits onto the outside of most tanks. It collects the first 60 litres of run-off. Ph 1800 062 064.

ANTI BIO TECHNOLOGY

Anti Bio Technology is a system which emits sound frequencies to control parasite and virus contamination in water. The System uses electro magnetics, and sweeping sound frequency waves, to purify water, making it cleaner and clearer. The System is currently in use in commercial swimming pools. For further information see web site <www.antibio.com.au>.

THE KATHRO RAINCATCHER

DRINKING WATER SYSTEM

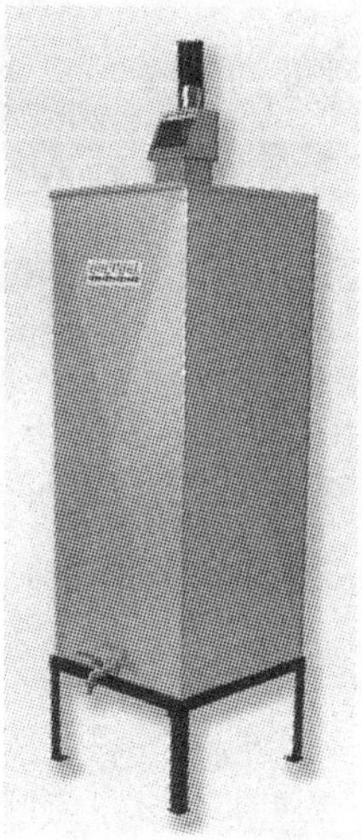

Incorporates a specially designed filter system to flush away the first rainfall so that the tank fills with clean water. The whole unit is made from stainless steel, resisting corrosion, staining and algae growth. Ph (03) 9706 6700, web: <www.harttohart.com.au>

HOUSEHOLD PRESSURE SYSTEMS

Davey and Marina are two of the companies producing household pressure systems. Pumps come in different sizes, can include fire-fighting ability and can be used with clean, grey or black water. Davey ph 1300 367 866, web: <www.davey.com.au>. Marina products are available through Bushman Tanks, ph 1800 008 888.

3

Conserve

A flourishing urban low-water garden

If you are faced with an unprepossessing garden and poor soil, and you want to reduce watering to a minimum, you needn't despair, as Liz discovered.

BY LIZ INGHAM, *YARRAVILLE, VICTORIA*

HERE IN Yarraville, in Melbourne's industrial inner west, gardens are "cottage style". Picket fences, standard roses, lavender, daffs, annuals with big glossy labels, and cumquats in terracotta pots. Front gardens have either a weeping tree with a spindly trunk clamped to a stake, or a silver birch. Back gardens are either an "outdoor room" with mondo grass, square pavers and little hedges (for yuppies) or a Hills hoist with patchy lawn and narrow garden beds (everyone else). Nature strips boast a tree-the-council-put-there with whipper-snipper marks around its ankles.

English cottage gardens made sense in olde Englande, where people chose the prettiest flowers from the surrounding fields and cultivated them. But why here? Why their wildflowers?

When we first moved here, our garden was tragic. Wall-to-wall couch grass, I'm afraid, with ivy pulling down the back fence, a pod of three silver birches out front and a bump on the nature strip where the tree used to be. Its saving grace was a grapevine growing over the shed. Hmm, a blank canvas ...

WHAT TO GROW

We considered a Jackie French-style garden with trellises, hanging baskets, nice messy beds and a wombat. Or a Jillaroo garden with old-style wooden gates, chooks in the orchard, ingenious things made of old inner tubes and a forest campaign. Then we went down the local creek and had a think. The local organic shop could feed us, but where did frogs, skinks, birds and lizards eat, since their homes were razed to build our suburb? Could we justify using Upper Thomson Catchment (hundreds of kilometres away) water to grow vegies? We decided to plant only indigenous plants – that is, those sourced from within five kilometres or so of our house.

It's been a fascinating journey. For a start, the lovely Trevor mattocked out all the couch grass by hand. And can I tell you, he found not one earth worm; just an inch of dust over potter's clay. The silver birches went to a neighbour, but after a quick conference, we decided the grapevine is actually native to Melbourne!

Next, a mate built us a 1,300-litre water tank, which we calculated would fill up on average once a week (in reality it's full or empty for months on end). Our rainwater was tested as safe to drink, despite our polluted location. As the garden now needs hardly any water, we've plumbed the water tank into the laundry, and use it for more interesting things, like home-brew. Later, Trevor linked three old hot water services together for additional rainwater storage.

THE FROG POND

After a few weekends of scraping pure clay off our boots, we decided not to bother lining the frog pond. It's held water for four years, though lately, now the trees are tall, it's beginning to leak a bit. We "seeded" the pond mud with mud from the nearby creek, and it was soon alive and kicking. These days there are dragonflies breeding in there, and their mud-eye larvae chomp everything that wriggles. You know, you don't need goldfish to eat mozzie larvae. Mozzies breed in blocked gutters and the like, not healthy frog ponds.

The garden looked pretty funny at first. It was a sea of mulch, and the dormant plants also looked exactly like mulch, only vertical. We had garden parties anyhow. I can't imagine what people thought. Stocking a new garden can be expensive, so it pays to propagate. Two jars of wallaby grass seed made half of the new garden, and were gradually replaced with other plants as funds permitted.

Many flowers need to be replaced every year or two, but can be grown from saved seed or cuttings. For example, all our golden billy-buttons come from a single plant purchased years ago. They can be struck by shoving cuttings straight into the ground at the winter solstice. All our common billy-button seed came from a bunch of flowers I gave my friend Riley when he was born.

Dozens of blue devils will grow from a single flower head; I discovered this from using their spiky seed casings as snail guards around little chocolate lilies (which also grow from seed). Cut-leaf daisies layer themselves in the mulch – rooted sections can be transplanted. Spreading

Tips

Advice for irrigation system design
Hand-watering too lightly and too frequently will result in shallow root systems and – in hot, dry periods – stressed plants. You can use water more effectively by installing an irrigation system.

Choose a water source
Most irrigation systems are supplied from the mains but you can use recycled bath, shower and laundry waste-water on established gardens, but not on edible plants or vegetables.

Measure water flow and pressure
To choose the correct pipes, sprinklers and spray patterns you need to know water flow and water pressure.

Select sprinkler heads
Sprinkler types are made to match garden conditions, and include adjustable, mechanical, spray, drip, bubbler, pop-up, and impact sprinklers.

Set time controls
Irrigation systems can use large amounts of water – use an adjustable timer that is programmed to turn the sprinklers on and off.

Select water-wise plants
Native plants are a good choice, but they should be indigenous to your area. For instance, rainforest plants are not well suited to the Canberra climate.

Avoid over-planting to ensure the water in the soil is well-utilised, reduce lawn and avoid planting large trees to save water.

lilies spread. Bog plants can usually be divided. Most grasses, bulbine lilies and native flax self-seed; you just have to transplant them, and so on.

Our flourishing garden makes us look skilled – but we aren't. We simply put plants into exactly the conditions they want to grow in, with the amount of sun and rain and the right soil structure to wriggle their roots into following thousands of years of evolution in exactly that area. We don't fight nature. When grasses began to rot in one spot, we planted cuttings from the bog garden instead. They took off. In dry spots we stick to grasses, shrubs or trees, and grow flowers everywhere else.

I've read well-meaning articles about "water-wise" gardening that say indigenous gardens only need to be watered in, then never touched again. This may be true, but if you don't water at all, everything will bolt to seed during a dry spring. Tank water augments the spring and autumn rains, prolongs flowering and shortens the summer dormancy.

The first frog

Our first frog moved in a month or so after we began the garden. We don't know where it came from: it just appeared in the shady front garden when it rained. I put a tray of water under the tap nearby, and sometimes it would swim there. Later that spring, we heard the first frog call. It was just passing through – we heard it at the neighbours' before and after. Even so, we sat on the back step and listened to it for ages, willing it to stay.

Four years later, it's difficult to imagine the garden was ever bare or new. We gather armloads of bottle-brush and wattle flowers, reeds and gum leaves for inside. We plant homemade seedlings into deep rich soil, teeming with bugs and worms. Grass inflorescences sway in the breeze. Birds have moved in to the tallest trees, and the frogs are here to stay.

We'll occasionally disturb a hibernating frog in winter, beneath the rotting fringes of a poa, or in the nardoo around the pond. In summer, pobble-bonk and striped marsh frogs call all day and all night, sometimes in plain sight. One humid night last summer there were two frogs on the garden path, one in the gully trap, two calling from the pond and one calling from under a cushion-bush! They've become part of our lives, but we'll never take them for granted.

Footnote: Flora for Fauna

Flora for Fauna is a new federal project aimed at inspiring people in urban areas to act to support their local environment. Flora for Fauna will show families, schools and other groups how they can change their own garden (and the way they garden) to attract wildlife using appropriate Australian plants. For more details contact the Nursery & Garden Industry <www.ngia.com.au> or <www.floraforfauna.com.au>.

Xeriscape gardening

HOW TO DESIGN FOR WATER-EFFICIENCY

The principles of xeriscape gardening can be used to save water in new and established gardens. Xeriscape is an American term derived from the Greek word *xeros*, meaning dry, and landscape – a dry landscape garden.

The seven xeriscape principles are:

1. PLANNING AND DESIGN
Practical design in xeriscape gardening should include the layout of garden and entertainment areas and the need for lawn areas. Avoid the temptation to have lawn over most of the garden.

2. SOIL KNOWLEDGE
Improve soil by adding organic material, compost, manure, chopped lucerne or sawdust.

3. CHOICE OF PLANTS
Choose plants for a purpose, such as privacy or shade. Group plants that have similar water needs. Where possible use native plants and shrubs that often need less water than exotics.

4. PRACTICAL LAWN AREAS
Plan lawn areas to match recreational needs and for landscape presentation. Aerate or core the lawn in spring or early autumn. De-thatch the lawn each spring. Keep the lawn long, cutting it no shorter than four centimetres.

5. WATERING
The time and length of watering depend on the soil and plant types in the garden. Watering should be done when it is cooler and there is little wind.

6. MULCHES
Mulch suppresses weed growth, reduces evaporation and run-off, and keeps the soil cool in summer.

7. MAINTENANCE
Weeding, pruning and adjusting irrigation systems help reduce water demand.

Visit the ActewAGL Xeriscape Gardens at Heysen Street, Weston, Canberra every weekend from September to April to learn more about water-efficient garden design.

Dry is beautiful in a water-saving garden.

Smart water management

HOW TO RETAIN 80 PER CENT MORE WATER

Jenny Allen is the author of *Paradise In Your Garden: Smart Permaculture Design*. In this article Jenny describes her own water management plan and the principles it was based upon. She shows how to create your own plan and use the techniques discussed.

BY JENNY ALLEN, *MALENY, QUEENSLAND*

DON'T WAIT until another dry spell hits or storm waters flood through – the backbone of smart water management is to plan ahead. It is best to plan before your land is planted up – but if this has already been done don't worry, you can still incorporate many changes that can increase the water in your landscape, changing it from hot and dry to a lush oasis.

The secret is to design your land so that you can go away for short periods and relax; and not fret about precious plants wilting away.

Following is our Water Management Plan and a description of how we incorporated it. After this I explain the principles of water management and show step-by-step how to create your own plan and how to integrate some of the techniques mentioned.

OUR WATER MANAGEMENT PLAN

When planning for water management we took every bit of our land into account. Each drop of rain that falls at our place is now destined to go where we want it – there's no hiding around here.

A lot of our rain falls in sharp bursts over short periods, so the plan aims to capture this rain and to help it infiltrate into the soil as soon as possible. Where there is too much to infiltrate in a short period we aim to send it to places where it is needed most and where we can have more control over it. I dread seeing any escape – maybe I should have been a prison warden.

A few things we took into account are:

- Water used to bank up behind the house and consequently one of the house posts had sunk 10 cm. Our house not only looked like a boat, but felt like one too. Potentially, this water could have caused a lot of

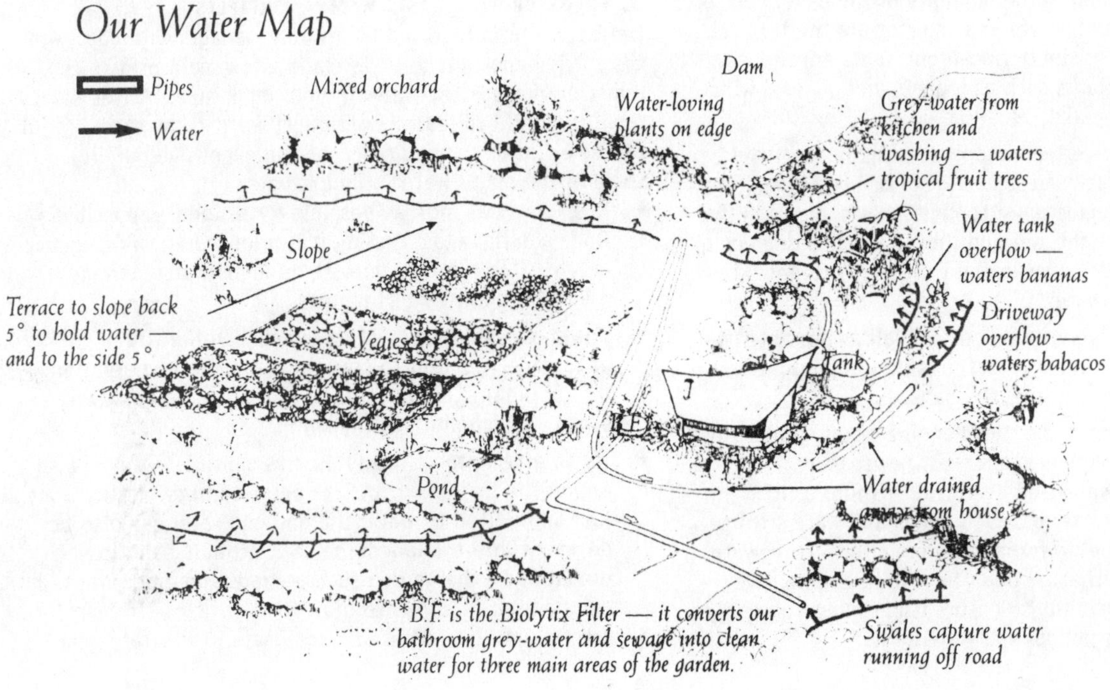

Our water management plan. (From *Paradise In Your Garden: Smart Permaculture Design* by Jenny Allen).

damage. So now we direct it away – from up the hill in a series of swales that feed the windbreak trees on the western side of the property. Any rain that falls below these swales is captured in diversion drains that spread it into agricultural pipes that irrigate the water-loving babacos and pecan nut tree. (I discuss swales more fully below.)

- Instead of the water run-off from the asphalt road causing potential storm water damage, we capture and spread it – the problem is now the solution. A series of swales take the water out to the ridges – preventing it from naturally converging in the gully.
- We created a one-metre ledge around the waterline of the dam to maximise the area of moist soil that can be planted up (many dams have straight edges where it is too difficult to grow things). When designed well, the merging of wet and dry areas can create abundant ecological niches with a different ecosystem from the rest of the property. On these ledges we grow plants that love moist soil such as cocoyams, river lilies and palms. We also planted a range of sedges as the water that comes downstream is a bit polluted with the neighbours' septic overflows. The sedges help to clean this out. We have a swinging chair under a mulberry tree overlooking the dam. We sit back, sipping lemon verbena tea, watching the azure kingfisher dart flashes of blue from the lateral branches above. The dam is designed not only to be functional, but to provide us with entertainment, wildlife shows and tranquillity as well. We have placed logs in it for the ducks and heron. Lilies are great landing pads for the dragonflies that eat most mosquitoes and the rocks around the edge attract our other main pest managers – lizards and frogs.
- By maximising different microclimates we can minimise water use. Basking in the humidity of the dam and the more moderate temperatures it creates are the tropical fruit trees. In the drier, wind-prone spots are the more Mediterranean plants such as loquats and guavas, which double as windbreaks.
- Storm water is diverted as soon as possible from the vegie garden as it can cause a lot of damage here. The vegie garden is made up of terraces that slope back five degrees to hold light rain and then slope five degrees to one side (towards water-loving fruit trees) to get rid of dangerous stormwater.
- The tank water overflow is kept as high as possible (we don't like to lose gravity) and runs into an agricultural pipe that passively waters the bananas.
- The Biolytix Filter is the silent engine of our garden. It converts our sewage, vegie scraps, newspaper, cardboard, greywater and even tin cans into a rich, odourless humus that passively feeds and waters thirty fruit trees (see below for more information). Greywater is such an asset that we don't let a drop escape. We also take responsibility to ensure it is cleaned on our land and doesn't pollute any waterways.

To avoid being a slave to your garden here are four steps for devising your own Water Management Plan.

1. Understanding your land

Many people rush out to make water-saving changes without understanding their land first – like getting married before knowing your partner. Careful observation is a helpful learning experience – never wasted. To do this, go out and feel the different dry and moist spots in the garden. Try and work out why this is so. Is it due to:

- soil type;
- time and rate of sun exposure;
- drainage zones in the area – maybe it collects water from a hard surface or water is diverted away;
- slope gradient; or
- trees in the vicinity, such as eucalypts, sucking up moisture?

Also, go out in really wet weather (if you get the chance) with a big umbrella and look at where your storm water flows – the all-important drainage lines.

2. Drawing a base map

The next step is drawing a base map showing all the important information you have gathered. To do this, draw a simple outline of the house and garden on a piece of paper – of what exists already. On this map mark:

- dry and wet areas
- heavy and light soil
- the path of winter and summer sun
- areas most and least exposed to sun
- gradients
- drainage lines
- where water banks up.

3. Incorporating basic water principles

The base map is followed by a water management map. But, first, it is important to understand a few main principles that can increase the water in your landscape. At the same time, it is vital to learn how to deal with storm water – so it can be an asset to the garden not an expensive liability. Some of the major water principles are:

- Keep water as high as possible for as long as possible. Once you have lost gravity it is a lot more work to get it again. This can be achieved through swales, terraces, diversion drains, mulching etc.
- The cheapest place to store water is in the soil – encourage your soil to contain it – with good aeration, lots of organic matter, lots of root zones to go down, swales, mulch and healthy soil.
- Try to give water as many uses as possible – this is also one of the main principles of permaculture. Rather than just being used to water the garden, water can also be designed into the landscape so it attracts beneficial predators to the garden such as frogs and dragonflies. It can be used in ponds to grow food or fish or to help create a more moderate microclimate. For safety's sake

fence ponds so children don't fall in.

- Deal with water problems close to the point that they originate. If not, the problem will only get bigger and there will be less room to distribute it. For example, it is best to prevent storm water from converging and to spread it over as wide an area as possible and to encourage it to infiltrate into the soil.
- For water that you can't spread out then send it to plants that can benefit from a lot of water – and will benefit you – like water-loving fruit trees, such as mulberries and pecan trees, and other water-loving plants, such as water chestnuts, lotus, coco yams and kang kong.
- Where possible take responsibility for cleansing and re-using your greywater – use it to feed fruit trees but not vegies as it may spread pathogens.
- Plant according to the wet and dry areas in your garden – so the plants can automatically handle the conditions they are given – rather than suffering or demanding a lot of your attention. Fruit trees that are more adaptable to dry periods include mulberries, Japanese raisin tree, date, fig, grapes, guava, olive, mango, cherry guava and white sapote.
- Grow many layers of plants to help shade the garden and to ensure the sun is less fierce. It is important to shade out the afternoon summer sun (especially from the more vulnerable vegie garden). This hot sun can drain the garden of vitality. On the whole the morning sun is softer and more forgiving.
- Plant windbreaks – ensure the plants used can handle dry conditions and you don't use up all your water watering the windbreak. If you are using fruit trees in the windbreak, such as feijoas, then expect less fruit.

Some techniques for incorporating these principles include:

- making a pond (see below)
- swales (see following)
- diversion drains
- terraces
- grey water management (see Biolytix Filter below)
- mulching
- groundcovers
- planting according to soil type, moisture level and microclimate.

4. Drawing a water management map

The principles and techniques mentioned can be entwined together to create a water management map. This can be done on top of your base map or on a separate piece of paper. To do this, sketch where you would like things to go, but don't get caught up in details at this stage as it is the concepts that are most important and you don't want to lose these.

If you have the energy it does help to go into the next, more detailed stage. For example, angles of terraces, where run-off water is to be shed, plant species etc. It sounds a bit overwhelming but it can make an enormous difference. As soon as I enter a garden I can detect whether water is managed well – or whether the hose and purse do the work.

Some water-saving techniques:

Making a swale

A swale can have a very positive impact on the garden.

Swales are ditches that run along contours (or, in some cases, slightly off the contour, taking water out to the ridges). They are used on sloping land, helping to prevent water simply running off to the neighbours or the creek. They slow down and capture the water. They are designed to encourage water to infiltrate into the soil so it passively irrigates water-loving plants. Over time it slowly infiltrates further down the hill so that all plants can benefit.

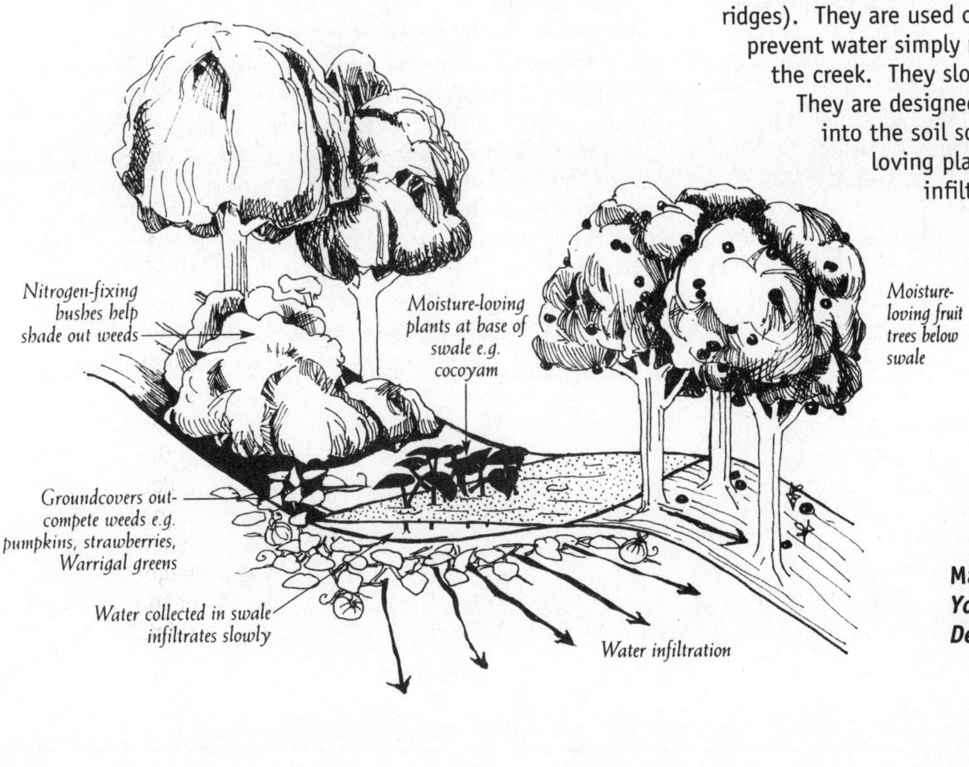

Making a swale. (*From Paradise In Your Garden: Smart Permaculture Design* by Jenny Allen).

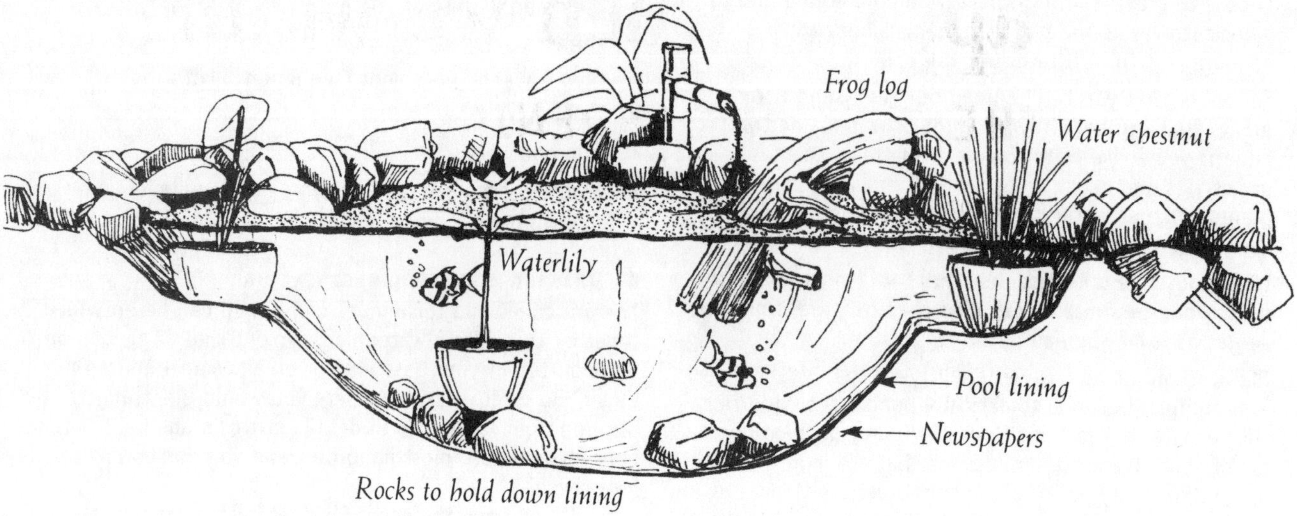

How to create a pond. (From *Paradise In Your Garden: Smart Permaculture Design* by Jenny Allen).

There may be many swales in the landscape depending on the slope, size, water requirements and maintenance needs etc.

Swales can be used either on a small-scale urban block or on a large property. They are becoming a lot more popular now with farmers. Water run-off, from a road, paving or tank overflow, can be diverted into swales. The diagram shows the layout of a swale. To reduce any tricky maintenance, plant it as thickly as possible so it becomes a little ecological niche in itself – often different to the rest of the landscape.

CREATING A POND

Rather than just being a wet hole in the landscape, a pond can be designed well so it has many uses as well as being attractive. Some features that make it multi-functional include:

- ledges to grow water chestnuts and lotuses (in pots so they don't take over);
- rocks around the pond that double up as a housing estate for lizards – they love the warmth and will help keep pests down in the garden;
- a frog log so that lizards and frogs can safely move in and out (this also helps prevent the pond turning into a stinky blood and bone soup);
- lots of little areas for plants such as water lilies (in pots). These then create habitat for fish and dragonflies that eat mossie wrigglers; and
- a place to sit and watch nature move in.

I hope that before long our sewerage, greywater and kitchen wastes can be major garden assets, not stinky problems that are hidden away and pollute the landscape.

Smart water management can be like playing a clever game of chess. Every piece is strategically placed to inter-relate and to support the whole team. It is about thinking ahead and planning to ride through potential hard times.

What happens when we water?

REDUCING THE COST OF GARDENING

Maintaining a garden and conserving precious water supplies aren't necessarily contradictory; and even a lawn can be sustainable!

BY KAREN THURTELL, *CREMORNE, NEW SOUTH WALES*

WHEN WATER is applied to the soil during either rainfall or irrigation, where does it go? Referring to diagram1 will assist in understanding the explanation in this article.

To begin, water, as it passes through the air, evaporates, especially in hot or windy conditions. This is normally in the order of three to five per cent, but can be 20 per cent or more if irrigation is carried out on a hot windy day. This is one of the many reasons to irrigate at night!

Next, depending on the heaviness of the rainfall or the pressure of the irrigation water, some of the water splashes from the surface. This is not a problem if the splash lands on other soil, but it adds to run-off if it lands on a hard surface.

Run-off is the big problem with all watering. If water is applied too quickly to be absorbed into the soil, it takes the path of least resistance to run away. You have not only lost this water, but it usually erodes some soil as well. It is impossible to change the rate of rainfall, but you can adjust the rate of irrigation to avoid run-off entirely. To do this you must know your soil, and observe your irrigation system in operation.

Now, most of the water applied has soaked into the soil, but not all of this water is available for plants. Gravity takes over and some of the water drains away from the root zone and is therefore lost. However, don't forget that the millions of animals and billions of micro-organisms in the soil also need water.

The amount of water that a soil can hold against gravity is termed the water holding capacity (WHC), and it is defined as the amount left after drainage has ceased. Most good garden soils have a capacity in the range of 20 to 40 per cent of volume, with clays being higher and sands lower. If you observe your soil during irrigation, you can quickly determine the rate at which water soaks in, and a simple test with measured amounts of water and soil in a pot will tell you the water holding capacity. Then you can calculate the right amount of water to apply so that the WHC is reached without any losses, except for some minor evaporation.

So, some easy observation and control will result in a great garden with minimal use of precious water.

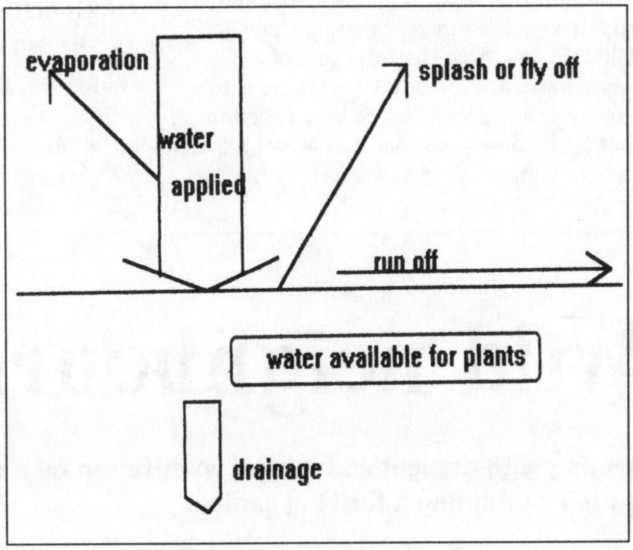

Diagram 1: destination of applied water.

REDUCED COST GARDENING

Water may not seem to be such a major cost, but some quick work with a calculator shows that water usage for gardening is between 100,000 litres and 150,000 litres a year per household. This is based on the current Sydney Water average figure (a few years old) of 350 litres a person per day, with approximately 35 per cent used in the garden. This still may seem minor, and includes flats and townhouses, but our water authorities continually assure us that the cost will only increase in the future.

There are many ways to reduce water usage in the garden, including heavy mulching and using drought-tolerant plants. Another important way is to avoid run-off entirely, by making sure that every drop goes on the garden, and not down the drain! It is surprising the number of times that a sprinkler is seen valiantly watering the driveway, when it is extremely unlikely that such a hard surface will grow anything! However, water can still run off from the garden if it is applied at a rate that exceeds the infiltration rate of your soil. Some simple observation during irrigation will quickly reveal any pooling, and your irrigation system can be just as quickly adjusted.

Reducing evaporation during irrigation also helps. Research in California reveals that using spray or floor irrigation during the day can result in up to 10 per cent evaporation before the water enters the soil, especially if there is any wind. Using drip irrigation at night is the most efficient form of irrigation, and there are many systems available to apply water in this way.

USING DRIP IRRIGATION AT NIGHT IS THE MOST EFFICIENT FORM OF IRRIGATION.

A lush, green lawn is a major user of water in the garden. If you feel that you must have a lawn in your design, there are still ways to reduce the total cost of maintaining it. One of the best ways is to select a lawn species that is best suited to your local climate, so that it does not require heroic efforts on your behalf just to survive. Planting cool season grasses in far north Queensland, or warm season grasses in Hobart would seem to be counter-productive, but both have been done! Once the correct species has been selected, all maintenance costs for the lawn will be reduced, including the amount of water needed by the grass.

Alternatively, you could eliminate the effort without sacrificing the appearance by using the new types of native grass on the market, or by using low-growing ground covers. You can still walk freely over these species, enjoying the feel and the fragrance, without ever having to mow and only rarely watering or fertilising them. The Australian Plant Study Group's *Grow What Where* has some excellent suggestions in this regard, or you could read some of Edna Walling's books for non-native species which fulfil the function of a lawn.

Wild neighbours in dry times

Dealing with drought and hungry wildlife can be a major test. Karen tells how she restricted water use while maintaining a thriving garden.

BY **KAREN SEDAITIS, *WYNDHAM, NEW SOUTH WALES***

LIFE'S TOUGH in dry times. Before breakfast it was 37°C in the shade. A hot wind's blasting through the eucalypts; the weather forecast is grim and what the marauding neighbours have left of the garden is bedraggled and limp.

There's the horrible possibility of bushfires; of death, destruction of native habitats, starvation and major upheaval. Even if you remind yourself that Australia always recovers, it's hard to believe. On the ridges of our land, huge eucalypts hundreds of years old began dying in September. Before spring was halfway along, the creek gave out, leaving disconnected pools surrounded by brackish sand and scum. Our pump-pool dried up yesterday. Who knows when the next rain will come?

Drought can be dispiriting. The wildlife are starving. Plants they wouldn't have sniffed a month ago have been eaten to the ground in the past week. In some cases, trees have been stripped of bark and branches eaten back to the trunk. In others, there's no trace of existence.

Drought can be confronting. Our impact on the land is huge. Is it right to pump up the last of a pool in order to keep your garden alive? Your household in water? To keep enough on standby in case the Red Steer comes through? It's painful to think of dying animals desperately trying to reach into your verdant jungle of edible delights, maddened by what they can't reach.

And there aren't any easy answers in a drought – just as always. You hope the rain will come. You cringe beneath the baking sun as the wind shrinks your skin. You watch the birds retreating and the night neighbours thin out.

It's tough, but it's not all bleak. There are ways of making it easier to endure a drought. Planning for drought is wise in Australia, where water is scarce and rain irregular. In our home, we use very little water simply because we have no plumbing. This sounds extreme, and it is, but at the moment it works better than any other precaution could. Every drop of water has to be fetched from the water tank in watering cans or buckets, and because of the effort required, every drop is used with respect. Here's how we do it:

A LONG DROP DUNNY

No water use. A deep hole outside, a platform made from hardwood decking, a toilet seat attached and an exquisite view of the forest...in a few years, another deep hole and a mass of rich humus. No smell, either, as long as the toilet

The flower and food garden with the food cage in the background.

A sawdust path winds through the flower and food garden.

Inside the food cage.

seat's down and the soil isn't flooded.

No plumbing

We have a 2,000-litre water tank close to the kitchen. A tank on the hill delivers only to the garden. Drinking water is poured into a porcelain water cooler; cooking water stays in two watering cans near the stove; water for washing up comes from a large pot on top of the stove; and clothes are washed in a large bucket (soaked overnight and prodded by passers-by bearing sticks). All water gets re-used in the flower garden, or on trees and climbers.

In summer, we wash in the creek (no soaps, but we don't use them anyway – a flannel washer is kinder on skin and environment) and shampoo our hair on the sand, using one-litre drink bottles to rinse. We supplement with warm water in a basin, at night. In winter, we wash in front of the fire from a large basin, and shampoo our hair in the sunshine. Children particularly like this more relaxed washing regime!

Managing the garden is less straightforward. To begin with, it's been impossible for me to restrict myself to growing only drought-tolerant plants, despite idealist intentions. For practical and aesthetic reasons, vegetables, fruit, berries and flowering plants had to be included. To make matters worse, our soil is a thin layer of gravelly loam over poor clay, which resists water before swelling up and drowning everything. Worse still, from a gardener's perspective, we've had to consider our otherwise very engaging neighbours: wallabies, kangaroos, possums, native rodents, wombats, big birds (although the lyrebirds seem to respect boundaries...so far) and even feral goats. My initial desire to plant enough to satisfy us all nearly broke my heart – nothing was allowed to establish itself before disappearing altogether. Fairly soon it became obvious that anything planted was dinner for the wildlife, and protection would be needed.

First of all – and before our first room was built – we erected a wire-enclosed food cage. Eight three-metre hardwood posts were set in holes 600 mm deep, tamped down and braced. Fencing wire was strung around the frame 600 mm off the ground, and a 300 mm-deep trench was dug underneath it. Rabbit wire was buried in this trench, leaving 600 mm above ground to deter wombats (everyone else follows a wombat, so keeping them out is crucial) and other burrowers. Nine hundred mm above this first wire, another line was attached; bird netting was hung off it and fixed to the top of the rabbit netting. Overhead, fencing wire was attached to the posts and strung diagonally to support the wire netting roof. Saplings or forked branches provide extra height. Alternatively, bird netting can be strung across the top, but this doesn't last as long and it isn't as strong a deterrent, either.

Next, it being winter, we planted fruit trees and berries, using compost and manures to improve the soil. We mowed the future vegetable areas close to the ground, covered them with newspaper, sprinkled with sheep manure and layered lucerne, manure, blood and bone and dolomite to create no-dig vegetable beds. This worked perfectly for our spring and summer crops, leaving a thick layer of humus within months, wriggling with worms and rich with microbial life.

Next, we built a garden fence using the food cage as a corner, and the same method without the roof. In places we laid the rabbit wire on top of the soil rather than beneath, and set rocks on top, hoping it would repel diggers. So far, it has, despite the rocks being rolled off at various times. Because the wombat has never been allowed into the garden, he hasn't developed an obstinate desire to break into it, hence the importance of fencing before planting.

By the time I was ready to plant, I had quite a bit of compost ready to use. I supplemented this with sheep and cow manure, and covered the mown grass with it. The grass never emerged. I'm a keen plant collector, and I wanted an oasis of leaf and flower, so I allowed myself wide beds and plenty of room. Paths were formed by close mowing, newspaper mulch and sawdust cover – it makes a soft, springy path that holds moisture and provides a moist, cooling area.

Tips

WASHING MACHINE

Washing machines are major users of water in the home. As with dishwashers, try not to operate them with small loads. If you are buying a new machine look for Standards Australia ratings which indicate good water efficiency: the more "A"s the better.

Consider buying a front loading machine. They generally use less water than top loaders.

This is how I keep the garden thriving:

GOOD SOIL

The ideal would be to green manure (with nitrogen-rich plants) every year, or before planting, but I didn't allow myself time. I've used compost and manures as the initial improvers, and mulch helps the worms continue the good work.

PLANT MATERIAL

Plan your garden so that ground covers spread and protect the soil and taller plants shield smaller, or more delicate ones from sun. I use sunflowers, hollyhocks, foxgloves and nicotiana for shade, and climbers trained over poly pipe hoops or tomato stakes (three together to form a pyramid) for others. Vines like clematis can ramble over and through the garden, and provide both horizontal and vertical focal points.

I plant vegetables in my flower garden. This makes the most of water and helps provide extra transpiration and shade, and you can use climbing beans and peas as well as silver beet (try the five colour variety) for both pleasure and food.

MULCH

Mulch with anything you can get your hands on. Best of all, invest in a chipper/shredder and use it year-round. Plant ground covers around the place to give added protection and cover the mulch.

IRRIGATION

Buy the biggest water tank you can afford, and fill it during wet seasons. In the garden, use drippers and soaker hose (try the new anti-ant dripper pipe). Cover with mulch to reduce water loss and keep the poly pipe cool. At intervals, erect sprinklers on risers for use during bushfires or desiccating winds. Water morning or evening, and never during the hottest times.

REDUCE PLANT STRESS

Don't over fertilise, as plants will get sappy and thirsty. Use a seaweed extract liquid feed, as it toughens up plants and increases resistance to extremes.

Shelter from hot sun using shade cloth, lattice, vines or taller plants. Alternatively, I use bracken fronds by shoving the sharp ends into the soil where and when most needed (seedlings or tender new growth).

But most importantly, remember that it will rain, sooner or later. And when it does, get amongst nature and relish every moment of it.

Fifteen mostly true hints to conserve water in the garden

There's nothing like the knowledge that comes from hard experience. Jackie covers watering and water conservation techniques, cultivation methods and includes lists of drought-tolerant plants and vegies.

BY JACKIE FRENCH, BRAIDWOOD, NEW SOUTH WALES

No biological system is ever simple! If you want simplicity, stick to engines!

1. Mulch increases the soil's moisture-carrying capacity, reduces evaporation and stops that thin crust forming on the top of your soil that can actually prevent moisture penetrating.

However, if most of your moisture comes from drizzle dripping down from the leaves, it may not actually penetrate the mulch. This doesn't mean don't mulch – it just means be aware of it.

Lucerne mulch is great; as is autumn leaves, pea straw and compost. We also chip the regrowth wattles that invade the orchard, or throw weeds under the avocadoes. Even a layer of pebbles is better than nothing at all. But avoid carpet, unless you are sure water can get through. And use only a thin scattering of lawn clippings as they can be water-repellent too.

PS I've started using eco-bag watering systems in some places. These are a UV-stabilised plastic container that mulch and water for up to 30 days. They're two for $22.50, or thereabouts – expensive, but great for spots up on the hill I know I'll neglect. They are really only useful for level ground though – no good at all on steep slopes.

2. Try drip irrigation or micro-jets. About 40 per cent of water can be lost in overhead watering.

However, overhead watering (and rain) washes the dust off leaves, and dust can kill young predators, which is why you get such bad pest outbreaks in a drought. Overhead watering will also kill pests like thrips and red spider mite, and when drippers are introduced these can really become a problem. Again, do go for the drippers or micro-jets, but remember you may need a good splodge of water for pest control.

3. Go for tough plants with a high oil content, or thick, fleshy or hairy leaves.

However, these plants usually need lots of sun, and if I put them in my deep valley garden a lot just go and die on me. Don't just bung hardy plants in willy-nilly – you need to find out a bit more about them than the fact they won't kark it in a drought.

You can be reasonably sure your plant will be drought-tolerant if it: has a deep, fleshy root system; tough, thin leaves to reduce evaporation, or a waxy or hairy coating; has small leaves that point up and down to reduce the surface area exposed to sunlight; sheds leaves when water-stressed and regrows them later; or if it opens its stomata (pores in the leaves through which water can pass) only at night, like cactus and pineapples.

Some of my favourite toughies include shrubs like Grevillea Robin Gordon and her descendants, hebe, hibiscus, hydrangea, dwarf pomegranate, China roses like Mutabilis, oleander, sacred bamboo (*Nandina* spp) – either the small or giant one, elderflower bushes, Sasanqua camellias, juniper, cistus, or masses and masses of lavender.

If you want smaller shrubs, try curry bush (smells wonderful in summer), ivy-leafed geraniums (pelargonium hybrids), erigeron, impatiens, most salvias as long as they are in the right spot, or darling daisies – single daisies are the toughest.

Summer bulbs are wonderfully tough, and survive long hot or dry periods by living on their hump like camels. Acanthus, agapanthus, dahlias (miniature or single ones that don't need staking), cannas, clivias, dietes, red hot pokers (I prefer the miniature yellow ones) and day lilies can provide a wonderfully hardy backdrop of colour all through the heat.

And if you want some tough, heat and drought-proof edibles (no, I don't mean they taste tough – they just survive), stick to artichokes, which also look stunning, cherry tomatoes, marjoram, apple mint (variegated apple mint isn't as hardy), rosemary, Jerusalem artichokes, bronze fennel (careful – it can become a weed!), lemon balm, garlic, garlic chives, New Zealand or warrigal spinach, and mitsuba, or Japanese parsley.

4. Plant natives.

However, in the last two bad droughts here my native shrubs were the first to die. Native plants are not necessarily drought-resistant. The plants that survive drought best are ones with big roots – not native shrubs like grevilleas, whose attitude to drought is to flower, seed and die, with their offspring popping up in ten or fifteen years when the rain comes again. In the last drought here 15-year-old roses and camellias survived a damn sight better than grevilleas.

Young natives survive better than young introduced plants, but do make sure your natives are native to dry parts of Australia, not wet forest or rainforest.

5. Install a greywater system.

However, greywater can also be extraordinarily dangerous!

Firstly, even without water from the toilet, small amounts of faecal matter and bodily wastes can be flushed down showers, laundry tubs etc. and, while most disease organisms are quickly broken down in the soil, some might be splashed onto vegetables. Greywater is probably safe if used only on trees and ornamentals.

Secondly, many kitchen wastes swept down the kitchen sink are no good at all in the garden – grease and oil, for example, that clog the soil and stop moisture penetrating, and salt.

Salt is also a by-product of soap and detergent, though soap, and particularly soap flakes, have far less sodium salt than detergents. If you plan to use greywater, avoid detergents, highly-perfumed soap and water softeners. If possible install a filter, and regularly clean out soap sludge. Try to avoid products containing boron or chlorine too.

If it's a choice of greywater or not enough, use greywater. Use it carefully, and never more than a bucket a week per square metre. Always use it combined with other moisture-conserving techniques.

6. Get hold of more water.

Put in a dam, more tanks, an underground cistern or collect water from the shed roof too.

However, make sure it doesn't breed mozzies.

7. Prepare the ground.

If you are putting in lots of trees, deep ripping will help roots penetrate, and large roots mean hardier trees. You can also contour the rips along and down the slope, so they collect water and feed it to the trees further down.

8. Water only as deep as the roots. Not all areas of the garden will need the same amount of water. Shallow-rooted plants like strawberries and lettuce will need more frequent but shorter watering than carrots or shrubs. If in doubt dig a trench near your vegetables to about the same depth as their roots. Stop watering when the moisture has penetrated to the bottom of the trench. Or buy a tensiometer, which will tell you the amount of moisture in your soil so you can time your watering accordingly.

I place a honey jar – normal size – under the hose or sprinkler when I water. When it's full the trees have been well watered; when it's half-full the shubs' soil should be moist; a quarter-full is okay for grass and most vegetables.

9. Time your watering.

Water before a hot spell, if you can predict it, so plants are more resilient, and not during the searing heat of the day when most will evaporate. Forget about watering on windy days. Try watering in the evening or in the early morning if you are worried about powdery mildew on damp foliage.

Contrary to lots of gardening advice, one good watering a week may not be best for your garden. Plants do best with a constant water supply – not a weekly waterlogging. Give as much water as is needed to penetrate to the roots and water again just before the plants start to wilt. This last is an art, but one that any person who closely watches their garden soon learns (see above).

10. Keep plants healthy. Strongly growing plants are better able to take up moisture and to cope with a temporary lack. Feed the poor things and watch out for weeds and pests and give them mulch.

11. Increase shade.

Shade will cool the garden generally. The more greenery, the less heat and light will be reflected, and in hot areas broken light will keep plants and soil below moist. Most flowers and vegetables will tolerate broken light. Shade can be from a pergola; a tall trellis facing the afternoon light (this is stronger than morning light); or from a tree or tall plants like corn, Jerusalem artichokes or sunflowers liberally planted through your flower and vegetable beds.

If most of your moisture comes from drizzle, this will collect on the leaves and drip down on the plants below. Many rain forests in fact don't get much rain, just a lot of drizzle and mist that's caught by the leaves. Few leaves means less moisture reaching the ground.

However, you can also get dry shade under trees, where moisture doesn't reach, and too much shade means stuff won't grow.

12. Protect vegies, young trees and shrubs with plastic shelters. This can make an extraordinary difference in very hot weather, and in hot, windy weather too. Often a little moisture will condense from the air at night and trickle down onto the soil.

You can buy water-filled plastic shelters that slowly drip water onto roots over two weeks or so. They are expensive, and we have had animals claw them open to get the water (yes, it has been an extraordinarily bad year), but on the other hand, some of our young shrubs in these protectors have actually grown in the past nine months, when we have had literally no rain at all.

13. Don't dig dried-up soil. If you must plant – and I'd strongly advise waiting till the drought breaks– only dig just enough to plant. I use a teaspoon in the vegie garden. Leave a slight depression around plants so water doesn't run off too fast from the hard baked soil, and mulch. Mulch will help soften the soil without resorting to digging.

Digging also spreads dust that coats plants and kills young predators, so you'll be making pest problems worse too.

14. Work out what you must save, and what you can bear to let die. Remember, grass will return when it rains.

15. Well, I could go on for pages. Plant your corn seed under a few inches of sand; condense water from the air at night between two layers of plastic and funnel it down to trees and garden; use tree guards in summer too, as they help slow down moisture loss from the trees.

But, basically, just think about your problem. We are supposed to be the brightest species on the planet (well, according to us anyway). There are hundreds of ways to get a limited amount of water most efficiently to your garden, and to make sure every bit possible is used well. And if you think about the problem you'll come up with the answers best suited to your area.

PS Mulch!

PPS And keep mulching!

PPPS And if anyone finds a never-fail rain dance, let me know!

Drought-tolerant edibles

Note: trees are not drought hardy at all till well established.

almond
apricot
apple
plum
quince
olive
loquat trees
carob (but not as drought-resistant as some claim)
pistachio
bunya nut
macadamia, if grown without irrigation when young
date (you need male and female)
Canary Island date palms (edible but pretty yuk)
cashew nut
carambola
hazel nut (lose their leaves but mostly return when it rains)
pine nut
fig
elderberry (lose leaves but mostly come back)
pomegranate
Eugenia aggreghata (Cherry of the Rio Grande)
kei apple
grumiochama (*Eugenia brasiliensis*)
Note: there are quite a few eugenia fruits, and all I have tried have survived drought.
Irish strawberry tree – *Arbutus unedo*
kiwi fruit – must be at least six years old to have any drought hardiness though – young ones needs regular watering
juniper– need male and female for fruit
Chinese jujube
prickly pear – avoid the weed species
most bramble berries, i.e., thornless blackberry, loganberry etc.– will die back in the drought but will shoot from their roots when it rains.

Also, look for yucca and cacti species with edible fruit.

Note: all citrus are shallow-rooted and needs lots of mulch and water, unless they are very old seedling trees – these may have more extensive root systems. Bush lemon – citronelle – is perhaps the most drought-resistant citrus.

Passionfruit and strawberries need lots of regular water.

Vegetables

Note: vegetables grown *in situ* are much more drought-tolerant than transplanted ones. And mulch!!!!!

artichoke (globe and Jerusalem)
asparagus – old large plants survive, but don't pick them unless you can water them too, or they may die.
burdock
cardoon – once established
beans – perennial scarlet runner and painted lady. I've found lazy housewife bean and zebra bean the best in nightmarishly hot, dry, gale-force winds – they actually survived and fruited! Mulch to half-way up the plant.
capsicum – I grow mini ones within a shield of flower pots with the bottom cut out.
cucumber
watermelon
pumpkin
dandelion – once established
cucumber
eggplant
leek – once half-grown
radish
spring onion
tomato – mulch to half-way up the plant
zucchini
Italian parsley
silver beet – once established
corn – if planted very deeply
kale

A nice place to sit

As Marian says, one does not usually talk about dunny meditation and dunny etiquette. But they are a vital element of the "McCain Method" of building an inexpensive, sweet-smelling composting toilet.

BY **MARIAN MCCAIN, *CLIFTON HILL, VICTORIA***

HOW MANY city-dwellers, returning home reluctantly from a rare and wonderful outback holiday, have not walked into their bathrooms and felt their sadness at leaving the bush offset, just a teeny bit, by a moment of sheer appreciation for that gleaming little Caroma throne? Followed, of course, by a stab of guilt for the gallons of water it takes to flush it.

When we make our permanent move towards a simpler lifestyle, especially if this involves living in the bush, the question of toilets often has to be answered immediately. Even if local regulations insist that we put a septic system into any new house we build, there is still the question of what to do in the meantime.

While the most common and obvious solution to the immediate dunny problem, if you wish to avoid chemicals, is some home-made version of a "long-drop", let's face it: they do tend to smell quite unpleasant after a while.

COMPOSTING TOILETS

Composting toilets are a wonderful idea. Nowadays, there are several excellent commercial models available and a number of designs for home-built ones. The disadvantage of the commercial ones, of course, is their cost. Some of the home-built ones are amazingly ingenious and even aesthetically beautiful as buildings.

I have seen, and tried, quite a few different types of composting toilets, both here and in the US, and I really like them – apart from the minor discomfort, in some of them, of having a cool draught blow strongly across one's fanny while seated! But they are virtually odourless, and of course environmentally impeccable.

So when we moved permanently into the caravan, in anticipation of building our mudbrick house, Don and I gave a lot of thought to the dunny question. I was keen to design and build a composting one, but the technology seemed complex. The compost unit itself needs a sloping floor or some other way of draining off liquid; there needs to be heat and air for evaporation; the resultant compost must be accessible for periodic removal; and the person generating all this raw material has to be perched up on top of it all somewhere, which usually means steps and platforms and stuff.

SIMPLICITY – THE FRY-TOL CAN

Then I went to a residential, two-week permaculture course, where the outdoor dunny was a funny old wooden chair with a hole in the seat and a Fry-tol can underneath. "How simple," I thought. But the tutor warned that with this method, to be quite certain no pathogens remained, the can should be kept sealed for a very long time – a couple of years, to be totally sure. I went home and thought about that.

Asking around, I discovered two things. Firstly, that Fry-tol cans were scarce (partly because the neighbours were using them too, but mainly because the cafes were switching to vegetable oil in cardboard cartons); and secondly, that most people emptied them out after a few weeks anyway, with no ill effects, like the Chinese do. But I was still dubious.

Put two ideas next to each other and cross-fertilisation may occur. What I came up with may not be new, but it is new for me and it certainly works, combining as it does the best of both methods. I call it the sweet-smelling, solar-heated, composting Fry-tol dunny design – or the McCain Method, for short.

THE MCCAIN METHOD

The secret to this method is that it divides up functions. It divides up – as much as possible – liquids and solids at source. I first saw this idea in a public toilet in the High Sierras in California, a solar composting unit where solid waste was baked to a dry powder under glass and users were politely informed that if they needed to pee they should go do it in the bushes.

In our simple little dunny building, which Don made from timber and fibro-cement sheeting, no-one has to go to the bushes as there is ample room for two receptacles side by side, well-labelled for visitors. One is the pee bucket, a tall plastic drum – the sort that pastry-cooks get bulk stuff in – with a small toilet seat that fits snugly on the top. This was from one of those camping toilets that we had years ago, which was hopeless because it used to collapse. The seat happened to be the perfect size. The lid of the drum, with a handle made from an old wooden curtain ring, sits on top to cover it.

The other is an old wooden chair that we found at the tip, complete with Fry-tol can. The plastic lid from a second drum fits over this. The second drum itself is open and filled with grass clippings and there is also a drum of sawdust on hand.

When the can is full, it is sealed with its own lid, stored outside in the garden and replaced by another. After all the cans are full – to date we have managed to scrounge

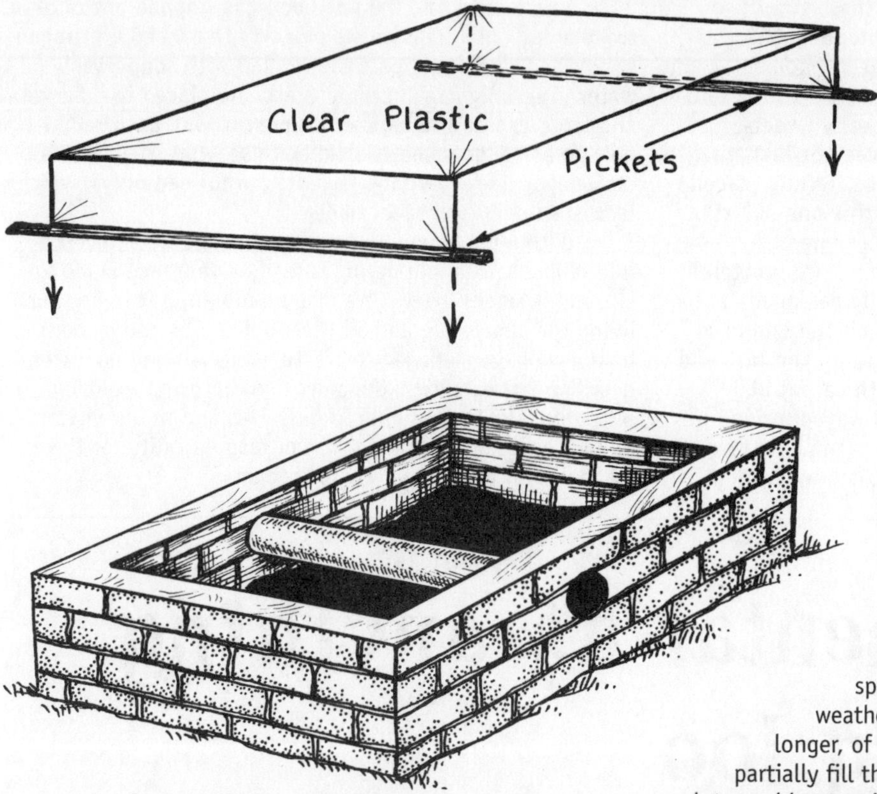

twelve – they are all emptied at the same time into the "bunker". So once again, for simplicity, functions are divided. The cans are filled in one place, right by the house, and solar-dried in another, way down in the garden.

The bunker

This is a rectangular structure built of mudbricks on a small concrete slab, with a sloped top facing north. It is aerated by means of a piece of slotted pipe that runs right through it, and covered by clear plastic. Originally it was going to be glass, but the plastic was cheaper and easier at the time and seems to work just as well.

The slope was achieved by building the mudbricks in a stepped formation and then finishing the tops of the walls with cob (handfuls of the same mud mixture, put in place while still wet). The tops of the walls were sealed with Bondcrete. The sheet of plastic overlaps a little at the sides, and is held in place back and front by the simple device of winding it on to a star picket so that it just rests on the ground. To make it extra secure, I often place small, heavy pieces of wood across the corners or, even better, some of the ubiquitous newspaper bundles that are waiting to go into no-dig garden beds. Because of the slope, rain runs straight off but maximum sunlight is caught.

There is a sheet of shiny tin against the inside back wall, to reflect and intensify the rays of the sun. The walls, of course, act as a heat bank to store and give out the heat trapped under the clear plastic cover, and on any sunny day, even in cold weather, the temperature inside ranges from warm to baking. (I first built the bunker in early spring and used it – topless on fine days and covered at night – as a greenhouse for all my vegie seeds while the twelve cans were initially being filled. It worked so well I almost changed my mind about emptying the cans into it!) I figured that the intense heat on very sunny days would be enough to kill any pathogens or parasites after a few weeks.

The contents of the first twelve cans went into the bunker in November and baked through the summer. By the end of February they had dried to a fine, powdery, sweet-smelling compost which was spread around the orchard. In cooler weather, the "cooking" process may take longer, of course, but since twelve cans only partially fill the bunker, there is no reason why several lots could not wait in there together until the warm weather rolls around again.

The "McCain Method": throne and spare container.

DUNNY ETIQUETTE

I know one does not usually talk about these things in great detail but they really are important. Besides which, they help us stay fully in the present moment. Dunny meditation, you could call it. Attention to detail, I have discovered, is what makes for a really sweet-smelling dunny. First, used toilet paper is not just dropped unthinkingly into the abyss but carefully placed for maximum coverage (Don baulked at this one at first, but he got used to it.) Secondly, sawdust, grass clippings and other carbonaceous materials are scattered thickly, and compressed with my specially designed "poo-squisher" (a circular piece of chipboard on the end of a long handle) so that the can does not fill up too fast and there is nothing left visible but a smooth carpet of sawdust etc. Thirdly, a match is lit and waved around a bit inside the can, to burn off methane. Finally, a few drops of eucalyptus oil are shaken on to a bowl of gum leaves on the shelf.

Needless to say, the pee bucket is slopped out once or twice a day onto areas of the property that need a nitrogen boost, and rinsed and partially refilled with soapy wash water. Pee-only paper, tampons etc. are placed in a basket and later go into the regular compost bins. For myself, I now do as my grandmother did and use what she called a "towelette" (a face-washer-sized cloth for pee-only), which is washed daily and saves paper.

With a rug, some nice pictures on the walls, even a pile of magazines, our dunny is really a very nice place to sit, and it smells lovely. We may be roughing it in the bush, living the simple life and all that, but this is one modern, luxury we have managed to create while wasting no water, using no energy except the sun's and our own, recycling nutrients, and maintaining in ourselves and in our visitors an awareness of body and sense of responsibility for the management of our own waste products.

An excremental-as-anything composting loo

"Every home-styled loo is an act of individuality and creativity," Linda maintains. Here she describes how she went about building hers.

BY LINDA ROBBINS, *UKI, NEW SOUTH WALES*

THE PRODUCTIVE use of our human wastes, the conservation and non-degradation of our precious water reserves, and the maintenance of pleasant, convenient and hygienic toilet facilities are a problem for every pioneering and financially-challenged alternate lifestyler. Lack of access to town sewerage and the questionable nature and cost of septics can be turned into an advantage with a well-designed home-built system.

My first loo was of the old thunderbox style, environmentally sound but arduous work when it came time to bury. After that I graduated to a combustion model – a decapitated 44-gallon drum two-thirds buried in the ground with a flue and chip heater-style "choofer" to permit periodic burn-offs. This was physically easier and perhaps more sanitary, but polluting, more costly (kero required) and not always convenient. Obviously it also has to be located some distance from the house.

The composting system I have now constructed I am totally satisfied (deliriously delighted) with, and it avoids all these pitfalls. My design was based very much on the composting toilet described by Jenny Ledgar (see "A homemade above-ground composting toilet" on page 74). To her I am very grateful and I recommend her article to all those seriously interested. I, however, adapted and modified her design in several ways which some may find workable and applicable.

Whereas Jenny built her loo on an elevated platform at some distance from her house, I was able to successfully incorporate mine into a verandah and so achieve easy, all weather and nocturnal access. My system also differs in that I used two wheelie bins as the "digestive receptacle", instead of Jenny's fixed, inverted plastic drum. The wheelie bins can be moved and rotated as required. Whilst one bin is being filled, the second stands quietly and obediently decomposing. Second-hand bins can currently be bought for about $60.

In retrospect, it may have been simpler to have the wheelie bin sitting directly on the ground with a drainage pipe attached, or some kind of absorption pit underneath. This may be necessary if the floor level is lower. The available height must be able to accommodate a full-sized wheelie bin (about 1300 mm). Small bins are not suitable, as efficient decomposition requires a larger volume.

Some composting loos have in-built fans, but I have not found this necessary. Providing the wheelie bin is fitted with a good sized vent, extending well up, and the heap is well oxygenated (via the two perforated poly pipes which pass diagonally through the bin), odour should not be a problem. However, it is not reasonable to expect it to smell always like a host of golden daffodils. The principal additive I use with this system is wood shavings, usually available from sawmills. Sawdust may also be used but it lacks the light and airy quality of the shavings, and so is not as suitable. Crumbled manure, kitchen scraps and wood ash are also beneficial. The bin is also an excellent way to dispose of doggie-do and grease trap sludge.

Tips

Too many flushes

The toilet is a big user of water in the home, with anything from three to eleven litres needed for every half or full flush. It is surprising how many people use the toilet to flush away cigarette butts, tissues and other rubbish. Apart from the potential to cause problems in the sewerage or septic system, this practice wastes large volumes of water.

As a single person I've found one bin to last about eight months and in that time a full bin decomposes to roughly one-third its original volume, when it is ready to use as a wonderful fertiliser for trees. Use on vegie gardens is not recommended. Families may find it necessary to introduce a third bin into the cycle. I believe it is good to water the contents of the standing bin occasionally to facilitate decomposition, and it should preferably be positioned in a warm spot for the same reason. I also add composting worms from time to time to hasten the process. This will flourish, providing water and temperature levels are maintained. A simple worm farm is thus a valuable resource.

Because oxygen is vital to the essential bacterial life of the excremental as anything loo, I have constructed beside it a separate system exclusively for liquids, thus avoiding the possibility of over-saturation. Some people may prefer to simply go bush fairly frequently. On the liquid side of life, I have simply used a sink, at floor level, with an S-bend.

In this arrangement the water from the hand basin nearby acts to flush the lower sink, or urinal. Because the S-bend below is thus filled with clean water, no smell can linger. In the garden the flow is distributed by an underground agricultural pipe, which has resulted in some abnormally prolific bananas.

If gravity prevents the installation of a hand basin, a tap only on the lower sink may suffice, or water might even be bailed in. Cleaning is simple enough if things are put together so they can be readily dismantled. The chute should lift out and likewise the chair.

The modern convention of using water as a medium for transporting human waste, and then perhaps struggling to separate the two at some later stage, is both inefficient and irresponsible. At last it is being recognized that composting treatments, whether of the continuous or the batch style as here described, are sensible, feasible and even preferable. Every home-styled loo is an act of individuality and creativity. For too long the magic flushing now-you-see-it-now-you-don't loo has been put on a pedestal.

Build your own composting toilet

It's taken a long time, but landowners and councils are starting to recognise the environmental benefits of composting toilets. "Guess what! No-one's died yet since councils relaxed their opposition to these water savers!" Colin shows how to build your own little water closet – minus the water.

BY COLIN WESTWOOD, *MURWILLUMBAH, NEW SOUTH WALES*

WITH THE many on-site toilet systems now registered and approved by the EPA and state government health departments, it is easier to convince local council building departments of the safety and environmental benefits of composting toilet installation. If you cannot afford to buy a commercial composting toilet system, you may like to think about building your own.

In 1985, long before the authorities approved of these things, I decided to clean up my act and replace the old "long drop" loo with a small composting toilet based on the Clivus Multrum design, also called a Clivus Minimus. Because of its very simple design it is the easiest for an owner builder to tackle.

Ideally, a slope of around 30 degrees with a northerly aspect will be the most suitable for ease of construction and efficient composting, but neither is essential to a successful outcome. My loo was actually built on an easterly slope of around 15 degrees so some digging was needed to get a 30-degree incline for the floor slab.

About one cubic metre of composting space per person is the ideal size to build. My unit was about three metres long by 40 centimetres high and 60 centimetres wide (less than a cubic metre) but at one stage, six of us were able to use the unit for a year or so without a problem.

DESIGN

My design consists of recycled concrete blocks, corrugated iron and lots of cement render. I first dug my

Pedestal area made with cement-rendered marine ply; sawdust and dolomite bin to the right.

Pickle barrel loo, with ventilation pipe to the right.

30-degree slope and poured a five-centimetre-thick concrete slab. The sides were then constructed using a combination of recycled slimline concrete blocks and bricks. The top and bottom ends of the box were made of standard-size "Besser" blocks with ventilation blocks in the centre for good aerobic composting. At the base of the bottom vent block is a six-centimetre space, which can be opened to rake out the completed compost from time to time.

The roof of the composting chamber is simply a length of old corrugated iron, wedged between the outside walls and rendered with a coating of three parts sand to one part cement. I see no reason why the entire structure couldn't be built using concrete-rendered corrugated iron for the composting box sides and top. The area around the seat is a piece of marine ply that has also been rendered with concrete. The only fancy bit not visible is two lengths of plastic pipe that run down the length of the box inside. These were made from a plastic downpipe cut in half lengthwise with a carpenter's saw. They are inserted into the top and bottom ventilation blocks by carefully trimming and bending to fit the half moon shapes (like an inverted U) of the vent blocks. Air will find its way through the centre of the compost pile with this in place.

To keep out rodents and insects the vent blocks have a layer of heavy-duty mesh placed over them. My biggest problem had been the accumulation of condensation on the toilet seat. Just adding a breather pipe near the seat would probably solve this. However, me being one to lift the lid and squat when using the loo, I never bothered to try this.

This design will work well provided that you keep urine input to a minimum. If you decide to use the system as a urinal as well, your best option here is to build a transpiration trench at the bottom of the composting unit. The really adventurous could try a reed bed system combining grey and black water, although I think that issues such as mosquito and midge control make this idea unacceptable. The simpler option, as I have always done, is to keep a bucket full of sawdust or chaff near the loo and pee in that. The vegetable matter will absorb the nitrogen and keep things smelling sweet for a week or two. This brew is ideal around trees and has grown the biggest, sweetest bananas I have tasted.

Tips

Dishwasher

Dishwashers can be thirsty items. Even a dishwasher with a low water-use rating can use the equivalent of two sinks of water a wash. Older models can use more – up to 50 litres. The way to save water is to operate your dishwasher only when it is full. This way you will also save on your power bills.

Getting started

To start a composting toilet system working, first add a bucket or two of good soil or compost. Add earthworms and composting worms to this, which is the most important ingredient in the recipe. They will multiply rapidly if you remember to add a sprinkle of dolomite or wood ash and a handful of sawdust or chaff, each time you use the loo. You might like to pre-mix these ingredients for an easy-to-use, visitor-friendly, one-handful application.

If this all sounds like too much for you to handle and you visit a bush site where an easy loo set-up is needed, a recycled plastic pickle barrel will make a great compost loo. Provided that you keep most of your urine elsewhere, like on the garden or in a separate bucket, your compost worms will love the environment if treated the same way as above with dolomite and sawdust added.

To create a worm-friendly aerobic environment all you need to do is cut a small hole near the top of the barrel and insert a short length of poly pipe with a fly-wire cover on the end of it. This can be held in place by slicing a small length of poly pipe lengthwise and slotting it over a bit of fly-wire. The worms will then remain inside and blowflies outside.

Seat

A wooden seat can be easily adapted to fit over the barrel and when not in use, the plastic barrel lid can be kept firmly on. When this eventually becomes full, a replacement barrel would be used while the first can be left to fully mature until barrel number two is filled.

Recently I came across another version of the pickle barrel idea: simply a collection of recycled 20-litre plastic buckets, a miniature version of the pickle barrel system.

Of course dealing with your local authorities can be time consuming, difficult and frustrating. You will need to provide detailed drawings and specifications if you intend to seek council approval. So whether you prefer to install one of the many brilliant commercial composting toilet systems or your own design, the rewards are great. Consider the environmental disaster of sewage outfalls into river systems and oceans, or the problems with septic system maintenance and the waste of water associated with these methods. You too can be a pioneer of a new age of environment-friendly responsible citizens!

Yes! – to sewer alternative

Michael Wilson and Fiona Buining have managed to convince the local council that their composting toilet and reed bed greywater treatment system was a valid reason for not connecting to the nearby sewer.

BY MICHAEL WILSON *AND* FIONA BUINING, *HEPBURN, VICTORIA.*

WE HAD always been unimpressed by the sewer. When we lived in Sydney we felt awful contributing to the 'floaters' in the water near the ocean outfalls. The Sydney solution, a long pipe to dump it all a few kilometres offshore, didn't reassure us in the slightest. We became quite convinced that wherever we lived, we were not going to contribute to nutrient problems in our seas and waterways. We wanted to find a good waste-treatment system that retained as many nutrients as possible, preferably in a form we could use on our garden.

In September 1995 we moved into our house on a one-acre block in the sewered township in Hepburn, central Victoria. And no, we have not connected to the sewer. After six months of negotiation with Central Highlands Water (CHW) and Hepburn Shire Council, our composting toilet and reed-bed greywater treatment system was approved.

When we first tested the waters by talking to senior management at CHW about an onsite system instead of the sewer, they simply said, "you have no chance". In addition we expected rigid legislation that required sewer connection. However, what we found was quite supportive legislation under the State Environment Protection Policy, Waters of Victoria (SEPP). This policy is under the Environmental Protection Act 1970, and the Water Act requires all water authorities to conform to SEPP.

A lot of homework led us to Terry Lustig from Environmental Management in Sydney.

We had already decided on a composting toilet, and we knew that most on the market had approval from the Victorian Health Department and the Environment Protection Authority (EPA). We needed help in the design for the greywater system to treat our kitchen, laundry and bathroom water.

Environmental Management had EPA and Health Department approval on greywater treatment systems, through its subsidiary Environment Equipment. So we used Terry Lustig and John Randles as consultative engineers to design a system and to talk directly to CHW. This meant they could not knock us back on technical grounds. We confidently submitted our plans with supporting documents and covering letters. They knocked us back! The reasons given were clauses 28 and 40(e) of SEPP. They read,

'The discharge of waste water from any sewered property where sewerage reticulation is available should be to the sewerage system, if that waste (with pre-treatment if necessary) is acceptable to the responsible authority.'

THE OTHER REASON WAS,

'In sewered areas appropriate steps shall be taken by sewerage authorities to ensure all premises are connected to the sewerage system for the purpose of domestic waste water disposal.'

We cried "foul"! When you read the legislation in full, there are clauses like clause 19. This read,

'. . . any technology which achieves the same or greater performance than the specified technology shall be acceptable.'

Furthermore, clause 37 encouraged both water conservation and reuse of waste water for irrigation, watering of gardens and wetland recharge. It became obvious that we needed some ruling on what SEPP requires.

The EPA administers the relevant Act, so we suggested they evaluate the whole matter. They wrote,

'Clause 28 and 40(c) of the SEPP (Water of Victoria) clearly encourages the connection of any premises to sewer where it is available. However there is no statutory power in the SEPP to require connection of any premises to the sewer . . . the responsible authority must determine which alternative is going to have least impact on the environment'.

Sorry to fill the page with legal babble, but we believe our system was the first of its kind in a sewered area in Australia. If others want to find sewer alternatives, then being well-informed, plus refusal to take 'no' for an answer, is probably the way to go.

The EPA ruling was the turning point. CHW approved the system after a full board meeting, and suggested a four-page, section-173 agreement be attached to our title. This agreement included a detailed monitoring program, indemnifying clauses, eventualities on sale of the property and so on. All this went back to the final authority, Hepburn Council, which would be expected to rubber-stamp an EPA, Health Department and CHW approved system. But, in its wisdom, it knocked us back on the basis of clauses 28 and 40 (e).

ABSURD

At a one-hour meeting with the commissioners, we pointed out how absurd it looked when the sewerage authority said they were happy for us to treat our own waste, but the council said they were wrong. We pointed out that by saying 'no', the council was implying that the EPA was wrong in ruling on its own Act. I think the council realised it

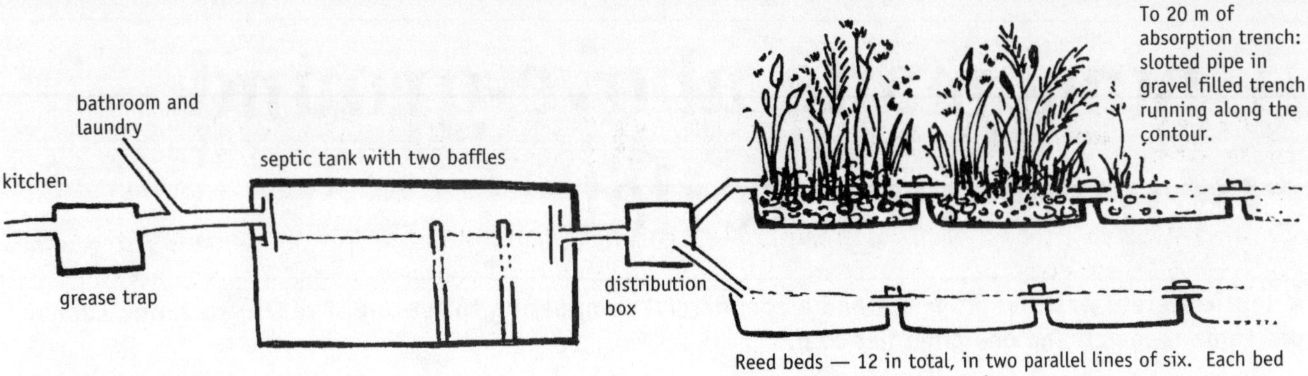

The reed bed treatment system. Not to scale

would look very silly at the Administrative Appeals Tribunal. It gave us approval the next day!

The system

A Rotaloo composting toilet sits under a conventional concrete slab floor. The slab is suspended over a cellar which has a glasshouse-like structure over the outside section that ensures dry warm air flows through the toilet. The compost, ready after one year or more, gets buried in our gardens.

The greywater system (shown in the sketch) includes a grease trap outside the kitchen, a modified septic tank, two parallel lines of reed beds, and final disposal into a 20-metre-long conventional absorption trench. Bacteria do all the cleansing work. Even in the reed bed, it is the bacteria living on the reed's roots that do the treatment work; the reeds take up nutrients and pump oxygen and other goodies down to the roots to help the bacteria do the job. The bacteria we want hate grease, hence the grease trap and the modifications to the septic tank, making it like another large grease and sludge trap. By harvesting the reeds (up to one-third each growing season), we can get the nutrients out of the reed bed and under our fruit trees as mulch.

Baffles

The reed beds were constructed by digging two parallel trenches each 18.5 m long, 600 mm wide and 500 mm deep, with a fall of one in 100. Ian Stares, our wonderful plumber, had concrete baffles made up with a hole in the top for a short length of round stormwater pipe to slide through. The baffles were placed vertically every three metres. We just needed to check that the outlet (that is, the hole through the baffle on the downhill side) was 30 mm lower than the inlet (the hole on the previous baffle) to give us the right fall along the beds.

Slab plastic is strong and comes off the roll already doubled in just the right size to line the trench. The plastic was rolled out down the whole trench. A bit of folding and pleating ensured a snug fit in each bed and up and over the baffles. A small hole could then be made to slip the outlet pipe through the baffle, and the plastic was sealed to the outlet pipe with either waterproof concrete, epoxy resin or Denso tape (a grease impregnated cloth tape that sticks very well to plastics). We are experimenting to see which is the best method. The trenches were then filled with 25 mm+ scoria/blue metal mix. The gravel can be quite large, up to 75 mm diameter, but shouldn't be smaller than about 25 mm. The gravel completely covers the outlets; no water is visible, hence there are no mozzies or risk of disease.

The final act to get the system going was the planting. Digging and planting into gravel is not pleasurable. In the end we used three main species, Typha (bullrush or cumbungi), Phragmities and Juncus, dug from a neighbour's dam or roadside drains. The Typha and Phragmities are growing best and will probably dominate for a while.

In summer, evaporation and transpiration from the reeds sucks out more water than we put into the system, so we have needed to use a bit of tap water in the last few beds to keep the newly planted reeds growing well. They need to be well-established for winter when evaporation and transpiration will be minimal. Even though the reeds die down over winter, the root mass is still alive and bacteria are still working away.

We are really enjoying dealing with our own waste. It is great not to flush good drinking-water down a toilet. When we pull a plug we think of it as watering our reeds. The reed bed is to the north, a useful firebreak, and provides a supply of mulch. When we go to the toilet we know the nutrients are going to go back on to our land. Ultimately it grows more food, which we eat to provide more waste and so on. We are using the nutrients from our waste to grow mulch and food crops, which is a damn sight better than using them to grow toxic blue-green algae in our rivers!

Cost

The greywater system cost about $3,500 — from the pipe leading out of the house to the reed bed, but minus the planting. This figure also included digging, installation and equipment — grease trap, septic, baffles, scoria/blue metal mix, and so on. The toilet cost about $3,000, which included the purchase of the Rotaloo, installation, plumbing attachments and various sundries.

A homemade above-ground composting toilet

A septic system was inappropriate and a commercial composting toilet out of reach, so Jenny Ledgar did some research and designed her own.

BY JENNY LEDGAR, *REPTON, NEW SOUTH WALES*

WHEN I FIRST moved out of town nine years ago, my two sons were living with me. Our dwelling had a canvas roof and bark walls and we carried water every day for drinking and washing. As the years went by life became more comfortable. We now have a tin roof, a water tank and dam water on tap. But we had a pit toilet – the shallow topsoil was unsuitable for a septic system and the commercially available composting toilets were beyond my budget. After reading a few articles about homemade varieties, I decided to design a composting toilet appropriate for my situation.

The composting toilets that I read about had the following things in common:

- a minimum chamber size of one cubic metre;
- the pile had to be aerated somehow;
- there was drainage for excess moisture;
- the chambers were flyproof; and
- a trapdoor or exit point was placed near the base.

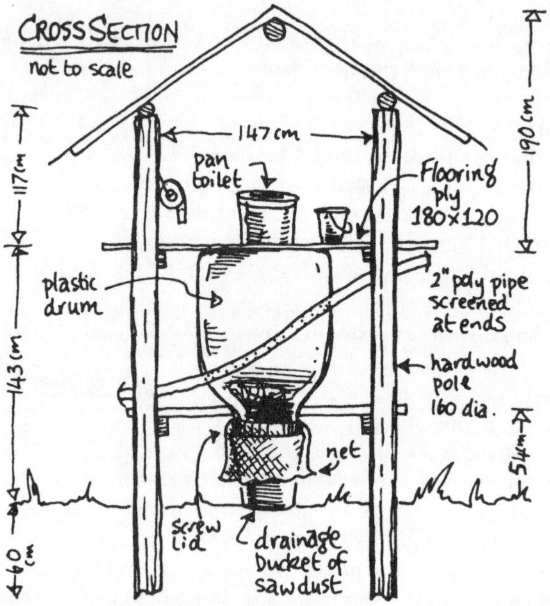

Jenny's toilet in its secluded setting.

PLASTIC DRUMS

I started looking for a second-hand container that I could use for the chambers and decided on large screw-top plastic drums that had been used to store concentrated orange juice. They were available locally for $30 each. So using the criteria listed above, two drums and a collection of building materials from a demolished shed, I drew up a plan.

Luckily, my neighbour and workmate, Andy, was also interested in the plan for a new toilet and agreed to help with the project, so work began.

We inverted the drums, making the lids the exit points and then drilled numerous holes in the lids to provide drainage. A piece of poly pipe with holes drilled along its length was fed through each drum from a point near the base across the inside and out again near the top. We spent a few days building a little pole-framed, tin-roofed structure to house the drums. This was positioned at the edge of the forest where the afternoon sun would provide extra heat and, we hoped, where breezes would whistle up through the length of poly pipes and aerate the piles.

In the base of each drum, we built a false floor a few inches high with chicken wire and straw – a bed to start the pile on. The drums were supported by sections of flooring ply with round holes cut in them. The lids of the drums fit through the holes and are high enough above the ground for a low barrow to be wheeled under at emptying time. Plastic buckets of sawdust sit under the drums to collect any drops. Netting "skirts" between the base of the drums and the buckets keep flies at bay, and the base of each drum and the ends of the aerators are screened too.

A sheet of flooring ply was used for the main platform. Round holes, slightly smaller than the base of the pan toilet, were cut to access the drums from above. The "throne" sits over one drum and the other is sealed with a wooden lid and left closed during the composting period.

NINE MONTHS

It takes about nine months for three of us to fill a drum. We keep the pile as dry as possible and have a bucket of extra goodies next to the loo. A cupful of these extras is added after each visit. This extra material helps with the composting and we add a variety of sawdust, grass clippings, seaweed or raked leaf mulch and dirt from the forest floor. A most important additive when the drum is full and being closed is worms. We get our worms, red wrigglers and tiger worms (they love manure and breed quickly), and castings from a worm farm. The worms move up and down inside the chamber eating, excreting and aerating the pile, helping it break down more quickly.

After nine months, or when the drum in use is full, it is time to empty the first drum, which has been composting, and move the pan.

Tips

SHOWERS

Showers typically use around 25 litres of water a minute. A minute or two less showering time adds up to a lot of water over a year.

EMPTYING

Emptying the loo is never a popular job, sometimes the screw-lid refuses to budge and needs a few taps with the hammer. Once the drum has been emptied we give it a good flush out with a hose and scrub the pan before starting afresh.

We barrow the contents of the loo to the favoured fruit trees, where is it covered with a thick layer of mulch. Providing you've fed your toilet a good diet, including the worms, the resulting fertiliser is a rich, dark, crumbly mixture with lots of healthy, red worms and it proves to be a fantastic treat for the trees.

Our composting toilet has been in service for three years now and, although councils are reluctant to approve or endorse such a display of practicality and initiative, we have had no health problems with ours and consider it to be a vast improvement on the old pit.

My pickle barrel composting toilet

This is a composting toilet you can build yourself from scratch.

BY GOVINDA SAILER, *LARNOOK, NEW SOUTH WALES*

AFTER READING an article on composting toilets in *Earth Garden*, I feel inspired to let your readers know about my own composting toilet. At Sundara Retreat in Billen Cliffs community, in northern NSW, we have three of these toilets, which have been working perfectly well for many years.

My model is based on recycled pickle barrels that are readily available at farming stores. Approximately ten cm from the base, 5 mm x 10 mm steel rods are placed across the drum and a strong galvanised mesh is wired on top of the rods, creating a second floor in the drum. Air holes are then drilled in to the barrel just below the mesh. My design uses 3 mm x 50 mm holes and these are covered in fly mesh. A fourth hole is drilled out to 40 mm to allow a PVC pipe urine outlet. This hole is close to the base of the drum.

To aid the removal of moisture from the drum, a 50 mm pipe is wired in from below the mesh to three quarters of the way up (to the level of the exhaust outlet) creating a passage for air movement while the seat is closed, thus reducing smells. A 75-mm hole is made and a 75-mm pop is rivetted into place, to which the vent pipe is connected.

This toilet is ideal for a floor height of 1 to 1.2 metres on existing buildings or verandahs. The height of the pickle barrels vary from 96 cm to 108 cm, so you can pick a size that is ideal for your place.

The aeration holes are covered by fly wire and on the top of the drum a foam seal (10 mm x 100 mm) keeps the flies out.

All you need now is a chute – either commercial or from a bucket with the bottom cut out, or a sheet of tin riveted or soldered into a cylinder, and a base with a seat. You can do away with the chute for a squatting toilet.

Once the drum is in place, with a 50 mm elbow and a 50 mm pipe connected to the urine outlet, a container is needed to collect the liquid, which can be used as a liquid fertiliser.

A 75 mm PVC pipe is connected to the vent hole and extends past the roof-line. Fly wire and a china hat are fixed to prevent rain and flies from entering the vent. If the vent goes through the roof, a roof seal will be necessary. To improve airflow, the vent pipe can be painted black, which absorbs solar radiation, or a larger diameter pipe can be used.

Now you have a wonderfully aerated composting toilet

The drum in its place with vent pipe and urine outlet.

Interior of the drum showing second floor, vent pipe and air holes.

that will get approval from most councils.

After each use, a handful of sawdust is thrown in. After around six months for two people, or when the drum is almost full to the vent hole, the drum is removed, capped with its lid and allowed to sit for another few months to complete the composting process. The addition of five to eight kilograms of dolomite and a stir will increase the composting rate. In summer temperatures, the compost may be ready for use on the garden in eight weeks. A second drum is put in place. Larger families will require a third drum. I have also witnessed wheelie bins being used effectively in the same manner.

So when you're up the creek get Govinda's composting drum. It has undergone a two-year trial and works perfectly, and is easily fitted under most houses, only needing one metre in height. One person can slowly rock the full drum out.

Composting time is four to five months after removing, but this can be accelerated by stirring. The system is easily enlarged by adding more drums. The urine outlet would be better made from thick PVC.

Commercial composting toilets

There are a number of proven, reliable commercial composting toilets available now in every state of Australia, each with their own strengths. Here are some to consider: contact each maker and assess carefully!

THE HYBRID TOILET SYSTEM

This environmentally friendly system uses no water or a mere 300ml for flushing. The Hybrid Toilet System is fully self-contained and comes in sizes 6 to 150 person. Contact the manufacturers for larger system designs.

This system delivers extremely high quality effluent and is capable of coping with over 100% overload situations. It requires minimal maintenance, you'll only need to pump-out once every 4-6 years dependant upon usage.

The system is easily installed in new or existing households, or for outdoor use, cubicle kits are available. Wind, solar or electric exhaust fan options are also available.

Web. <www.hybridtoiletsystem.com>
Ph. 1800 308 302.

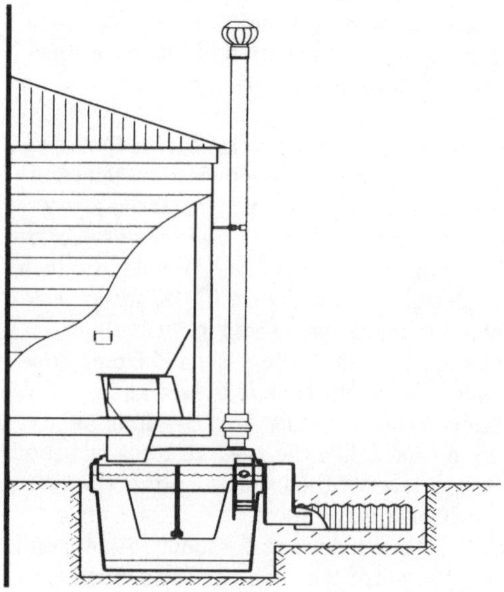

NATURE LOO

When Brisbane City Council developed the environmentally-sensitive Boondall Wetlands, they chose Nature Loo for the toilet and greywater solution. Nature Loo Classic model composting toilets are installed in the male, female and disabled facilities, and the Nature-Clear greywater treatment system treats the non-toilet water before it is reintroduced into the wetland surrounds.

Nature Loo works on exactly the same principle as a compost bin, only faster. Except in the case of the Compact model, the waste is collected in a chamber directly beneath the toilet pedestal. A low-powered electric fan continually circulates air through the chamber, evaporating liquids, speeding the composting process, and eliminating odours. A typical family of four will fill the Classic chamber in about six months. Once it's full, you move it to one side and replace it with your second chamber. By the time the second chamber is full, the composting process is complete in the first. You then remove the compost, put it in your garden and re-use the chamber. Nature Loo toilets are designed for self-installation. Even complete novices can install a Nature Loo in about half a day. The Compact can be set up more or less anywhere since the whole unit simply sits on the floor. To install a Classic or Ensuite you will need a clearance of about one metre beneath the floor.

If you're using a concrete slab, you'll need to allow space beneath the slab for the Classic or Ensuite collection chamber and for access. If the slab is already poured, the chamber can sit on the slab and can be boxed in with a couple of steps leading up to the pedestal. You can place an upstairs toilet almost anywhere you want, completely independent of your downstairs unit. If you are building your house and living in a shed or caravan you can use a Nature Loo Classic now, then install it in the house when it's finished, or you can buy the Compact and use it until the house is completed, then use it as a second, or outside, toilet. The Nature Loo Compact includes two small composting chambers (which double up as pedestals), a black plastic seat, a vent cap, a 12 volt 2.8 watt air fan and housing plus connecting flexible hose and insect screen, a moisture trap, a regulated transformer for 12 volt power to the fan, and a manual.

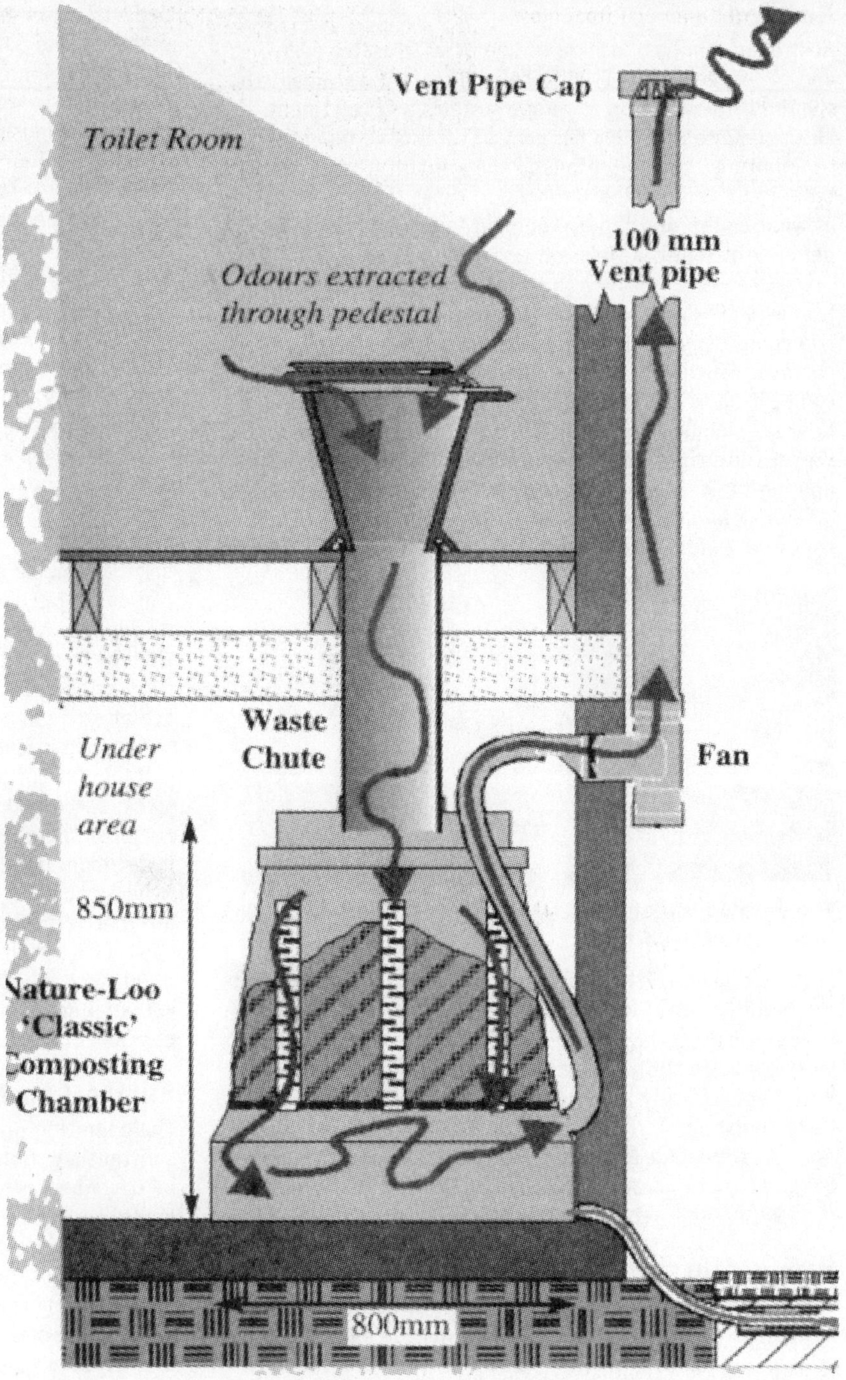

Complete novices can install a Nature-Loo in about half a day.

Nature Loo, PO Box 2157, Toowong, Qld, 4066. Phone: (07) 3870 5037, fax: (07) 3870 5088, email: <info@nature-loo.com.au>, web: <www.nature-loo.com.au>.

ROTALOO

Australian families flush 78 billion litres of water every year, and in 11 years from 1980, local and state governments had spent $10.6 billion on sewerage systems and treatment. This accounted for 11.6 per cent of total government expenditure. Concentrations in the effluent from a septic tank are in the order of one million times the concentration of what comes out of a composting toilet, and roughly 50 per cent of septic systems do not work properly.

One person using a flush toilet will produce eight tonnes of waste water in a year. In the same period a Rota-Loo composting toilet produces about 20 kg of disease-free compost which can be used as organic fertiliser. Some composting toilets are cheaper than the Rota-Loo because they are simpler to construct. Rota-Loo has a minimum of six separate compost bins contained on a turntable, inside a holding tank. The bins remain inside the tank, safely shut off out of harm's way. There is no need to remove any container holding fresh waste for storage elsewhere.

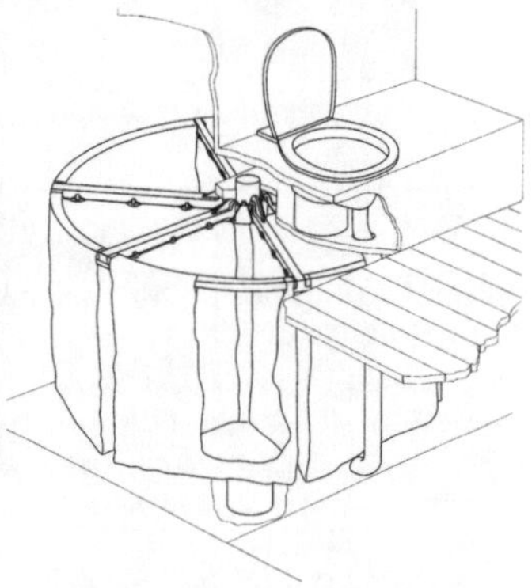

The Rotaloo Biolet is a mini, portable unit.

Rota-Loo is designed as a composting system without the requirement of earthworms, cardboard or organic matter to make it function. However, if a user wishes to add earthworms to the composting process, this can be done. Rota-Loo is factory assembled and is easily installed by a handy person.

Environment Equipment Pty Ltd, 41A Jarrah Drive, Braeside, Victoria, 3195. Freecall: 1800 250 950, phone (03) 9587 2447 website: <www.rotaloo.com>.

CLIVUS MULTRUM COMPOSTING TOILETS

Clivus Multrum composting toilets use absolutely no water or chemicals. They are the only continuous composting system. This means the lowest maintenance and the most efficient composting of any composting toilet. Clivus systems are designed for easy cleaning and easy operation. They require no heavy lifting or changing over of bins, nor do they rely on the use of worms. They are widely accepted by councils and government departments in all states. They have a proven track record after more than 20 years of supplying composting toilets.

The most popular model, the CM8 (suitable for the average family) reduces household water consumption by up to 60,000 litres a year. It is available with one polymarble pedestal, with an optional vent and drain kit available. Excreta accumulates in the tank along with carbon-rich material added for bulk (wood shavings, finely chopped garden clippings and leaves, and other biodegradables). A small fan in the vent pipe draws off odour continuously and keeps the toilet cubicles odour-free at all times. The fan can be powered by a solar system or by mains power.

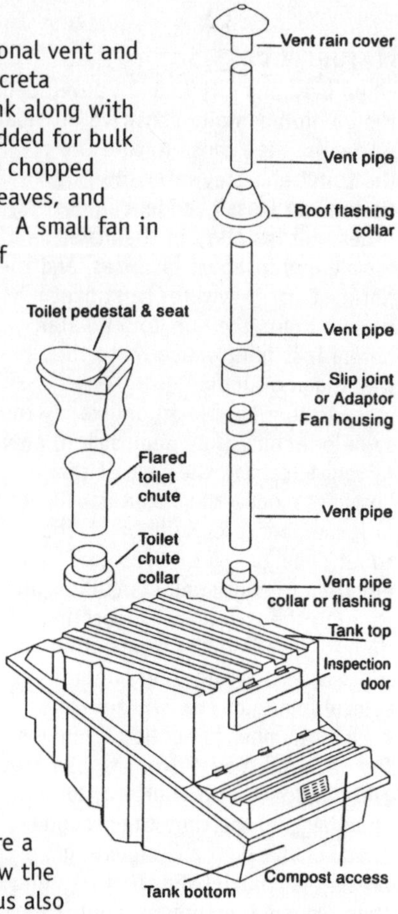

Decomposed wastes will be reduced by 95 per cent of their original volume and can easily be disposed of by shallow burial in the garden. The Ecolet range of toilets is particularly suitable for concrete slabs: they don't require a compost chamber below the toilet room floor. Clivus also have a compact, low budget alternative for intermittent use in a shed or weekender.

Clivus Multrum Australia, PO Box 126, Strathpine, Qld, 4500. Phone (07) 3889 6144, fax (07) 3889 6149, email <clivus@ats.com.au>, and website: <www.clivusmultrum.com.au>.

ENVIRO LOO EVAPORATION/DEHYDRATION TOILET

The operating principles of the Enviro Loo differ substantially from standard composting systems: it can best be described as an evaporation/dehydration system. The Enviro Loo System separates the solids and liquids upon entering the holding tank. The liquids make their way to the bottom of the container, and the solids are captured on a specially-designed drying tray that is suspended at an angle approximately halfway down the holding tank. The unit evaporates the liquids and dehydrates the solids via an accelerated ventilation process. The solids are between 95 per cent and 97 per cent liquid, and in time the dehydration activity reduces the waste to between three and five per cent of its original mass.

The constant ventilation keeps the air flowing through the Enviro Loo in such a way that any odour generated is discharged by the Windmaster-driven vent pipe. The ventilation is also assisted by the black polyethylene unit that increases the temperature within the holding tank. The warm air rises and creates a constant upward draught,

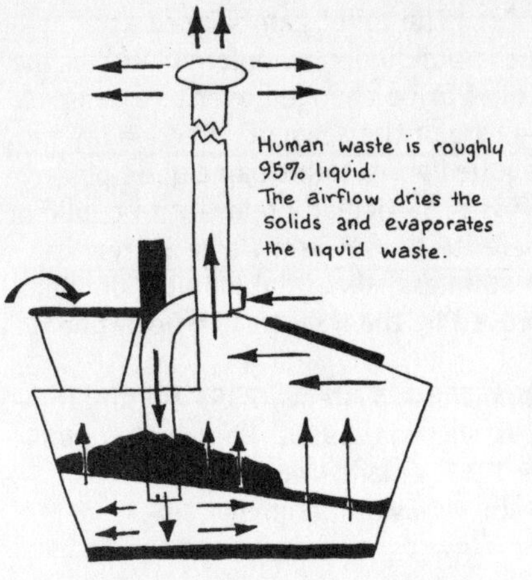

The ventilation circulation stimulates aerobic conditions for rapid dehydration – decomposition.

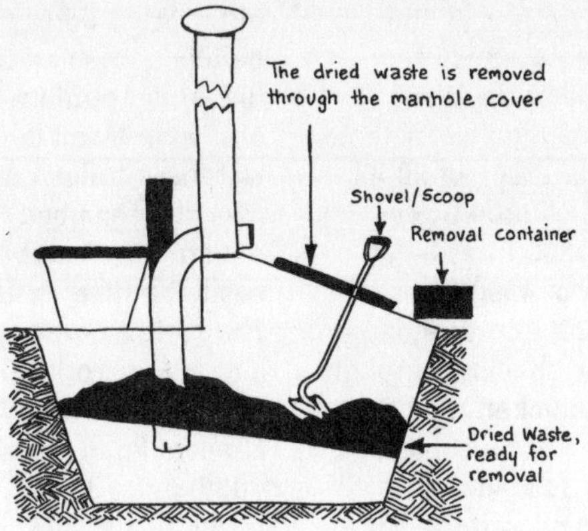

It is only the dried waste that requires removal after an extended retention period of approximately 2-3 years. A shovel or scoop and container are all the tools necessary for removal of the dried waste.

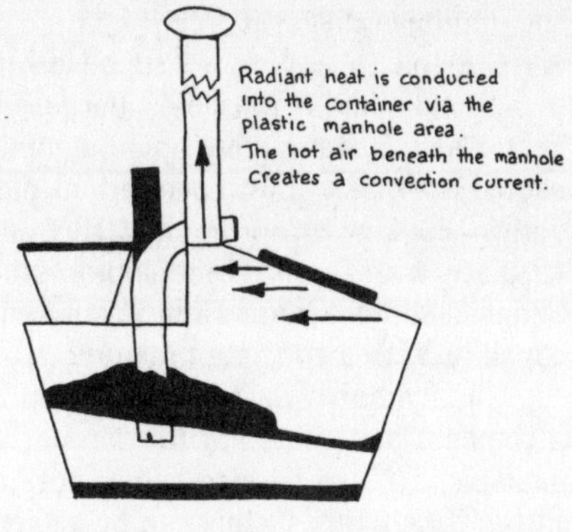

The increased internal temperature speeds up the rate of evaporation – dehydration and therefore decomposition of the solid waste.

driving the Windmaster, even on rainy and windless days. The continuous ventilation evaporates the liquids and dries out the solids. Oxygen itself is also a very powerful deodoriser. Foul odours considered normal in many composting, pit and septic systems due to the chemical reaction from faeces and urine do not occur in the Enviro Loo due to the early separation of liquids and solids. The end result is an odourless, dignified system for the user.

Whereas standard composting toilets actually increase the bulk of the waste by adding wood shavings, and other bulking agents, the Enviro Loo does not. The Enviro Loo actually works hard to reduce the eventual amount of waste. In a domestic situation the likelihood of having to remove any waste in the first two years of operation is extremely low. The more common reality is between four to five years. Importantly, when the waste is ready to be removed it will only be a small amount of inoffensive dry material. At this point the waste is either pathogen-free or has a very low count, suitable for further composting. The Enviro Loo 2010 Domestic Model has a capacity for eight to ten people times three uses a day.

Enviro Options, PO Box 219, 23 Gooraway Place, Berowra Heights, NSW, 2082. Phone (02) 9456 0172, fax (02) 9456 0173, or mobile 0415 605 5762, email <allan@enviro-options.com.au>.

A & A Worm Farm Waste Systems

A & A Worm Farm Waste Systems process rubbish, sewage, showers and kitchen waste into a clear, aerated liquid which is absorbed into soils better than septic liquids due to the worm activity and naturally-occurring organisms opening up the soil. The system takes greywater, black water and garbage into one chamber, and can also be fitted to existing septic tanks. The process is similar to that which occurs naturally on the forest floor. Series 1100-L is a Worm Farm Waste System of 3000 litres in a polythene tank processing 1100 litres per day. This system used on a sloping site can take liquids out by gravity to an EPA-approved disposal area, or, on a flat site, a small sump pump is added to move liquid to

SERIES 1800L

Series 1800L is a Worm Farm Waste System of 3300 litres capacity concrete tank processing 1800 litres per day

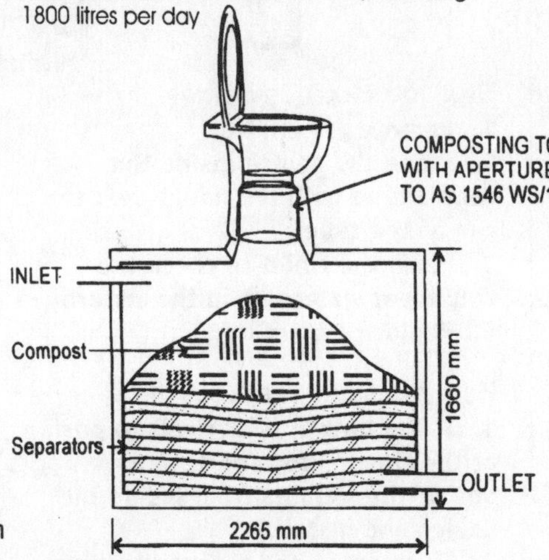

SERIES 2000L

Series 2000L is a Worm Farm Waste System of 4500 litres capacity concrete tank processing 2000 litres per day

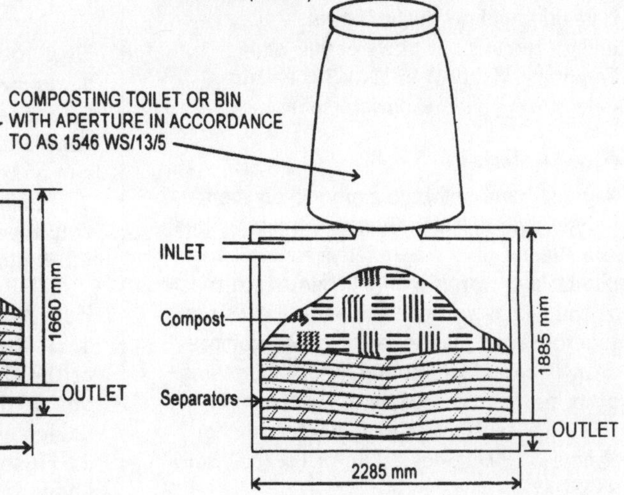

the approved disposal area.

All pump systems are supplied with an alarm system, and all plumbing is standard. Because none of the Worm Farm Waste Systems store liquid, land with a high water table should use one of the concrete tank models 1800L or 2000L. Series 1800L is a Worm Farm Waste System of 3300 litres capacity, with a concrete tank processing 1800 litres a day. Series 2000L is a Worm Farm Waste System of 4500 litres capacity, with a concrete tank processing 2000 litres a day.

The rubbish waste is poured into the chamber through a compost bin located at the top of the chamber. As an example, a 20-kg hessian bag of potatoes will be consumed in ten days. This system can be attached to standard Australian sewerage pipes with either a compost toilet or bin located on top of it. The toilet can be used as a builder's toilet until the building is completed. It can then remain an outdoor toilet or be changed over to a compost bin while also taking care of the sewage. Where a dry or waterless toilet is required a dry toilet pan can be placed over the chamber. This is particularly relevant in public or remote locations where the Worm Farm Waste System can easily be fitted with stainless steel or aluminium dry pans. The systems are approved by the NSW Health Department and EPA Victoria.

A & A Worm Farm Waste Systems, 2353 Mornington–Flinders Road, Flinders, Victoria, 3929. Phone: (03) 5989 1088, fax: (03) 5989 1155, email: <wormfarm @pacific.net.au>, web: www.wormfarm.com.au>.

Conserve products

TOILET FLOW CONTROLLER

Designed to fit single flush toilets with centrally-located overflow chambers, the Toilet Flow Controller allows you to control the amount of water flushed through your toilet. The unit can deliver the water savings of a dual flush toilet without replacing the entire system.

Sold by Melbourne company, South East Water, ph. 131 694, web: <www.sewl.com.au>.

CISTERN CONVERTOR

This is a simple device that converts cisterns to controllable flow. Normally when you flush your toilet all the cistern water empties into the bowl: this device allows you to control the amount of water used (see details at right).

By adjusting the weights and pressing the button once or adjusting the amount of time you hold down the button, you can release the amount of water you want. Enquiries: Ph: (02) 9519 0433, email: <enquiries@energyandwatersolutions.com.au>.

MULCH GUARD

Ray and Sandra Mitchelmore reckon their polypropylene Mulch Guards will last 20 years. The Mulch Guard slowly releases water to plants, and worms work nutrients into the soil as the mulch breaks down. The guards pin together with plastic canoe clips, promote growth, retard weeds and deter rabbits and other pests. "Tests show a water saving of up to 70 per cent," says Ray. Contact Ray or Sandra on (03) 5461 3000, or fax (03) 5461 3145.

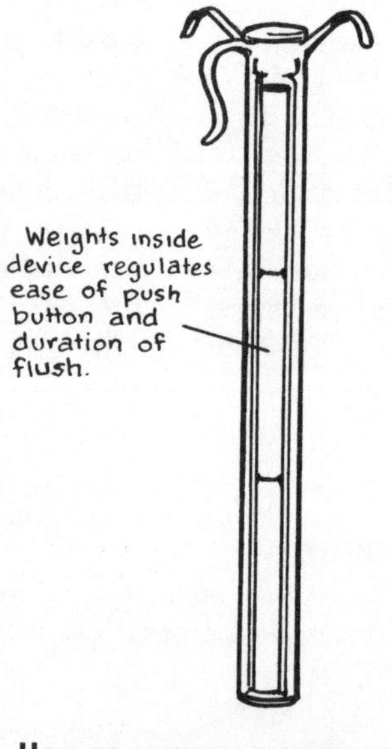

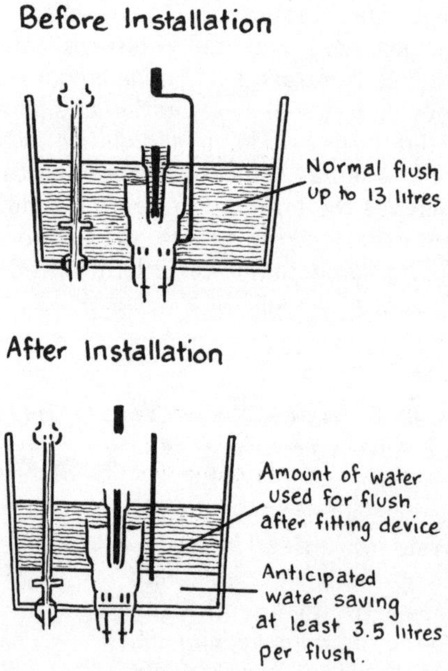

HOW TO INSTALL CONVERTOR

1. Remove cistern lid.
2. Stand the device inside the centre tube with the hooks over the rim of the tube.
3. Flush the toilet to check the volume of water left in the cistern.
4. Replace cistern lid.

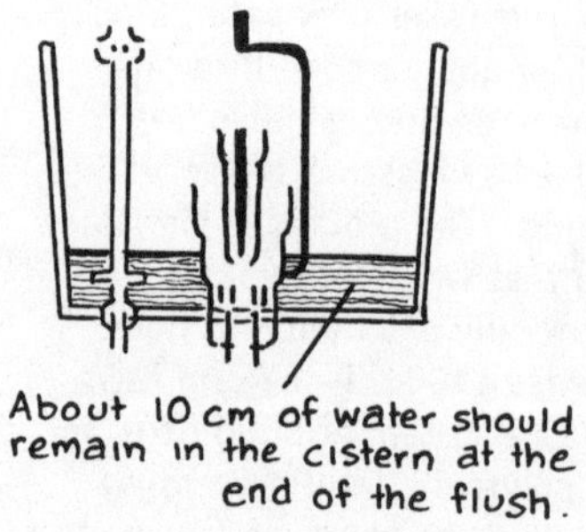

HOW TO ADJUST THE FLUSH

1. If the button is difficult to push or the flush is too short, remove one of the weights from inside the device and install.
2. Flush again and repeat the steps above if necessary.

Leeaky Hose

Many Earth Gardeners rave about the Leeaky Hose as a brilliant way to water vegie gardens and raised beds. The hose is made from 100 per cent recycled rubber and plastic and is designed so that water "sweats" through its walls at a controlled rate over long distance at low water flow. This is claimed to save 70 per cent on garden water use, and there are then no drippers or jets to block. At pressures of 4 psi or below, the hose will deliver moisture to the surrounding soil through capillary action.

The hose can be installed either above or below ground, but below ground installation gives the maximum water saving and soil improvement. Recycled household water or dam water can be put through the hose, and the maker recommends that the end of the hose is easily accessible (that is, not a buried loop) to flush it several times a year. The Leeaky Hose uses standard hose fittings and may be cut to any length for any configuration. The unit works efficiently from a one-metre-high head, so it's perfect for city gardeners who attach it to the open valve of a rainwater tank. Standard 13 mm joiners can be used to insert sections of ordinary hose where watering is not required, and the hose can be bought by the metre from shops such as Going Solar, The Green Building, 60 Leicester Street, Carlton, Vic. 3053, Ph. (03) 9328 4123.

Leeaky Hose, 86 York Street, Richmond, Vic., 3121. Phone: (03) 9429 2977, fax: (03) 9429 8811, email: <leeaky@leeaky.com.au>, web: <www.leeaky.com.au>.

E-Co shower

This is a new Australian shower water-saving device that actually gets you wet! The E-Co shower uses around 7.5 litres of water a minute compared to the 20+ litres going down the drain with a normal showerhead, and works differently to most water-saving showerheads. The water passes through a tiny hole that makes the air bubble droplets cling and flow over your body. The shower spray head may not be suitable for use with some instantaneous water heaters, and it operates in the range of 150 kPa to 650 kPa.

Sink Hand Shower fits on the end of bathroom and kitchen spouts in place of a tap aerator. The sink hand shower is designed to save two thirds of normal water usage as a spray rather than a straight stream of water. It is made from dezincification-resistant brass, chrome plated, and has an AAA-rated shower fitting.

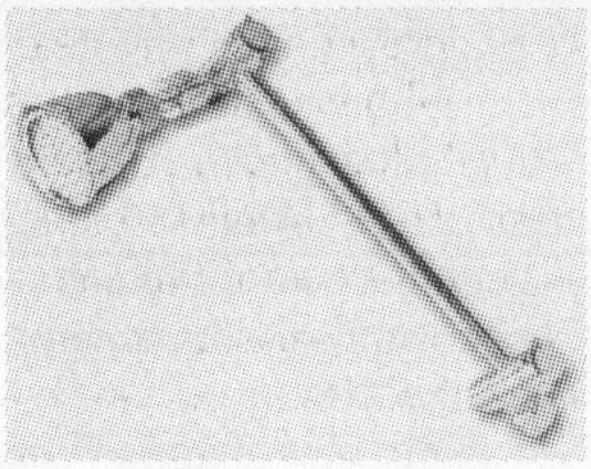

The products are made by Westson Pty Ltd, PO Box 82, Currumbin, Qld, 4223, ph: 1300 133 376, web: <www.ecoshower. com.au>.

Low pressure country sprinkler

"All our country customers rave about this unique design," say the wonderful people from The Digger's Club, who sell this sprinkler. It will not block up on even the dirtiest tank, dam or creek water. The sprinkler covers a diameter up to ten metres. It's not for high pressure supply, but great for gravity feed or washing machine water.

Hand-held spray nozzle

This is the best hand-held spray because you can adjust the flow rate without going back to the tap. It offers a choice of seven settings, from a jet spray to the finest mist for seedlings. "The best we have seen," says The Diggers Club.

Water saver sprinkler

This sprinkler can adjust from a full to a part circle with a distance control knob, so water only falls where you want it to. It covers a diameter of ten metres. From The Digger's Club, 105 La Trobe Parade, Dromana, 3936, phone: (03) 5987 1877, fax: 5981 4298, or the Garden of St Erth, Simmons Reef Road, Blackwood, 3458.

Watersavers Water Level Alarm

Has your washing machine ever overflowed the laundry trough? Have you ever left the bath running, only to return and find it too full? The Water Level Alarm can help you avoid overfilling the basin, sink or bath and may save you money. You set the flexible sensor arm to the depth required and turn on the alarm. The unit has a long life battery and is waterproof.

Sold by Melbourne company, South East Water, ph. 131 694, web: <www.sewl.com.au>.

Deluxe Showerhead Kit

The Deluxe Showerhead Kit offers a choice of six settings (including massage) and is "AAA" rated by Standards Australia. In recent surveys conducted by a major consumer association, the Deluxe Showerhead was rated the best by users. The Deluxe Kit features the Waterpik six function massaging showerhead, and comes with high rise arm, a five year product warranty and a 14 day money back guarantee. The showerhead kits are not suitable for gravity-fed hot water systems.

Sold by Melbourne company South East Water, ph. 131 694, web: <www.sewl.com.au>.

WATERSAVERS SHOWERTIMER

The ShowerTimer can help get kids or housemates out of the shower more quickly. It encourages shorter showers, and can save money on water and energy accounts. By shortening daily showers by two minutes you can save up to 10,000 litres of water a person a year. That's a potential annual saving on your water and energy accounts of nearly $30 a person if you're on town water. The ShowerTimer also comes with a ready reckoner to help you calculate your water usage and savings.

Sold by Melbourne company, South East Water, ph. 131 694, web: <www.sewl.com.au>.

WATERSMART AUTOMATIC WATER SAVER

The WaterSmart soil moisture control system introduces "set and forget" watering as the control system senses the water requirements of the garden and then cancels the pre-set start times if the soil moisture is adequate. Studies undertaken at the University of Western Australia indicated a 60 per cent water saving over an 80-day trial on average (30 per cent in a hot week, 50 per cent in typical summer conditions). The sensor is permanently calibrated and does not drift in time. It must always be located under healthy turf as this provides a uniform leaf area and a dense root concentration.

For information contact Holman Industries, 463 Scarborough Beach Rd, Osborne Park, WA 6017, ph: (08) 9204 1011. In Melbourne, ph: (03) 9357 9991.

WATER FLOW PRODUCTS

WATER FLOW CONTROL DISCS

Can be fitted to existing tap or showerhead to reduce the amount of water flow without affecting your water pressure.

On average 18 to 28 litres of water flows out of a household tap every minute, which the disc can reduce to only 9 or 12 litres a minute.

INLINE WATER FLOW CONTROL VALVES

The Inline Water Saver is designed to be installed in shower heads and hand-held showers to reduce water consumption by more than 50 per cent. They are available in both 9 and 12 litre a minute regulator rates and are installed between the showerhead and supply pipe.

TOILET WATER SAVER

This device is fitted to your cistern and ensures your toilet only flushes while the button is held down, potentially reducing the water usage by up to 70 per cent. Installing the Toilet Water Saver can eliminate the need to install a dual flush system.

WATER SAVING SINK SWISH

This device transforms the kitchen tap from an aerated stream to a spray with a simple push. The Sink Swish also has a built-in water saver to reduce water consumption. The swivel area on the Sink Swish is 360 degrees.

WATER SAVING AERATOR

When installed onto an existing tap the water flow is reduced from 18 to 28 litres a minute to only 8 litres a minute. It can improve water pressure by oxygenating the water that flows from the tap.

FLOOD STOP SAFETY VALVE

This valve is designed to prevent water flowing from your tap by shutting off the water flow if your hose (washing machine or dishwasher) slips off or breaks.

INLINE WATER FLOW CONTROL DISCS

These discs, fitted to an existing garden tap adaptor, are designed to equalise the water flow from your outdoor tap, improving water pressure while reducing water flow.

Available from Water Wizz Products Pty Ltd, PO Box 574, Camberwell, Vic, 3124. Ph: (03) 9833 5530, fax: (03) 9833 5587, email: <enquiries@waterwizz.com.au>, web: <www.waterwizz.com.au>.

NO-FLUSH URINALS

No-Flush Urinals offer total water conservation as they function on gravity flow and use absolutely no water. They resemble conventional wall-hung fixtures, but do not require a water supply or flush valve. They connect to standard 50 mm drain lines. They are easily retro-fitted in existing installations. The dry surfaces are hostile to bacteria that require water to live. The unit uses an Eco Trap that helps to eliminate odours. The Eco Trap principle works by urine flowing down into the Eco Trap drain insert. Within this device the urine passes through a floating layer of BlueSeal liquid, which forms a barrier that prevents sewer vapours from escaping to the atmosphere. Urine under the barrier layer overflows into the central tube and runs down to the conventional drain line.

Further information from Environment Equipment Pty Ltd, 41a Jarrah Drive, Braeside, Vic., 3195. Ph. (03) 9587 2447, fax (03) 9587 5622, email: <enquiry@ rotaloo.com>.

4

Re-use Recycle

A wetland garden for recycling waste water

A wetland waste-water garden can be sized to fit a backyard or a small city. Pam Andrews describes the model used at Birdwood Downs in the Kimberley.

BY PAM ANDREWS, *BIRDWOOD DOWNS, WESTERN AUSTRALIA*

WELL, I FINALLY returned to the Kimberley. After a 14-month absence it was good to be back at Birdwood Downs station. This time I experienced the dry season; last time it was "the wet": dramatic also, but in a different way. The stars, sunsets and the boabs are just as beautiful whatever the season.

One of the first projects I was involved in was helping to construct a waste-water garden behind the homestead. I worked with Dr Mark Nelson, a partner in Birdwood Downs. Mark was in Biosphere 2 in Arizona as part of the eight-person crew during the two-year closure experiment from September 1991 to September 1993.

While in the Biosphere, Mark was in charge of the constructed wetland used for waste-water treatment. His wetland system produced flowers, food for the Biospherians and animal fodder. It was then Mark realised the huge untapped resource going to waste. When he left Biosphere 2, Mark went to the Yucatan Peninsula in Mexico to fine-tune this waste-water system, in collaboration with the Planetary Coral Reef Foundation and Professor H T Odum of the Centre for Wetlands at the University of Florida.

"Waste-water garden" is Mark's term for an ecologically diverse, sub-surface flow, constructed wetland for sewage recycling and treatment. (The term is now trademarked in the USA.). It is such a simple yet brilliant concept. A pit is dug, lined, filled with gravel, and a wide diversity of wetland plants, including grasses, flowering shrubs, wetland palms and trees are planted. This is then connected to the septic tank and the "treatment" of household waste-water commences!

Solids are separated from the liquid in the septic tank. A final filter ensures no solids pass into the wetland, maintaining the gravel's ability to hold and treat the waste-water. Primary treatment occurs here as solids remain and are broken down, leaving sludge that can eventually be composted. The nutrient-rich waste-water is fed into the wetland garden where it is kept five to ten centimetres below the gravel surface, preventing accidental contact and also preventing odour or breeding of mosquitoes.

Each particle of gravel is colonised by the natural variety of microbes that are effective in utilising and treating waste-water. Water and nutrients are also taken up by the root systems of the wetland plants. Faecal coliform bacteria are reduced by more than 99 per cent, biochemical oxygen demand is reduced by 85 to 90 per cent, and the removal of phosphorus and nitrogen is substantial. Treated water can be used for irrigating lawns, shrubs, flowers or trees.

The system is so effective that only 20 per cent of the area is required compared to a surface-flow wetland. A wetland waste-water garden can be sized to fit a backyard or cater for a town or small city. Studies have shown that in tropical conditions as little as three to four square metres of wetland will effectively treat the black and grey water of one full-time resident. Depending on local climate, water usage and level of treatment required, the area needed per inhabitant may increase. The system permits extension by creating an additional treatment compartment to accommodate development and increased loading. The wetlands are low cost and easily maintained. Many systems can be designed to rely completely on gravity flow, thereby eliminating the need for electricity or pumps. The only maintenance necessary is regular filter checks and gardening as required.

The waste-water garden consistently cleans water to levels better than municipal standards and is now fully endorsed by the United States EPA and by many European countries. Studies are now being carried out on the waste-water garden at Birdwood Downs, a pilot project under a program monitored by the WA Health Department.

Waste-water gardens are now operating in over sixty sites, including the Yucatan Peninsula in Mexico, Bali, Indonesia and New Mexico in the USA. In all these areas they have proved extremely successful. They are particularly effective in preventing pollution damage to offshore coral reefs so are ideal for coastal resorts. They are also recommended for areas where groundwater is too close to the surface, or where density of population has resulted in contamination from too many septic tank systems.

Climbing a giant boab tree on Birdwood Downs: the perfect place to survey the wetland waste-water garden.

As the system relies on the activities of plants and microbes, it performs even better in mild and tropical or sub-tropical conditions. With higher temperatures and increased sunlight, effectiveness is high year round. Originally developed in the US and Europe, this refined concept is ideal for Australian conditions.

These gardens are beautiful. As a landscaping feature alone, they add beauty to any environment. To know they are treating sewage rather than pumping it into the ocean or groundwater is quite amazing!

Having been involved in the building of a wetland waste-water garden I can testify to its simplicity and effectiveness. In my six months at Birdwood Downs the plants grew at an astronomical rate although this was the dry season. All other garden plants survived because they were irrigated. The potential for such a garden is immense when you think of plants for fibre, timber, fuel, animal fodder or simply for cut flowers and landscape beauty. Local biodiversity is enhanced, increasing the habitat for wildlife and birds. Added to this is the water that flows out of the system, ready to be used for irrigation.

Dr Mark Nelson is usually based at Birdwood Downs from December to June, and is available to deliver talks on his wetland systems. He or Robyn Tredwell (manager of Birdwood Downs) can be contacted for more information. Phone: (08) 9191 1275, fax: (08) 9291 2072 or email: <marknelson1@cs.com>.

He is a very good man to spend time with, not only for his wealth of knowledge but he has one of the driest senses of humour I have experienced! This remains a magical place for me. In the midst of the magnificent Kimberley lies a place where people are transformed. I've seen this happen often. Whether you get involved with animals, plants, machinery or the land, (usually all of them!) you grow. Robyn arms you with enough knowledge to get started, then guides and encourages you to work the rest out. As before, people who come for a short visit usually stay longer. When they leave it's with a greater sense of both who they are and that there is no limit to what they can do.

World-beating natural waste treatment

A tenacious Australian inventor has solved the waste treatment riddle with a world-class system to turn all household waste – kitchen, bathroom, laundry – into irrigation water, without chemicals.

By Jenny Allen, *Maleny, Queensland*

MOST PEOPLE would have given up. Eleven years ago Dean Cameron, influenced by his mother's passion for organic gardening, began his quest to turn sewage into "organic" irrigation water.

He was also influenced by necessity. Dean had selected a well-known composting toilet system but became disillusioned by its poor performance. He soon discovered that some other systems also didn't work effectively – they would break down or let out an awful smell, emanating through the house and garden just as a party began. He knew there had to be a better way, a way that stopped his friends clearing out before dessert arrived.

As an ecologist and environmental scientist, he looked to ecosystems for the answer. While other scientists were studying oxygen diffusion into waste water in their laboratories, Dean was out in the paddock getting dirty, reflecting on the breakdown of dead cows and cowpats. He observed the succession of organisms that moved in to break up various decomposing materials – and quickly found sponge-like patterns in the architecture of decomposition.

He also studied the breakdown of forest litter in rivers and in roof gutters. He observed that the fastest breakdown did not occur in the water, as most engineers have assumed for well over a century, but was occurring on the waterline where the organic matter was moist but surrounded by air.

"I have never seen anything as simple and as natural as the Biolytix system. The concept behind the process is truly novel."

— Professor Ted Loudon, 25 years in the waste water treatment industry.

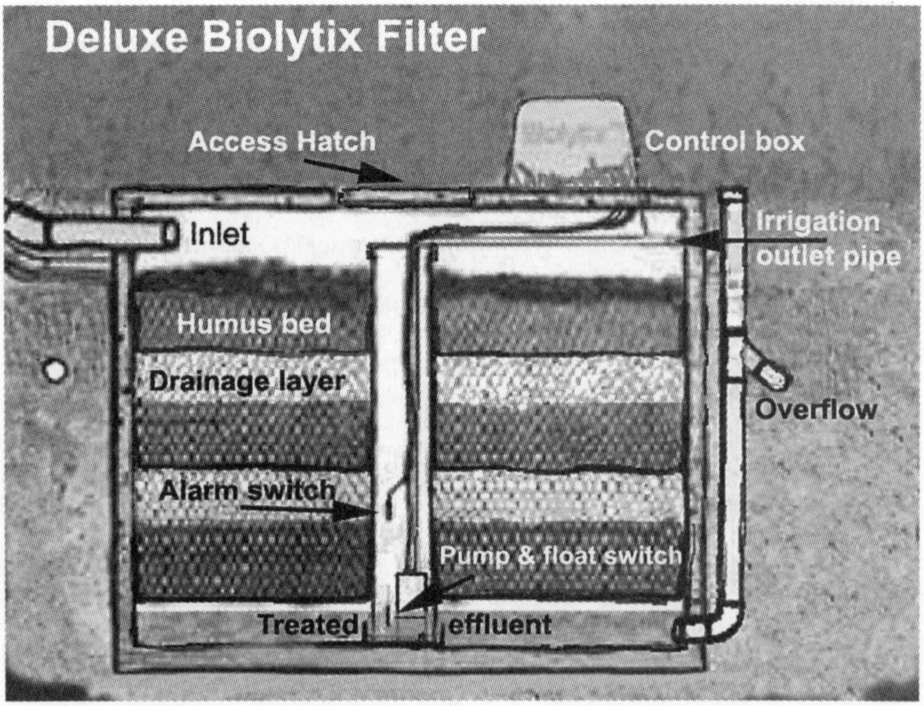

The Biolytix system will accept food and toilet wastes, wastewater, tampons, sanitary pads, drinks and milk, cleaning products, and vegie scraps.

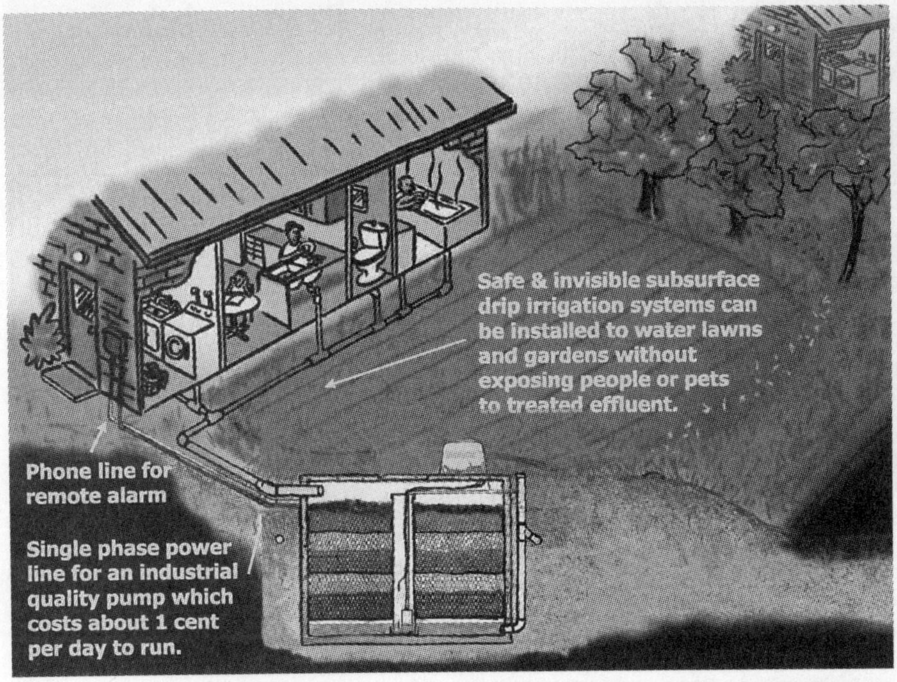

Above: within half an hour the Biolytix can turn sewage into high-quality irrigation water.
Left: the Biolytix can safely process waste from the kitchen, bathroom, laundry and toilet.

From these observations he knew intuitively that human waste and waste water treatment were based on the wrong principles. Waste should neither be left to pickle in a dry heap, as in many existing composting toilets, nor left in the water to rot very slowly, like a septic. The waste should be removed as fast as possible from the water and stocked with worms, beetles and other soil invertebrates, not just micro-organisms. Organic matter should be allowed to break down rapidly and aerobically in a moist, organic, soil-like environment, created by burrowing invertebrates vital to this natural "biolytic" ecosystem.

Biolytix waste treatment system

His hunch turned out to be correct and his organic breakthrough had just begun. So he designed the Biolytix waste treatment system, which immediately separates the solids from the water using a structured humus bed.

Biolytix, with the help of the Co-operative Research Centre, GHD engineers and Murdoch and Queensland universities, has produced a world first in waste water and organic waste treatment. A South African company, Spier Estates, tracked down the technology as a solution to the high fat waste water problem they had at their chef training school. They were so impressed they invested $3 million in Biolytix to further this ground-breaking research.

After three more years of research and development they got the outcome they were hoping for: the Biolytix system achieved the best results in the world for the most compact system.

How Biolytix can benefit your garden

- Over 70 per cent of septic systems fail and pollute the environment, including sensitive waterways. Biolytix is the only system compact enough to upgrade an existing (non-leaking) septic. This therefore improves the garden, rather than polluting it.
- Most other secondary waste treatment systems use potentially toxic chemicals, such as chlorine. These can harm the garden and are costly to keep replacing. If sub-surface irrigation is used, the chlorine can degrade the drip irrigation emitters. Biolytix copies nature, in that all the worms and microbes in the system clean up the waste without any chemicals ... and so rather than potentially harming the garden, it benefits greatly.
- Biolytix is the only secondary waste treatment system that works with an "in-sink-erator" food disposal unit. While other systems can't handle high organic loading, the Biolytix thrives on it. This means that, instead of being discarded or composted, food scraps can go into the "in-sink-erator", which automatically feeds the Biolytix, without you having to do a thing. The worms and microbes prosper on the gastronomical delights and break them down quickly. The system then irrigates the garden and helps it to flourish.
- Surveys show people use about as much water in the garden as they do inside the house. Using the Biolytix means that instead of all the house water being sent

CHECKLIST –
VITAL FOR SELECTING ANY WASTE TREATMENT SYSTEM

1. To what level does the system treat? And how is it able to benefit your garden? There are three main levels of treatment, which determine the quality of water that is produced and how this water can be used.

A. Primary treatment can be dispersed in trenches only.

B. Secondary treatment can be used for sub-surface drip irrigation — for lawns and trees.

C. Tertiary treatment can be reused to flush the toilet and to wash clothes. It can also be used to irrigate above ground with sprinklers through a lilac tap outlet.

2. How much does it cost and what do you get for your money? Check to see if there are any extra costs — and if so, what are they? Get a signed quote in writing so there aren't any hidden surprises. Does the quote include freight, installation and irrigation?

3. Are there a lot of big tanks that complicate installation? The more big tanks there are the greater the freight and installation costs, as well as more disruption to the garden. Check if the tank or tanks can be installed sub-surface — so they aren't an eyesore and take up less valuable garden space.

4. What guarantees do you get? Can it be replaced if you are not happy with it? Check to see if you can get a money-back guarantee if you are not happy with the system and service. The longer the guarantee, the more confident the company is with its product, and the stronger, long term relationship you can have with the company.

5. How many times per year does it need to be serviced? What does servicing involve and could it mean extra costs to you? The cost of servicing a waste treatment system adds up — and if it needs a quarterly service this can come around very quickly. A system needs to be serviced often if it is likely to break down a lot, or has a lot of vulnerable mechanical parts. Also, some companies make a lot of money simply from frequent servicing. Better to buy a system that is built to be sturdy and more independent.

6. Does it have to be periodically desludged — at a cost to you? If the system is designed well it can convert the waste into valuable nutrients that help the garden flourish, rather than sending the potential nutrients offsite as sludge.

7. How much electricity does it use per year? Like new white-good appliances, systems should now be designed to use a lot less energy and therefore have less impact on the Greenhouse effect. But unfortunately, most aren't. Ask how much the system will cost to run per year. If it uses more than 100 watts per kilolitre treated then it is too much of an energy-guzzler.

8. Does it have many parts that can break down and are expensive to fix, like pumps and blowers and so on. Does it rely heavily on mechanical operation? How many pumps does it have? How long are the pumps designed to last? The more pumps, the greater the risk of breakdowns.

9. Can you hear the system operating? Get a guarantee that you can't hear the system operating. There's nothing worse than moving away from the noise of the city — only to hear a noisy waste treatment system.

10. Can it also treat food scraps after they have been through an in-sink-erator? Rather than throwing out or physically composting your food scraps, check if the system can work automatically in conjunction with an in-sink-erator.

11. Does it help improve the environment or deteriorate it? Does it rely on chemicals, such as chlorine, that could be harmful to your family and garden?

12. Does it ever smell? Can it handle peak loadings and parties — without putting up a stink?

13. How will you know if it is not working? Does the alarm go straight to the company so they can be responsible for it — or do you have to find it and deal with it?

14. How resilient is it to the use of everyday household chemicals? Could it handle a bit of bleach? What about antibiotics?

15. Do you need to change your lifestyle to adapt to it? Does it need to be physically emptied by you.

16. Are you getting an up-to-date waste treatment system? Check it is not an old model, which has been superseded by new technology.

The Biolytix needs only standard sewerage plumbing connections, and no grease traps are required.

down a drain and away, or into trenches where it is mainly lost, it can all be reused throughout the garden. Not a drop is wasted and there is no need to pay for extra water for the garden. This can save gardeners around $200 a year in water bills.

- The Biolytix irrigation can be strategically placed below the surface to irrigate either the lawn or the trees, or both. So while the neighbours' gardens are browning off in the dry weather, yours can be green and abundant all year round.

DESIGN YOUR GARDEN TO MAXIMISE YOUR WASTE TREATMENT SYSTEM

Whether you are doing your initial garden design, or updating an existing one, you can design to make the most of your valuable waste treatment system. Parallel to, and about one metre to the low side of the irrigation lines, plant fruit trees that thrive with a lot of water. Make sure they are species without overly aggressive roots. (However, there are some clever innovations available for root intrusion control now; fortunately these don't involve restrictive root control herbicides.) If the trees also need good drainage, then plant them in raised beds. It's best not to waste this valuable space with native trees that are adapted to drier conditions.

Run the irrigation lines as well as the water-loving trees along the contour. You can also run simple pathways in between to manage the fruit trees, and for collecting fruit. The Biolytix also works well on gradients because it is a pressure compensated system. This means the drippers only open to irrigate at a certain head of pressure, and, with the supplied high specification pump, they can operate over a surprising height difference of more than 15 metres.

The irrigation system can also go under the lawn, watering it without the need of wasteful above-ground sprinklers. It can handle mowers going over it but not heavy machinery, such as earthmovers. From a gardener's perspective, the earlier the waste treatment system can go in the better.

MORE INFORMATION

The Biolytix has a detailed website: www.biolytix.com. There are two main models: the Biolytix Rugged for treating to primary standard, and the Biolytix Deluxe, which treats to high secondary standard and can be used for sub-surface irrigation. The gravity version of the Biolytix Rugged is $2830, and the Biolytix Deluxe is $4080.

Septic upgrades cost slightly more because they need to be built on-site in the existing (sound) tank.

To talk to Biolytix further about their system, or to order one, you can ring their toll-free number: 1300 881 472.

Growing herbs using household greywater

A general view of the system showing the three wetland areas and the pump to oxygenate the water in the lower tank. Note the increased growth in the growing tank.

Tim's concern about the amount of greywater being wasted led to some extensive research and ultimately to his design for a wetland filtering system.

BY TIM SAVAGE, WOODSTOCK, QUEENSLAND

I LIVE AND FARM in the dry tropics of north Queensland and although the annual rainfall is around 1000 mm, this tends to fall all at once, or at least over a two-month period, just after Christmas. For the rest of the year it is very dry and, as we live fifty kilometres from the nearest town, we have to rely on bore water. Luckily this is available in good quality and quantity. We have lived here for about eight years and during that time all the used household waste-water has been collected into a tank and when this was full, pumped to a soak away. This household waste-water is called greywater, mainly because it turns a grey colour shortly after being released. Water from the toilet is called black water because...well, I never discovered that and anyway it's not relevant here. In our situation this is collected in a septic tank and kept separate from our greywater.

The only thing I knew about greywater was that it was excessively smelly. Every time I pumped the tank out the whole area smelt very bad. Our septic tank for the disposal of toilet waste has never smelt, even when we had it pumped out!

I grow organic produce for sale at the local Sunday market and wasting thousands of litres of water has always been a worry. Of course, working for myself and attempting to make a living has never left much time for the development of new ideas. However, as part of my masters degree in Sustainable Agriculture, studied at Orange Agricultural College, I decided to research greywater with a view to using it, safely and cheaply, to irrigate a small herb garden.

The first thing I learnt about greywater was that its re-use is banned in every state of Australia where municipal sewerage systems exist. This is, of course, a brilliant idea. For example, according to Jonathan Berry from ECO Design, Brisbane City discharges 240 million litres of greywater into the river every day. It must also use at least that amount of water to irrigate its public gardens and this is quality, potable water of which supply is always finite. Just imagine how much water could be saved all over Australia, if all greywater was re-used!

Greywater is indeed very smelly and, in many people's minds, this is associated with disease. It is also a fact that it is a product of what the household discards. Who is to know if some clever inhabitant pours the contents of his car's sump, or the leftover weed killer he has been using, down the drain? This may be why municipal authorities are reluctant to use greywater. They fear being sued if someone gets sick from its use.

After my initial research, which mainly involved searching the web, I was beginning to think greywater was indeed dangerous. However, there is a lot of misinformation and uninformed comment about. According to Glen Marshall, research done in Los Angeles perhaps summed it all up when it stated that tests of greywater failed to find any harmful pathogens in the water or soil irrigated by it, and that no one in either Britain, America or Australia has ever been reported as getting sick from its use.

However, greywater is not as innocent as all that if released into the environment. The most common way of disposing of it is to flush it into a local watercourse. Just remember Brisbane's 240 million litres being released into the river! What does it do in these circumstances?

Greywater contains large quantities of organic compounds from the cleaning products you use and the food scraps you discard, all of which go down your drain. Thank goodness the sink garbage disposal unit has not become a standard here, as in the United States! This organic waste is acted upon by micro-organisms, which use it as a food source. This is good for the micro-organisms as they get fat and happy, but it is very bad for the environment. This is because the micro-organisms require large amounts of oxygen to process waste and they take this from the water. Algae also love these nutrients. They feed so well on it that they can multiply rapidly and form algal blooms. The result of all this is that the naturally occurring organisms in the water, such as fish, are starved of oxygen and food and either die off or emigrate. The final result is a dead river, which will take years to recuperate. This is not what we want. So instead of

Right: the main growing tank showing the drain at the front taking water back to the settling tank.

Far right: the in-ground settling tank showing the greywater supply pipe. The pump is suspended by the chain.

wasting this resource, let's re-use it for the benefit of all.

For a single household there is no problem, as you know what you are putting down your drain. The larger the number of households, the greater the risk from some irresponsible dumper of nasties. However, this is still not a great problem, as the average Australian household disposes of approximately 150 litres of greywater every day and this will dilute any harmful ingredients to such an extent that they have little effect.

This does not mean that greywater can be used without caution. Every household puts items such as phosphorus, sodium and boron into their water every day. "I use phosphorus-free washing powder", I hear you say. Well, perhaps you do, but remember that the majority of household cleaning products have added phosphorus as a water softener. Phosphorus is not a real problem if the greywater is to be used for irrigation. Indeed it can be an asset, except for native plants, which are sensitive to phosphorus. However, it is a real problem if the greywater is to be dumped into a watercourse!

Sodium forms the basis of most soap. It is also a problem once in the soil, as it can lead to a salt build-up which will eventually kill plants. But it can be controlled by using sufficient water to flush out the salt. Boron is another common ingredient of household cleaning products and this can kill some plants. Greywater is also very alkaline, which can adversely affect acid-loving plants.

So there are certain treatments which need to be carried out before greywater can safely be used for irrigation. Things to watch out for are: suspended solids, such as hair, human pathogens and certain metals.

I have designed a simple treatment system, which can be constructed by anyone with a little bit of ability. It has two main components, a settling tank and a wetland, which sounds very grand, but in reality is any waterproof container with a minimum of 150 litres capacity.

I already had a settling tank, the tank into which all my greywater is channelled. In this tank the pre-treatment occurs. The greywater sits in this tank for a few hours to allow it to cool and for any heavy material to settle to the bottom. At the same time micro-organisms contained in the water will begin to react. They will feed on the organic waste and produce energy while releasing carbon dioxide and water. As I have already said, they require oxygen to do this which they take from the water. Over time the oxygen is depleted and their reaction slows and eventually stops. This is when the anaerobic micro-organisms take over. These are bugs which should not be encouraged, as they take the oxygen they require for their reactions from inorganic salts, such as nitrate, sulphate and phosphate. These reactions result in the release of wonderful gases such as methane, phosphine and hydrogen sulphide, giving the greywater its distinctive aroma.

I use a sump pump to move the water from the settling tank to the wetland. Ideally the system should be as simple as possible and without mechanical pumps. The more complicated the system the more likely breakdowns will occur and the greater the need for maintenance. Unfortunately, unless you live on the side of a steep hill, or in a high-set house, this is not always possible, so I have to use a pump. The pump is automatic and controlled by a float system, which switches automatically as the water level rises and falls.

The wetland is simply a tank of water in which I grow floating waterweeds. The weeds play a very important role in the system so the choice of species is important. Wetland systems such as reed beds are designed to remove as many nutrients as possible before the water is released into the environment. The majority of nutrients removed in a wetland system are held in the soil. However, as I want to use the water for irrigation, I do not want the nutrients to be removed and have chosen water hyacinth because of its rapid growth rates and its massive root system. Although this is a listed noxious weed, it is being grown in a controlled environment and great care will be taken not to allow it to pollute any local waterway. The excess weed will be removed from the tank and fed to my pigs. Unfortunately this weed dislikes frost, so you will have to choose your weed to suit the area in which you live.

The roots of the water hyacinth act as a filter, attracting suspended particles by being electrically charged. The particles stick to the roots and are slowly digested by the plant. The wetland, therefore, filters the water and allows for the removal of other nasties, such as pathogens, bacteria and viruses. These either die off naturally, are filtered out, or settle to the bottom of the tank.

The greywater leaving the wetland is safe for irrigating food plants and is fed into a growing tank. This is a sand–clay mix to ensure good nutrient holding capacity and drainage. The water is fed to this area by buried pipes, which deliver the water to the root zone where it is taken up by the plants. Feeding the greywater into the root zone prevents it ever coming into contact with the plant leaves, which is just an added precaution. Any excess water is drained away and is either fed back into the settling tank ready for a second go around the system, or used to irrigate other plants.

The system is designed to be as maintenance-free as possible and to provide both water and nutrients to the growing plants. It is hoped it will produce an economic crop and is far better than wasting all that scarce water.

Double dipping: getting the most from your water

Short of water? Use it twice. Fabienne discusses techniques especially suited to tenants.

BY FABIENNE BAYET-CHARLTON, *MYLOR, SOUTH AUSTRALIA*

STUDIES show that the average house in Australia (those on the quarter-acre block) can use up to 80 per cent of their water on the garden. With summer around the corner, and the term "Adelaide drinking water" being an oxymoron, water use has proven to be an issue of concern to gardeners here. (Drinking a glass or tap water in Adelaide is like drinking a glass of hair.)

The first summer that Adelaide's supply became a "utility" and residents had to pay for their water caught me unawares. I watered our backyard at Goodwood and brought in a water bill for over three hundred dollars. It was a harsh lesson for me to learn.

It pays to double dip. Tenants rarely have the luxury of purchasing and installing permanent water-saving or recycling structures. Double dipping is my strategy for watering the garden without wasting precious fresh water. There are so many ways to use water at least once or twice before it can go on the garden and there are many strategies for a rental situation as well.

Use your bath water on your roses or fruit trees. Mild soapy water is a great deterrent against aphids and some mites. If using a bucket is too much strain buy a small bilge pump and grow something outside the bathroom window. Put a bucket in the shower cubicle with you, or a baby bath to stand in. You'll be amazed at how much water is wasted down the drain while we stand waiting for the shower to warm up. The bilge pump will pay for itself by reducing your water bill in the long run.

Attach a hose with a redirecting valve to your washing machine and water the lawn or fruit trees. If you use a washing detergent that has phosphates in it at least re-use the rinse water. If your garden is desperate for water consider using a softer detergent or mixing up bucket of soap flakes instead. (My girl, Ashlyn, was born with chemical sensitivity to just about all detergents, perfumes and soaps. New clothes needed to be rinsed out before she could wear them so I used to wash everything with diluted Velvet soap and scrub stains with eucalyptus and vinegar. It wasn't much fun but at least all the washing machine water could be re-used on the garden.)

Fabienne surveys her garden, flourishing after using her water-saving methods to maximum effect.

When water restrictions are really tight, I use the babies' bath water to wash their really grotty clothes, then put it on the garden. This is the ultimate in double dipping.

A neighbour confided that her washing machine is connected to the toilet cistern so that the rinse water is used to flush the toilet, saving fresh water for the shower, drinking and dishes. If the layout of your house doesn't allow this, put a recycled 1.5 or 2-litre soft drink bottle, filled with water, in your toilet's cistern. It will not have an adverse affect on your toilet's ability to work, trust me, and you'll save yourself two litres of water every time you flush. In many rural towns it is compulsory for all septic tanks to be replaced with Envirocycle water recycling units. The water from the toilet is treated within the unit and then used to water the garden. But it is not recommended for use on the vegie patch and it's not a great idea for kids to be near the sprinklers. If you are really concerned about water pollution and sewage treatment in your area, don't flush your toilet paper! Put it in an airtight bucket and dispose of as solid waste instead. It's a little known fact that toilet paper is the hardest matter to break down in a sewage treatment system and if the system overloads, it will have to be flushed out to sea and break down there. If you don't believe me, check out Adelaide's St Kilda mangroves at low tide. That ain't seaweed draped along the trees.

Get a rainwater tank. Small square ones are easy to install and transport for a rental situation. Our tank paid for itself within a year with the drinking water we didn't need buy in. Rainwater is the ultimate tonic for a mains or bore-watered garden as it gives your vegie patch a reprieve from the build-up of harmful salts, bacteria and residual pollution that's unavoidable in our cities' water systems. If you're worried about air pollutants dissolving in the water or leaves from the roof, lay netting over the incoming pipe and attach a water filter to the tank tap.

If you can afford it, install a dripper or seepage irrigation system with a timer. If you can't, buy a transportable seepage hose to move around the garden. Water first thing in the morning, or last thing at night. Do not be obliged by urban fashion to have the lawn permanently green. Water once a week if you must. If not, let the bloody stuff die off. Unless it is specifically stated in the lease agreement it is not compulsory for tenants to water the lawn. Mow it if you're really embarrassed maybe once a fortnight. Do not be bullied into urban mediocrity.

Mulch has become the byword of successful summer gardening and everybody has their favourite garden topping. Some people swear by pea straw, others love newspaper; some can't get enough council clippings, and succulent lovers get off on gravel or colourful rocks. I reckon diversity is the spice of life and the life of organic gardening. Mulch, for god's sake, mulch. If you can, nab your local lawn mowing service and ask for clippings. Chances are they will love you for it, as most lawn mowing services have to pay dumping fees to get rid of the stuff. Most progressive inner city councils will drop a truck load of mulch in your driveway for a reasonable fee. It will consist of shredded branches and probably have a high eucalyptus component so don't chuck it directly on the vegie patch or near acid-hating plants. Straw bales are the ultimate mulch for the vegie patch, better value for the dollar compared to loosely packed bags sold at the mainstream nurseries. Find your local fodder or old-fashioned landscaping store. You'll be surprised how many "historic nurseries" continue to survive and serve inner city suburbs.

If you have a small balcony garden or lots of terracotta pots grab yourself a peat or coconut fibre brick from the local hardware store for about two dollars. Break it in half and soak it in water until it resembles a bucket of hairy monster. Using a cup, or your hands, slosh it onto the soil of your pot plants and water in well. The fibre will act as a good water retainer and mulch, helping your plants through dehydrating days. If your pot plants have dried out and the soil has shrunk away from the sides of the pot you can rejuvenate them by plunging them in a bucket of water for an hour. (Do not leave them any longer as many delicate plants may drown.) Old one-litre soft drink bottles can also be used to water pot plants. Cut the bottom off and push the bottle upside down into the soil. The bottle will act as a slow release funnel reducing the effect of dehydration and shrinkage. Don't forget to take the lid off first though.

My Nanna used to have a bucket under her kitchen sink as there was no plumbing in her Coober Pedy dugout. Every day the fern and jade plant she had outside her front door got a bucket of dishwater. Her shower consisted solely of an aluminium bucket with a valve attached to the shower nozzle. Once that water ran out bad luck.

Grossed out? Try living without water for more than two days. I mean really try. Buy yourself a four-litre cask of drinking water and turn off all the taps, cisterns, washing machines, dishwashers, showers and hoses and see how it affects your family, house and garden. I'm sure Sydney-siders will remember what that's like. Double dipping for the garden doesn't seem so insane.

Tips

SAVE WATER

Use recycled bath, shower and laundry waste-water in the garden, but not on edible plants or vegetables.

Do not rinse dishes under a running tap. Instead, partially fill a sink or bowl with rinsing water.

Do not peel or clean vegetables under running water.

CATCH THE COLD WATER

Water is wasted each time cold water is flushed from a hot water pipe. Keep containers near the sink and shower, and use this excess on the garden or indoor plants.

The Greywater Re-use Standard System

For those wishing to tackle disposing of greywater and putting it to use in a systematic fashion, Ross details his method and supplies guidelines for building your own.

BY DR ROSS MARS, *MIDLAND, WESTERN AUSTRALIA*

THE GREYWATER Re-use System (GRS) Standard system was formerly called the "Candlelight System" after the original system was designed and installed at Candlelight Farm in the hills east of Perth. Since this time ten years ago, many people have used this greywater system to complement their use of a dry or wet composting toilet.

The GRS Standard greywater dispersal system is an alternative to conventional leach drains and for general greywater dispersal. It was designed for people who wished to install an environmentally-friendly greywater dispersal system that deals with all waste-water from the kitchen, laundry and bathroom. A separate system dealt with toilet (black) water.

The GRS Standard system comprises two parts. Initially, all greywater passes into a sedimentation tank (see Figure 3) and then the waste-water is dispersed throughout an interconnecting sub-surface drain system (Figure 2). The drain cross-section is shown in Figure 1.

Guidelines calculating the required length of drain based on soil type, loading infiltration rate, size of house and number of bedrooms are included here, and are taken from Australian Standards 1547-2000. These calculations are subject to the soil being suitable as per Schedule 8 of the *Treatment of Sewage and Disposal of Effluent and Liquid Waste Regulations* (1998).

The loading infiltration rate is a measure of how well water moves through the soil. Water moves most easily through sandy soils and least easily through heavy clay soils. Essentially, this means that any sub-surface drains which are used for waste-water dispersal can be shorter in sandy soils. How you test what type of soil you may have, and what the loading infiltration rate could be, is discussed below.

METHOD OF DETERMINING ABSORPTIVE CAPACITY OF SOIL

Dig a hole 300 mm square and 400 mm deep. Remove all loose material such as roots and stones. Carefully scarify the sides and base of the hole to provide a natural surface into which water may percolate. Add 50 mm blue metal aggregate to protect the bottom from scouring. Fill the hole with water and allow it to soak overnight. The next day, fill again and allow it to soak away. Record the time for the water level to drop at least 25 mm. Use the table below to classify your soil type.

While the drain area will rely on absorption, it should also be planted out with small shrubs and trees to increase the dispersal by transpiration. Some examples of suitable plants are listed at the end of this article.

CALCULATIONS OF DRAIN SIZE FOR A COMPLETE GREYWATER DISPERSAL SYSTEM

To calculate the total length of drain required for greywater dispersal you will need to know how many bedrooms the house will contain, the loading infiltration rate (LIR, as determined from the test and table below) and the proposed drain width and height (such as that shown in Figure 1).

Time for drainage (minutes)	Soil type	Alternating system Loading infiltration rate L/m^2 per day	Alternating system Permeability m/day	Non-alternating Loading infiltration rate L/m^2 per day
less than 5	sand	30	1.2	15
5 - 60	loams or gravels	20	0.3	10
more than 60	impervious clays	5 * see below	0.06	* see below

*This soil type is generally unsuitable for the proposed drain system. Other systems such as evapo-transpiration systems (which include reed bed systems) may be more appropriate. Contact the Health Department to discuss an appropriate system design or site modification.

The general formula is:

L = V / LIR x A

Where L = length of drain (in metres), V = volume of greywater per day (litres) and A = surface area of the trench (add sides and base) in metres.

The following calculation is used as an example of a four-bedroom house with an LIR = 20 (alternating system, gravel soil). Greywater volume is estimated at 112 litres per person per day.

- A: surface area of trenches 400 mm (D) + 300 mm (W), but the stone matrix is 250 + 250 + 300 mm = 0.8 m/ lineal metre length
- V: house contains four bedrooms (5 people) @ 112 L per person = 560 L (greywater volume)
- LIR: loading infiltration rate = 20 L/m2.
- L: length of drain required = 560 / 20 x 0.8 = 35 m
- Design proposed has a total length of drain = 35 m. This comprises a series of shorter interconnected drains, as shown in Figure 2.

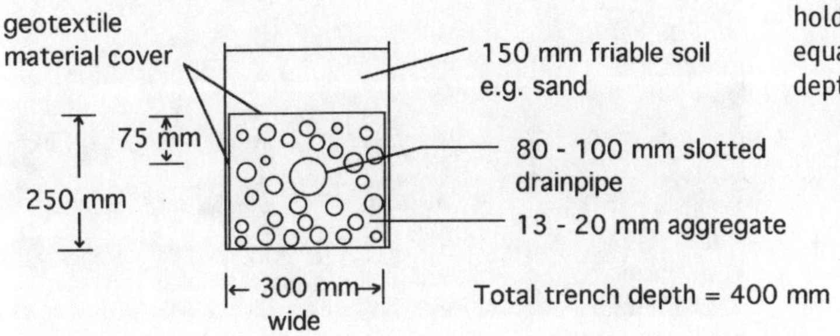

Figure 1. Typical construction and cross-section of GRS Standard drain.

DRAIN INFILTRATION AREA

Figure 2 is a typical infiltration area layout showing the size of drains and the arrangement of these drains to achieve the recommended total drain length for dispersal. A system of the dimensions shown will give a drain length more than that required.

The piped trenches should be laid level to ensure an even distribution of effluent. The installation of the piped trenches should also satisfy the same groundwater separation requirements as specified for other conventional drain systems. That is, a minimum 0.5 m separation between the base of the trenches and the highest known groundwater level.

If the drains installed are non-alternating, then the Loading Infiltration Rate (LIR) permitted is half that allowed for alternating drains. For example, for sandy soils, 30 L/m2 for alternating and 15 L/m2 for non-alternating is permitted. Consequently, twice the length of drain will be required if drains are non-alternating. An alternating system, where one half of the trenches are rested for a short time, is the preferred design, as less surface area is required for the dispersal area. The normal practice for leach drains is to change the diverter valve in the direction box each year (say on your birthday) so that one drain system is used and the other is rested. However for piped trenches , it is best if you can change the direction every month. Periodically resting half of the piped trench system allows the system to function more effectively.

SETTLING (SULLAGE) TANK

All greywater from the household should initially pass into a settling (or sedimentation) tank before being pumped or gravity fed into the dispersal area.

This tank is essentially a standard septic or sullage tank. A baffle may be incorporated into the tank but it is not essential. However, if a baffle is placed inside, the opening will need to be located so that sludge build-up does not block the opening. Typical commercially-produced baffles have the opening at the bottom, which may be unsuitable in this system. One type of tank which is suitable and available is illustrated in Figure 3.

For all greywater re-use a tank with a minimum holding volume of 1820 litres should be used. This volume equates to a tank size 1200 mm diameter and 1200 mm depth or height.

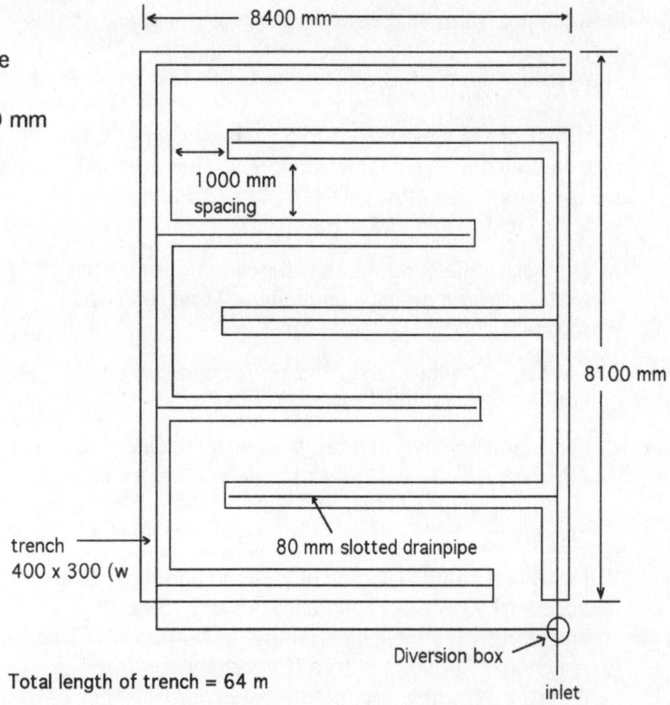

Figure 2. Typical alternating greywater dispersal trenches in gravel soil.

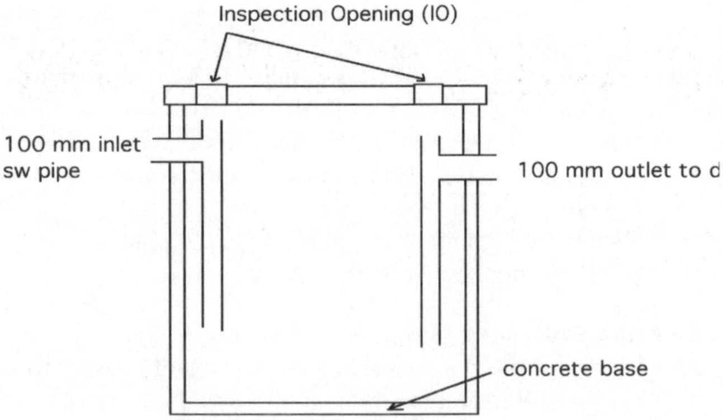

Figure 3. Typical settling tank required for complete greywater dispersal.

Should waste-water need to be pumped to an infiltration area, it should first pass from the settling tank into a small pumping tank. This is nominally a tank 600 mm in diameter and 600 mm in height which contains a submersible pump with a float valve. In addition, a safety warning device should be included in case the pump is not working and the tank begins to fill. An audible signal and glowing LED light indicate a rising water level.

PLANTS SUITABLE FOR GREYWATER INFILTRATION AREA

These plants, mainly natives, can tolerate wet soils. It should be noted, under current health regulations, that no below-ground food crops can be planted in this area. Fruit and nut trees are permissible.

Most of the species listed below have other useful functions, such as screen and windbreak, firewood and timber sources, bee attracting (and honey producing), aesthetic looking and bird attracting.

(a) Climbers – Black coral pea *(Kennedia nigricans)* Native wisteria (*Hardenbergia comptoniana)* and *Hibbertia scandens.*

(b) Grasses – Common reed (*Phragmites australis)* and Vetiver grass *(Vetiveria zizanioides)*

(c) Reeds and rushes – Jointed twig rush (*Baumea articulata)*, Pale rush (*Juncus pallidus)*, Lake club rush (*Schoenoplectus validus)* and Water ribbons (*Triglochin huegelii)*.

(d) Herbs and shrubs – Canna lily (*Canna flaccida)*, Swamp paperbark *(Melaleuca ericifolia)*, Lemon scented bottlebrush (*Callistemon citrinus)*, Spearwood *(Kunzea ericifolia)*, Tantoon tea tree (*Leptospermum flavescens)*, Astartea (*Astartea fascicularis)*, Coastal rosemary *(Westringia fruticosa)*, Comfrey (*Symphytum officinale)*, Grey honey myrtle *(Melaleuca incana)*, Sydney wattle (*Acacia longifolia)*, Western tea myrtle (*Melaleuca nesophila)* and Bog sage *(Salvia uliginosa)*

The greywater re-use system being installed; in the background is the trench system.

(e) Small to medium-sized trees – Swamp sheoak (*Casuarina obesa)*, Snowstorm *(Melaleuca linariifolia)*, River sheoak (*Casuarina cunninghamiana)*, Swamp oak *(Casuarina glauca)*, Bracelet honey myrtle (*Melaleuca armillaris)*, Blackwood (*Acacia melanoxylon)*, Broad-leaved paperbark (*M. quinquenervia)* and Mountain oak *(Casuarina stricta)*.

WHAT NEXT?

This article has covered only some aspects of greywater re-use strategies. There are many other factors to consider. For example, you may choose to use a non-alternating system, or you might like to split the system and disperse water in two different areas. Furthermore, the drain size can be changed and the length of the drain system adapted accordingly. You might only have a three-bedroom house or only wish to re-use the bathroom or laundry water. In these circumstances, the calculations of greywater volume, the sedimentation tank size and length of drain need to be adjusted.

Natural household water solution

Tony Camilleri was researching the use of composting toilets and greywater systems for his sustainable house design when he stumbled across a brilliant waste water management system, invented in the Top End to treat the bottom end of your household greywater.

BY TONY CAMILLERI, *CASUARINA, NORTHERN TERRITORY*

COMPOSTING toilets have been successfully used in Australia for a number of years as an environmentally-friendly method of disposing of human waste. They not only conserve water, but also transform the human waste into fertiliser that can be used in the garden. However, one drawback in using this system and avoiding a septic system altogether is how do you dispose of your greywater, that is, the waste water from the laundry, kitchen and shower?

H20 Solutions in Darwin have developed a waste-water disposal system that not only disposes of all the household waste water, but also allows the water to be treated and then recycled into the garden as irrigated water.

HOW DOES IT WORK?

Their system is known as an Aerated Wastewater Treatment System (AWTS), and uses two tanks. The primary tank receives the waste water from the household and is designed to retain it for one to two days, which allows some biological breakdown of the solids to take place through anaerobic (no air) digestion. The settled water in the primary tank then overflows into the treatment tank, which consists of an aeration chamber and sedimentation chamber. Aeration is achieved by the use of a linear air pump that is above ground and transfers compressed air into the chamber.

The aeration process enables nutrients present in the primary effluent to be digested by the bacteria. It usually takes about one day for this process, in which time the treated waste water enters the sedimentation chamber. Any excess sludge that entered the aerobic chamber is returned to the primary chamber by the pump or air lift. The primary tank is designed so that it does actually require disposing of excess sludge about every five years.

Once the waste water is treated through the aerobic process, it is then automatically pumped out as irrigated water. The Northern Territory, Queensland and New South Wales health authorities have approved the system for use in their states. The approvals specify that the waste water be dispersed using sub-surface irrigation on land with vegetation.

The beauty of this unit is that it eliminates the need for septic tanks altogether and recycles all your household water back into the garden.

Installation of the primary tank and the treatment tank.

THE H2O SOLUTIONS UNIT

H20 Solutions manufacture systems in either concrete or fibreglass, and they can be produced to any specifications. The fibreglass domestic unit can accommodate up to ten people in a household and is easily transportable. Safeguards in the system include alarms and warning lights if any problems occur with either the air or irrigation pump. H20 solutions have exported the technology for use in East Timor, South Africa, Italy and the Philippines.

RE-RECYCLING

This system allows the recycling of your entire household waste water. In areas of limited water supply, or if tank water is used, the addition of a Wattworks system could save an average household about 300 litres of water usage a day by diverting your bath and shower water to the toilet cistern.

Featured in the December 1996 edition of *Earth Garden* (EG 98), the Wattworks system stores the greywater from the bath and shower in a holding tank and then pumps the water into the toilet cistern for flushing when required. It features safety devices such as a cut-off switch, which prevents the pump from operating if the tank is empty. Put simply, your household water is used first in the shower or bath, then in the toilet cistern and then in the garden.

CONTACTS

H20 Solutions can be contacted by mail at PO Box 1034, Nightcliff, NT 0814. Phone: (08) 8922 9505, fax: (08) 8922 9555, email: <jim.lombard@octa4.net.au> or visit the website at <www.h2osolutions.com.au>.

Make a $15 movable sink drain

Who said ingenuity was dead? Owen's greywater recycling device couldn't be much simpler.

by Owen "Bert" Paynter, *Katanning, Western Australia*

DO YOU RUN free range chickens? Do you have fruit trees or grapevines to water? Are you tired of forking out for huge water bills or on limited water supply? Do you suffer blocked leach drains and all-too-frequently have to pay to have your septic tank pumped out by a contractor? If you can answer yes to even just one of these questions, then read on and see how I overcame them by diverting my sink waste-water into an easily movable drain.

Easy to do

I simply removed the sink drainpipe that ran from the kitchen to the greywater tank and connected a length of 25 mm rural poly pipe to the sink "S" trap. All I did was fit a short piece of PVC into the "S" under the sink, to which I fitted a normal PVC elbow, to which I fitted a cast iron reducing joiner, to which I fitted a poly pipe connector and poly pipe. I place the end of this poly drain at the base of a fruit tree or grapevine for a week and then shift it to another. It is very simple to set up. The advantages are numerous and reduce pollution as well as save money. Read on and you will be amazed at the benefits coming from putting your sink waste-water to good use.

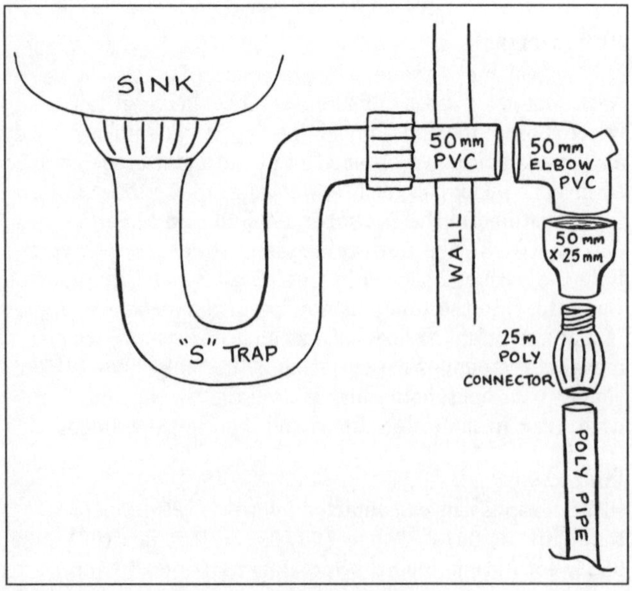

Fittings used for the moveable drain.

Healthy trees and vines

Because the sink waste-water is released steadily in small but frequent amounts the water penetrates deep into the soil and promotes strong root growth. I place the pipe around 150 mm away from the tree or vine trunk as the pipe gets very hot in warmer weather and could burn them if directly placed too close, plus the chickens need room for their snacks. In winter the sink pipe waters some of the tagasaste trees that it can reach and these are now twice the size of the others.

Water saving – time saving

The fruit trees and grapevines that are not situated around the grey water leach drains haven't been hand-watered since I connected the poly pipe to the sink. My annual water consumption has been visibly reduced – I estimate by 15,000 to 20,000 litres. I also save time by not needing to do watering. It is now just a simple matter of shifting the sink drainpipe once a week. I used to leave the watering hose trickling slowly on each tree or vine for about a day. I did forget to move it sometimes and some trees and vines got too much – costly! The need for installing reticulation is not required with the sink poly drain – I was considering installing drip irrigation when I came up with this idea of using the separate sink drain.

Free wetting agent for sandy soil

The washing up detergent may be a good wetting agent as the lawn around the base of the trees and vines watered by the sink stays green and lush for many weeks after only a week of sink watering. If you use a fairly safe environmentally-friendly brand of detergent, why have this valuable and useful resource disappear down the septic drain or sewer when it will benefit your soil? Because the pipe is only in one spot for a week, there is no problem with overloading the soil. I also place the sink pipe where I want to plant vegetables, for about a week before planting.

Free food for the chickens

Kitchen sink waste-water contains a four-course meal for chickens. They love snacking upon the food particles and fats that are washed down the sink, and run to the poly sink outlet as soon as they hear dishes being moved on the sink! One rooster in particular seems smarter than the rest (his name is Boris) and seems to get to the pipe first. Boris is the brownish rooster snacking on food particles in the photo. Small seeds such as tomato, cucumber and pumpkin (that always seem to stick to plates and end up washing down the sink) are a delicacy to the chickens.

Clean sweet greywater

The laundry, bathroom and kitchen waste-water had been going into the greywater tank for four years when I made the separate poly sink drain. I had noticed the waste-water in the tank stunk and it had a layer of fats and seeds floating on top. The soil around the leach drains smelt stagnant. I was concerned because the greywater is released into two very long leach pipes irrigating the main orchard. I figured out that it was likely to be the sink waste-water solids creating such stagnancy, rightly so it seems – now the greywater is sweet smelling and there are insects swimming in the tank.

Longer leach-drain life

Sink waste-water contains food particles, and these do not break down in a septic or greywater tank – they simply putrefy and are released from the tank and eventually block up the leach drains.

Reduced tank emptying

Washing-up water contains seeds, oils and fats which form a layer on top of the waste-water in a septic or greywater tank, and this builds up and must eventually be removed by a septic tank emptying contractor. Now only minimal bathroom and laundry solids such as dirt and lint are released into the tank. I think this will probably extend the period before pumping out at least thirty-fold for the greywater tank and at least double the period between pump outs for a combined toilet–greywater septic tank, which is a huge saving. It costs around $150 to have a tank pumped out where I live.

Connecting the sink to poly pipe

I used a hacksaw to cut the 50 mm PVC drain just before the point where it enters the greywater tank's pipe. I fitted a 50 mm PVC cap over the cut pipe, without using any glue (so it can be removed later if need be).

I loosened the sink "S" trap where it sleeves over the 50 mm drainpipe that goes out through the wall and removed the old drainpipe section in one piece. Then I slid a piece of 50 mm PVC pipe through the wall and into the "S" trap under the sink, to which I fitted a 50 mm PVC elbow, and connected this to the exit pipe.

Next I fitted a 100 mm piece of 50 mm PVC into the bottom of the elbow and screwed on to it a cast iron galvanised 50 mm x 25 mm (female thread) connector. It screwed on snugly and made its own thread on the PVC pipe.

I fitted a 25 mm poly joiner (female thread) to the cast iron connector and joined the one inch ID poly (rural grade) drain pipe. I used a 25-metre length that I already had laying around in the shed, but any length will work.

The total cost was about $15 not including the poly.

Boris enjoys his four-course meal.

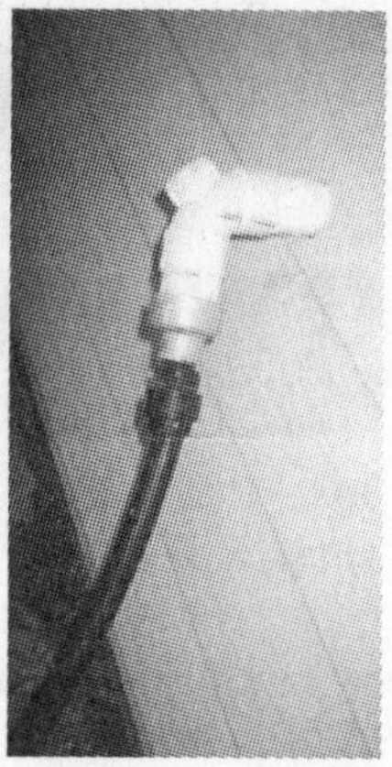

Right: keep the original parts so the waste pipe can revert to the conventional form.

The rural grade one inch ID poly is very common and you may be able to pick some up from a friendly farmer or neighbour if you don't have any – the only other option is to buy a full roll, but it comes in 200-metre rolls. If you are lucky enough to have *Earth Garden*-reading friends or neighbours, perhaps buy a roll together.

Save the original pipes

I kept the kitchen drain piping that I removed just in case I ever sell – I can imagine a few potential home buyers would be deterred by a poly pipe sink drain. Put the piping you remove in a safe spot and all you need is a cheap PVC joiner to reconnect it if you ever need to sell.

Cleaning the pipe

Every few months I unscrew the poly connector and run high-pressure water through to clean it. I use a sink plunger if a blockage occurs. I did not want to go to a poly size any larger than 25 mm as it would be too hard to move and walk over.

Footnotes

I imagine when eventually my greywater tank needs emptying (probably in another 20 years) it could be pumped out and dug into the soil as an enricher. It will mostly just be soil and lint that makes up the solids and not putrefied and smelly food particles. I envisage that one could borrow or hire a pump and do such emptying oneself by inserting the pump suction pipe into the inspection holes without even having to remove the tank's lid.

I have a separate 1800-litre septic tank and leach drain just for the toilet – a real water waster! – and I wish I had a composting toilet.

I have a website up and running. It contains articles on saving resources, energy and money. For those with access to the Internet my web address is: <www.wn.com.au/paynter>.

(Owen's site also has a handy link to the *Earth Garden* website – <www.earthgarden.com.au>).

Waste not: a simple greywater system

Jose treats light greywater and dark greywater separately, and gets multiple use of it by means of simple devices.

BY JOSE ROBINSON, *WILD CATTLE ISLAND, QUEENSLAND*

SUSTAINABLE water management is a high priority in this neck of the woods. We have no piped water system as we live on a tiny island. Our rainfall is poor, averaging 800 to 900 millimetres annually. We live in a very dry belt of Queensland. We have no soil for gardening, only sand.

Being born and raised in the city, neither of us had any conception initially of what it was like to rely only on rainwater for everything. However the years and countless droughts have educated us to realise every droplet of water is precious, even greywater. Waste-water comes in several categories.

LIGHT GREYWATER

Light greywater generally means water from the shower, the bath, the bathroom basin and the washing machine. Normally this is safe to re-use on gardens and fruit trees, as long as there isn't too much contamination from hair colouring treatments, strong soaps or bleaches. In the vegie garden I prefer not to use this water on root crops such as carrots and beetroot, for example. However, it should be fine for all other crops, as long as it is alternated with clean water. I make my own soaps, and sometimes shampoos, so rarely does anything too strong or undesirable go through my greywater system. Some of my household cleaners are home-made and we try to be eco-friendly with everything we use.

DARK GREYWATER

Dark greywater is from the kitchen sink, which I consider contaminated, mainly from grease. Although I use a natural herbal dishwashing liquid which contains no caustics and alkali builders, there is still contamination from solids and fats from foods, for example, so this water gets channelled out to gardens also, but definitely not food gardens.

BLACK WATER

Black water is water from toilets and waste-water from soaking babies' nappies, for example. Untreated, this is considered pathogenic (capable of breeding disease). So unless treated properly and professionally, this water is better off down the sewerage pipes.

In practice, ordinary light greywater may occasionally contain undesirable organisms, but the risk is minimal. Let's face it, water you've just washed your face in, or showered in, or washed your clothes in, shouldn't be any great risk. My greywater is not used in a sprinkler, but is only hosed without a nozzle straight onto the ground around the roots of fruit trees and some vegetables. It is not advisable to use any greywater close to wells, creeks or dams. Probably about 15 to 20 metres clearance should be sufficient. Greywater should not be stored for more than a few days, so that there is little chance of any bacteria multiplying.

Some councils still frown heavily on using greywater but many are now coming to realise how useful it can be. In some cities and towns it's not so easy to convince health authorities of legal uses for greywater. I feel that using untreated greywater is simply a matter of common sense.

Initially I began by bucketing out the washing machine water onto the garden; later I connected a hose for the job. I felt I was achieving a little towards re-using this valuable asset.

We now have a successful but simple system. Here on outstations it's a must to utilise every litre of water for at least two or three different uses. Our aim was for the simplest possible system with nothing complicated to go wrong.

Our light greywater is simply piped from the house through an expandable 50-mm flexible poly pipe. There is only just sufficient fall in the lay of our land. It then flows through a frequently changed nylon mesh filter. The nylon cloth is tied straight onto the end of the poly pipe. This takes care of any hairs and soap particles, for example. The greywater runs into a 200-litre heavy duty plastic drum buried to ground level.

The drum has an easily removed wooden lid. In the bottom of the drum we installed a small 12-volt submersible bilge pump. The cost was approximately $26, four years ago. We tied the pump inside the nylon bag to stop any gunking up of the pump inlet. A small 12-volt switch was installed at the top of the drum and an eight-mm hose was connected to the outlet of the pump.

On alternate days, I hose this water, without a nozzle,

onto the vegetable garden, where there are no root crops, and fruit trees. In two days (without visitors) the two of us have filled the 200-litre drum from four showers, plus hand washing, and teeth cleaning. All good, very light greywater. When we have guests staying over, I sometimes find it necessary to pump it out more than once a day. It just shows how much extra water unthinking people waste.

Our washing machine greywater is on a separate line. It pumps straight onto the paw paw and herb gardens using a nine-mm poly pipe. This has soaker holes, and, as well, I can relocate it.

There are several ways of successfully treating contaminated waste-water by running it through filters of stones, gravel, mesh, sand and reed beds, all of which apparently work very successfully. However we haven't found the need to resort to that effort and expense. We feel we are taking full responsibility for our own waste-water and consider it not waste-water at all. We could call ours three-times-used water.

For more complicated greywater systems than ours there is a small American booklet on the market called *Create an Oasis with Grey Water* written by Art Ludwig, published by PIP Printing, Santa Barbara, California,1984. It's well worth reading.

MY BATHROOM GREY WATER SYSTEM

200 LITRE HEAVY DUTY PLASTIC DRUM

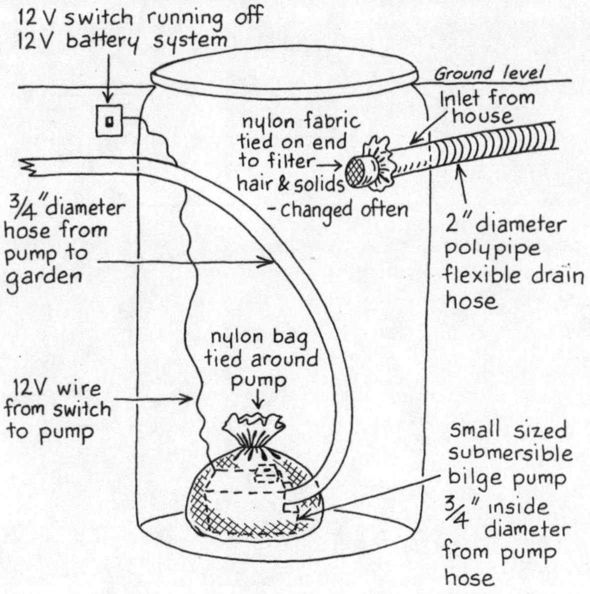

Installing a worm farm waste system

A leaking septic problem and uncooperative plumbers turned out to be an unsuspected benefit.

BY **GREG HOLDING,** ***ARTHURS SEAT, VICTORIA***

LIVING AT Arthurs Seat on the Mornington Peninsula comes with no natural gas, town water or sewerage. To some people this is often too much to bear. Not having the creature comforts of city living can cause some discomfort.

However, some flexibility and adaptability is required if you plan to stay! Since moving to the peninsula in 1992 we have installed a solar hot water system, a Worm Farm Waste System, and are now in the process of installing a solar air heater. Next year we plan to go totally solar.

Recently we installed a Worm Farm Waste System which takes greywater, black water and even garbage into one chamber (the cleaned and refitted septic tank), distributed through our half-acre indigenous garden.

Our sand-filtered septic, installed ten years ago, and approved by the local shire, began to leak with run-off dribbling down the road! An anonymous complaint (aren't they all?) was made to the shire and we were asked to fix the problem in 60 days.

This gave us the exciting opportunity to look around for an environmentally-sound waste disposal system that was cost-effective and easily installed, and would enable us to be responsible for our own waste.

A number of local plumbers visited our property and were keen to install another sand-filtered septic system, rip up my indigenous garden, charge me a lot of money, but they could not guarantee that I wouldn't be facing the same problem in ten years time. Some were cynical about "these greenie, newfangled systems that don't work" and "cost the earth to install".

I have never accepted this "can't do" attitude, so I went to the local library and was flicking through *Earth*

The compost bin sits over the old septic tank. The pipe cools the compost and is fitted with an alarm if the compost overheats.

Garden and there it was! – A&A Worm Farm Waste Systems. When I got home, feeling rather happy, a letter from the shire had arrived with a lot of information on this system. Having the support from the shire and the EPA encouraged me to call for a site inspection.

My first site meeting, then a visit to a property in Red Hill that had installed a Worm Farm Waste System (and since featured on *Gardening Australia*) convinced me to install the system.

OPERATION

The system works by using naturally occurring organisms found in a rainforest floor. These include worms, slaters, slugs, etc. They process the waste solids into material that is easily taken up in the soil.

Worms have the ability to convert a wide range of organic material including sewer waste presented in a varied form. Therefore, for the efficient operation of the waste system it is desirable to include carbonaceous materials such as paper and cardboard as well as other organic materials such as vegetable food scraps.

The objective of adding diverse organic waste is to deodorise and aerate the waste and adjust the system's carbon–nitrogen balance, the pH and salinity. The system is able to recycle all household organic wastes.

During processing, the waste liquid from the kitchen, shower and toilet (if a flushing toilet is used) enters the chamber where the solids are separated from the liquids. The liquids drain through the organic pile, and is polished. This process is similar to that which happens on the floor of a rainforest. The liquids then continue out of the chamber to an approved closed disposal system. No liquid is stored in the chamber.

The design of the Waste System has created a suspended bed of organic material, which allows for a continuous flow of material. Waste is fed to the surface. The worms, slaters and naturally occurring organisms, which are seeded into the system, live on and multiply with the food source available and stabilise the material. The material is harvested from the base and flushed to the trenches alongside the Waste System.

Worms eat 50 to 100 per cent of their own body weight each day. The grinding and tumbling action within the worm gut reduces material to sludge particle size, exposing a greater surface area to a range of enzymes and a host of bacteria. After excretion, the particles continue to be exposed to an aerobic environment in the suspended bed with very high bacterial and fungal populations. These particles are ready to be taken up in the trenches – incredible!

Installation of the system was professionally done, with my Land for Wildlife indigenous garden in mind. My thoughts and comments were always taken into consideration by the company. The distribution pit and where the pipes connect can be altered at any time, which allows you to control the flow of water around the garden.

It probably takes a few months before the system is working to its full capacity, but there are no major nasty smells. My only issue is that the water going to the distribution pit could get away a little faster. Six months on, the Waste System is working very well and my garden is looking very good. Anybody contemplating ridding themselves of their septic system should seriously consider a cost-effective and environmentally-sound Worm Farm Waste System.

Looking back, I am very happy that the shire received that anonymous call about our septic!!

Greywater use

Waste water from the bathroom, laundry or kitchen can be collected, filtered, diverted and distributed on to the garden.

Lightest greywater: water from bath and shower which contains few solids and fats.

Light greywater: from washing machine and basins and usually has more grit and scum that sinks and clogs.

Dark greywater: from kitchen and contains food scraps, oils and greases that require longer treatment.

GREYWATER PLUMBING RULES:

- First, always check with state plumbing regulations.
- EPA stipulates that installation of a greywater diversion system must be carried out by a licensed plumber.
- Greywater must not contaminate drinking water.
- It must not become contaminated with sewage.
- Rainwater (stormwater) must not enter the sewer.
- Greywater or sewage must not enter stormwater drains.
- Divert greywater back to the sewer when the soil is saturated.
- Choose carefully the products you use. Some, such as laundry detergents, can have unacceptable levels of salt and alkalinity for gardens.

All the following systems are usually used in conjunction with a waterless toilet. When approaching a geotech engineer for specifications, advise if you are using a waterless toilet as the size and length of the pipes will be greatly reduced.

NATURE-CLEAR SYSTEM

Nature-Clear is a greywater system designed to treat domestic waste water excluding toilet waste. Councils are increasingly reticent to allow new homeowners to dispose of greywater without treatment. The days of being allowed to spray waste water untreated onto the garden are coming to an end. Each state and council have their own regulations and you will need to speak to your local council to establish what they will permit alongside a waterless toilet.

In order to satisfy the new council requirements Nature Loo has developed a greywater system that cleans waste water via a natural grease trap and gravity fed sand filtration. They currently await approval for use of the system to treat water to the primary level, and will subsequently seek secondary treatment approval. In the interim they request that customers propose the system to their geotech engineer and/or council. If you would like them to do this for you they will be happy to do so. You will probably require site plans and soil tests.

Some Queensland councils allow this system; however, the EPA in Victoria, for instance, requires an 1800-litre septic tank in advance of the system.

If your site is suitable, the only excavation work required to install the system will be the trenching. The ongoing costs will be less than those of a standard septic system. The filtration tank, which is less than one cubic metre in size, consists of a natural grease trap on top of a sand filter. The grease trap is designed to catch scraps from the kitchen sink and lint from the washing machine. The sand filter traps any finer materials and cleans the water. The grease trap consists of a filter bag containing pine bark. The filtered material and bark will compost over time and should be removed once a year and replaced with fresh bark. If your distribution area is down hill from the filtration tank your engineer should be able to design a distribution system without the use of a pump. If this is not the case you will need our pump well and pump. If desired, and the pipes from the house are at a suitable height, the tank can sit on the ground. If this is not the case it will require a pit 700 mm deep.

The 225-litre pump well contains a submersible pump with a float valve capable of lifting water to a height of five metres. The tank, which measures 850 mm in height and 820 mm in diameter, can be located on the ground alongside the filtration tank but performs better if put in a shallow pit such that its base is 400 mm lower than the base of the filtration tank.

The system has been approved by a number of councils as a secondary treatment system, but has not yet been approved by any state regulators. It could, however, be used in conjunction with a septic tank to improve its performance in treating greywater.

REED BEDS

Reed beds are becoming increasingly popular in many parts of the country for treating either all domestic waste or greywater only in conjunction with a waterless toilet.

People wanting a flushing toilet, but who are concerned that a septic tank alone will result in pollution of their ground water, and cause odours, can add a reed bed to overcome these potential deficiencies. In most areas of Australia the water from a reed bed can be re-used with sub-surface irrigation lines without chlorination.

Reed beds to treat greywater only are also available. They are frequently used with composting toilets.

Not only do reed beds produce secondary treated water but they also reduce nutrient levels. Nutrients are responsible for blue-green algae and must not exceed restricted levels in certain areas of the country.

Reed beds offer a natural solution to waste water treatment and blend naturally with garden landscapes. They do not use pumps, electricity, chemicals or aerators. They do not require expensive quarterly inspections.

Nature Loo offers a packaged reed bed system that should be acceptable to most councils.

Nature Loo, PO Box 2157, Toowong, Qld 4066. Phone (07) 3870 5037, fax (07) 3870 5088, email: <info@nature-loo.com.au>, web: <www.nature-loo.com.au>.

ROTA-LOO

Absorption trenches that use an arrangement of soil types to absorb and purify greywater. Perforated pipes keep your greywater aerated and hungry solid microbes consume nutrients in the water. Trench lengths depend on the climate, soil types and number of people using the system.

ROCK PLANT FILTERS

The rock plant filter system is a series of stepped reed beds. Selected aquatic plants help filter and cleanse the greywater while creating habitat. Reed beds are best suited to wet climates or for reducing the length of absorption trenches. Again, the size of the system depends on where you are, and how much water you need to treat.

ROTA-LOO GREYWATER SYSTEM

2000 litre polyethylene baffled settling tank
Distribution chamber
Design and installation manual
Has EPA approval, but need to contact council.

CLIVUS MULTRUM GREYWATER PREFILTER

The greywater treatment principles that the Prefilter is based upon are well known, and are used extensively in the USA and other overseas countries and increasingly within Australia.

Instead of using gravel as the filter medium, plastic coil filter media are used to trap particles in an aerobic environment. This prevents the waste water turning anaerobic and prepares the water for disposal by any of the following methods, subject to suitability for the site and council approval:

- absorption trenches
- evapo-transpiration beds
- reedbed or wetland systems
- mounds
- sub-surface irrigation
- sand or soil filters followed by surface irrigation

This filtering greatly reduces the risk of clogging leach lines or sand filters. The Prefilter reduces surge flows. It uses aerobic processes and is compatible with further treatment by soil organisms. The unit drains promptly, either by gravity or switched pump.

The Prefilter is vented to ensure optimum oxygen levels within the unit, and to control any odours that may arise within the Prefilter or the drains.

Kitchen water can be directed into the Prefilter after first running it through a grease trap, but the Prefilter cannot be used in conjunction with a garbage grinder due to the high solids loading. Full access to the tank is provided by the removable lid.

As greywater enters the Prefilter, solid particles such as hair, lint, soap and other sediments are filtered by two long nylon socks, supported by a moulded plastic grate, that run the full length of the filter box. As liquid passes through the filter sock it is distributed to drain evenly down through the Aerobic Filter Media. This filter medium has a high surface area to which tiny particles and oils and so on adhere. This material is then processed by the aerobic bacteria growing on the surfaces. When the filter socks become full, they can be emptied into a compost or garbage bin and then re-fitted or replaced.

Clivus Multrum Australia, PO Box a126, Strathpine, Qld 4500. Phone: (07) 3889 6144, fax: (07) 3889 6149, email: info@clivusmultrum.com.au, web: <www.clivusmultrum.com.au>

GREYWATER SAVER

Jim Bertram, from Perth, Western Australia, is the sole inventor, developer, manufacturer, marketer and promoter of a system he has called the Greywater Saver.

The Greywater Saver provides a viable and acceptable means for recycling greywater. It has nation-wide plumbing product authorisation through the National Certification of Plumbing and Drainage Products Scheme, administered by Standards Australia. It is authorised and accepted by state health, waste water and plumbing regulators. It is inexpensive to purchase and free to operate. It is a miniature system with no tanks, electrics, or expensive maintenance contract requirements. The stainless steel filter should be regularly cleared of trapped lint and hair and it has a failsafe feature so greywater automatically flows to the sewer if the filter blocks or if the system becomes overloaded.

The Greywater Saver system is used to recycle laundry and bathroom greywater. It connects to a vertical wastepipe where it operates purely by gravity.

It has a manual gate valve, which users can open or close to select whether greywater is diverted for garden irrigation or disposed to the sewer or on-site waste water system. It has a removable stainless steel mesh filter basket that requires cleaning regularly by users via the unit's removable gas-tight screw cap access cover.

Filtered greywater flows by gravity from the unit in 50 mm pipes to a number of piped irrigation trenches located just beneath the surface of garden beds. Even distribution of filtered greywater to each irrigation trench is achieved by use of the purpose-made Greywater Saver Flow Splitter Y junction fittings. These fittings are specially designed to split a single stream equally in two, which in turn may be further split as needed for a particular garden layout. The Flow Splitter fits standard 50-mm DWV pipe, and can be used wherever there is a need to evenly split a liquid flow into multiple equal streams by gravity.

Greywater Saver, ph: 040 331 9410, web: <www.greywatersaver.com>.

A Wattworks water recycling system that was recently installed in inner Melbourne (above). With its cover, it's just another feature of the garden (right).

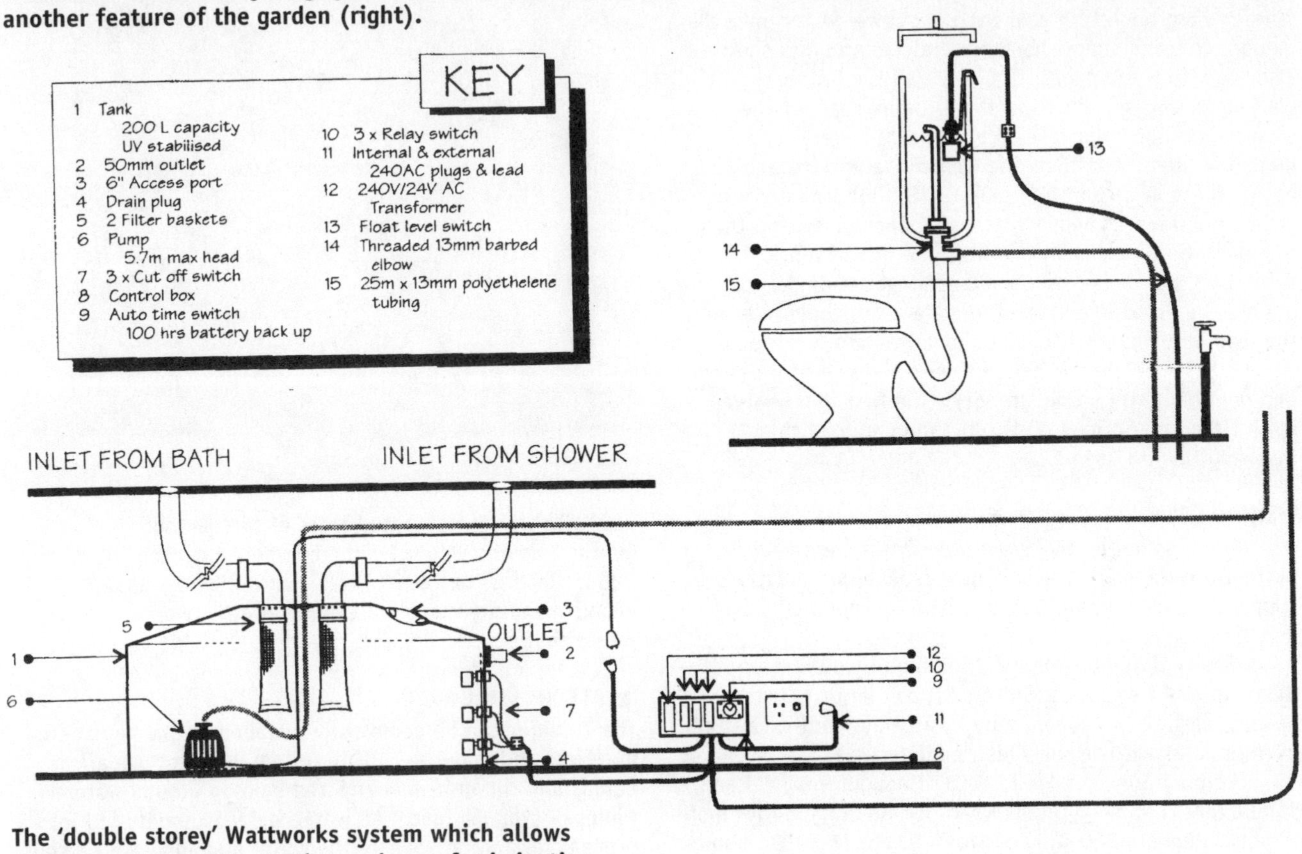

The 'double storey' Wattworks system which allows diversion of greywater to the garden or for irrigation.

WATTWORKS

Featured in the December 1996 edition of *Earth Garden* (EG 98), the WattWorks system stores greywater from the bath and shower in a holding tank, and then pumps the water into the toilet cistern to flush when required. It features safety devices such as a cut off switch, which prevents the pump from operating if the tank is empty. The tank automatically empties each day, according to a set time, to prevent the water sitting for longer than 24 hours and becoming contaminated. Put simply, your household water effectively is used first in the shower or bath, next in the toilet cistern and then in the garden. The Wattworks system is suitable for all households in city, country town or remote bush locations where flush toilets are installed.

The Wattworks system does not require approval if it is a closed, bath or shower water-to-cistern-to-sewer or septic set up. The system needs to be installed by a plumber. The one-toilet system, which includes the tank, 240 volt pump with seven metres of head, cistern connections, electric controllers, solenoids and float switch, costs $1,560, and the two-toilet system costs $1780. *Earth Garden*'s publishers, Alan and Judith Gray, have run a Wattworks system for more than seven years, and are "utterly delighted" with its performance. Distributors of Wattworks products are ARI Pty Ltd on (03) 5941 4967 or visit <www.wattworks.com.au>.

Greywater and sewage treatment products

IF YOU ARE connected to town water, your local water authority or company may require a permit before you start using greywater. There are many options for people who wish to use their greywater on their garden, ranging from bucketing your bath or shower water onto the garden, to using simple homemade diversion units shown elsewhere in these pages. There is also the brilliant Wattworks system, as well as large commercial sewage treatment plants that take all your waste water – and human wastes – and spray the treated water onto garden beds. These large units ($5,000 to $8,000) are becoming cheaper and more commonplace as councils insist on them in areas where previously people could install septic systems. Most modern sewage treatment plants do not require the use of chlorine. There are also people following the lead of Michael Wilson and Fiona Buining, who fought the Victorian EPA and installed their own greywater system and reed bed (still going strong!) – the first in a sewered town (Hepburn Springs, Victoria). You can read their inspiring tale on page 72.

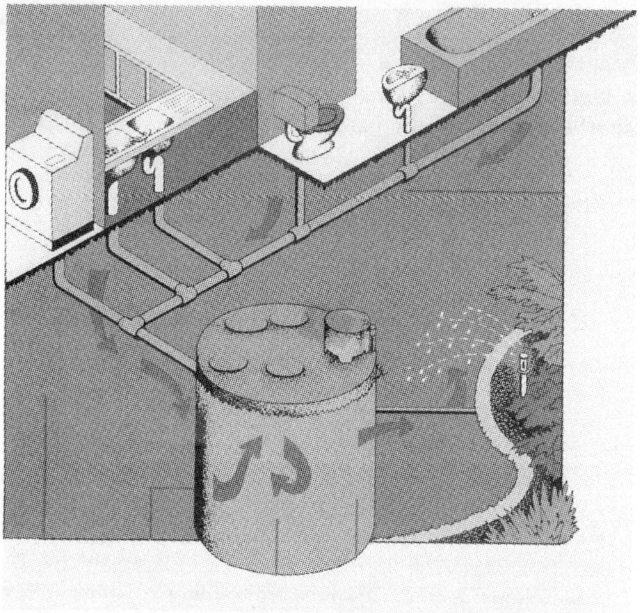

OZZI KLEEN

Ozzi Kleen is another AWTS (Aerated Waste Treatment System) on the market, and is now expanding operations to supply customers in most states. It is 100 per cent fully aerobic.

The Ozzi Kleen is only 2.35 m high by 1.95 m in diameter and weighs just 350 kg. It can be installed quickly, easily and economically by a single mini-excavator, even on sites with severely restricted access.

Contact Suncoast Waste Water Management (Mal and Sandra Close) at 6–40 Olsens Road, Ilkley, Qld 4554 for more details. Phone: 1800 450 767, fax: (07) 5478 8088, mobile: 0419 960 069, or email: <info@ozzikleen.com>, web: <www.ozzikleen.com>.

ENVIROCYCLE

Envirocycle is an alternative to sewerage, septic tank and pump out systems. It is based on the principle of separating solids from liquids to allow anaerobic bacteria (bacteria which do not require oxygen) and aerobic bacteria (bacteria which do require oxygen) to break down domestic waste. With an Envirocycle system, household waste from bathrooms, kitchens and laundries is treated in underground tanks to a level of purity approved by the relevant health authorities throughout Australia. The water is then dispersed automatically through irrigation lines and spray points to water designated areas of the garden.

Contact: Envirocycle, 61 Robert Street, Argenton, NSW, 2284. Phone: (02) 4958 7188, fax: (02) 4958 5512, email: <envirocycle@hunterlink.net.au>, web: <www.envirocycle.com.au>.

SEPTECH TURBOJET

The Turbojet can be completely installed in one day and is noiseless and odourless. This system does not use air pumps and the unit is unaffected by high ground water tables or swampy land. All waste water is gravity fed into a primary sewage tank where the waste undergoes settlement and digestion during a retention period of approximately 24 hours. The settled waste water then flows into the Turbojet unit. This unit is divided into two distinct chambers: submerged contact aeration (SCA) tank and humus tank. Effluent from the primary septic tanks then flows into the SCA tank. During regular time clock intervals, water and air are pumped into the SCA tank by strategically placed jets. Effluent entering the SCA chamber is forced into a spiralling flow pattern. A biomass develops within the sludge particles tumbling through the tank. This biomass assimilates nutrients and oxygen from the water leading to a gradual reduction of impurities as the effluent passes through the tank. The effluent and sludge particles then flow into the humus tank where the sludge particles settle

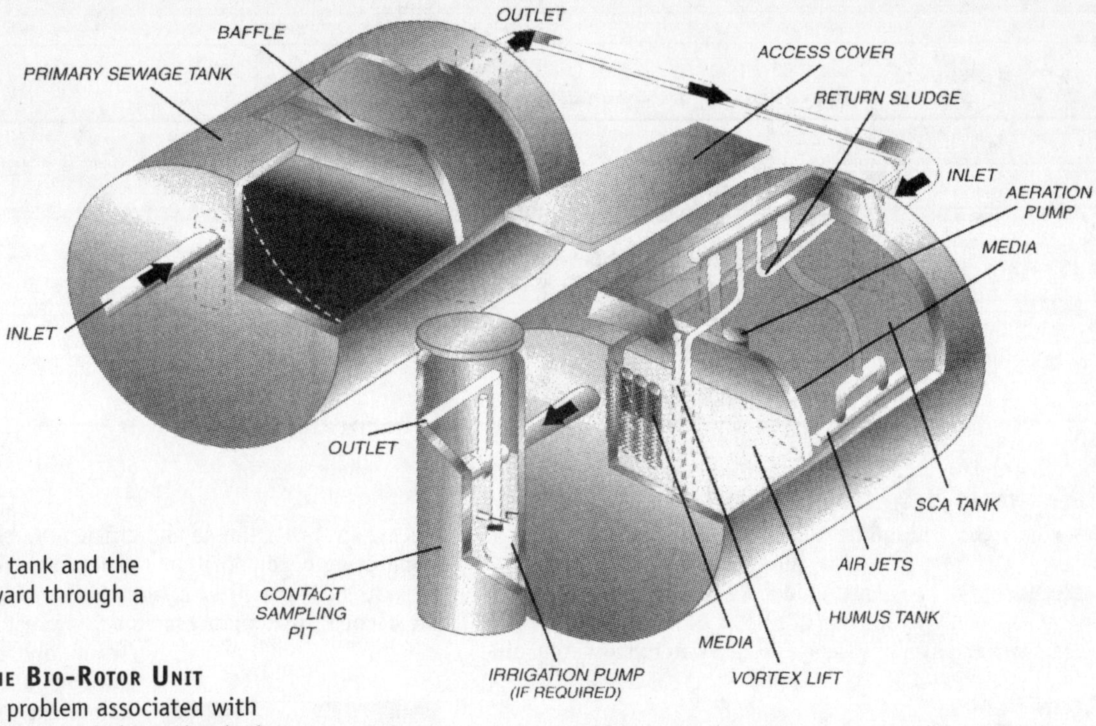

to the floor of the tank and the effluent flows upward through a contact media.

ADVANTAGES OF THE BIO-ROTOR UNIT

1. Eliminates the problem associated with clogged sand filters and absorption beds.
2. Utilises less valuable land space than sand filters or absorption drains.
3. Saves on expensive excavation costs in rocky or sloping terrain.
4. Unit is unaffected by ground water infiltration.
5. The Bio-Rotor has a very low power consumption and maintenance rating.
6. Bio-Rotor does not exhibit the same tank flotation problems as other STPs.
7. Mechanical components in contact with waste water are either galvanised, PVC or stainless steel
8. Effluent discharge is of a consistently high standard.
9. Plant operation is noiseless and odourless.
10. Plant has a low ground profile.
11. Installation can be carried out by client or manufacturer.
12. Bio-Rotor provides for a deep sewer invert at 850 mm below ground level and a shallow discharge outlet at 420 mm below ground level. This will allow connection to most sewer points and stormwater drainage systems without needing to be pumped.
13. Bio-Rotor is supplied with an extra large capacity: primary sewage tank 3,200 litres and final settling tank 1,000 litres. Consequently this unit requires less frequent de-sludging than comparable forms of STPs.
14. All units are backed by twelve months warranty and servicing, with the option to continue the servicing contract at the end of the warranty period.
15. Unit is unaffected by high ground water tables or swampy area.

Alternative Installation Configurations

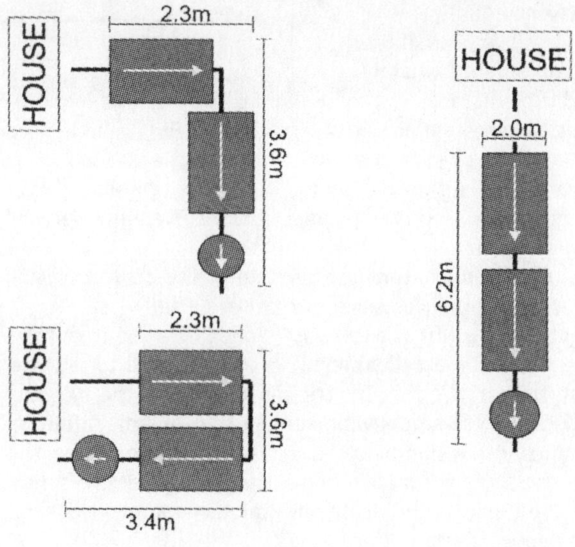

The Turbojet is EPA-approved, Health Department-approved and Australian Standards-approved. For more details contact: Septech Industries Pty Ltd Australia, 14 Burgess Rd, Bayswater Nth, Victoria, 3153. Phone: (03) 9729 0966, fax: (03) 9720 5534, email: <ken@septech.com.au>, or website <www.septech.com.au>.

Central Victorian Septics are now servicing around 100 such systems and can be contacted for advice on (03) 5472 3195.

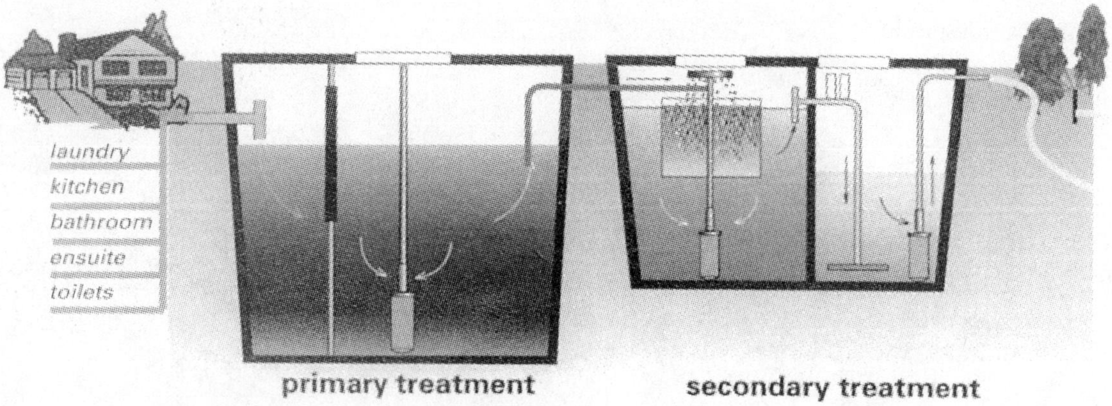

CLEARWATER SEWAGE TREATMENT

The Clearwater Sewage Treatment system is another automatic system that treats all household waste, and can be contacted at: 101 Cattai Ridge Rd, Glenorie, NSW, 2157, phone (02) 9652 2733, fax (02) 9652 2415, email: <clear@acay.com.au>, web: <www.clearwatersystems.com.au>.

AQUA CLARUS

The Simply Natural Wastewater Treatment System comprises a treatment tank that is connected to a vegetation cell and an appropriately-sized sub-soil land application system of a type approved by the relevant local authority.

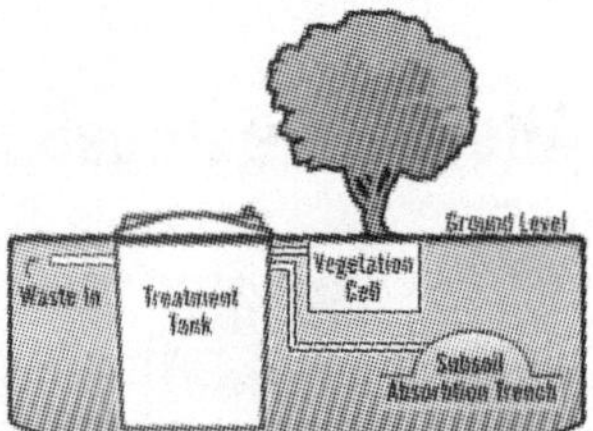

The treatment tank is a compact unit with very low service requirements.

The Simply Natural uses a state-of-the-art treatment process that produces enhanced primary effluent of exceptional quality at a low cost. Solids removed from the system make an excellent fertiliser and are used to fertilise vegetation on the site. The treated water from the system is applied to a sub-soil environment such as an absorption trench, transpiration mound or sub-soil irrigation system.

The Simply Natural automatically separates the solids from the liquid in the treatment tank using a revolutionary, patented separation device.

Most of the liquid (approximately 90 per cent) that is removed from the solids passes through a biological trickle bed and flows to a collection chamber at the base of the treatment tank. The aerobic trickle bed consists of alternate layers of coarse and fine media. The coarse media is passively ventilated to promote aeration.

Periodically, the liquid in the collection chamber re-circulates through the trickle bed. When the liquid in the collection chamber reaches a predetermined level, it is automatically pumped to the land application system.

The system breaks down the solids (toilet paper, faeces, etc.) in a simple and efficient vertical wet composting decomposition chamber using a mini-ecosystem. The mini-ecosystem works in a similar manner to the decomposition process on a rainforest floor and includes worms and other invertebrates. Unlike a rainforest, the Simply Natural is a closed system – the entire decomposition process is contained within the treatment tank.

The decomposition process is aerobic, in that the solids are exposed to air. Also, the surface area of the solids in the decomposition chamber is maximised, enabling efficient treatment within a relatively small space. When the solids are completely broken down, the resulting vermicast (worm manure) is pumped with a small quantity of liquid (approximately ten per cent of the influent) to the vegetation cell, where it provides nutrients for a growing plant.

The liquids and solids removal pumps provide a backup for each other in the event of a pump failure.

The Super Natural system is currently under development; contact the company for availability. The Super Natural Wastewater Treatment System will process domestic sewage in the same way as the Simply Natural system, although it will further treat the waste water to produce very high quality water that can be recycled. This will be achieved using advanced processes.

Simply Natural models can be retro-fitted with the Super Natural modules when they become available. The Super Natural modules will enhance and further treat the effluent to a tertiary level. The treated water can then be used for above ground irrigation and other approved domestic non-potable reuse such as toilet flushing, clothes and car washing, garden watering and hosing pavements.

Ph: 1300 368 158, web: <www.aquaclarus.com>.

Toilet priorities

Carol surveys the view from the interim toilet.

Nolan describes his family's steady progress from a primitive 'thunderbox' to a state of the art, worm-driven, composting toilet and greywater system.

BY NOLAN TYRRELL *AND* CAROL CARTER, *TYLDEN, VICTORIA*

WHAT DOES comfort begin with? Is it warmth, food, a roof? Carol wanted a toilet on-site; a place of relaxation a bit removed from prying eyes. The bushes I used were terrifying to her – snakes!

Carol and I wanted to have a dunny we could be comfortable in and please the neighbours. When we first arrived I used the bushes. However, we didn't want to be the cause of introducing killer pathogens to the watercourses.

I became used to taking the shovel and toilet roll and going for a walk each morning down to the patch of gorse, blackberry, sticky weed, and African boxthorn and digging a shallow hole. This is the only spot that is not in direct line of sight from at least one of the houses around Tylden. I expect the neighbours know what this early morning stroll is for.

I think Carol just thinks SNAKE; she doesn't feel safe, and nor do I for that matter. We discussed "long drops" and other such toilet matters; but one thing I wanted was to not have the dunny flooded. I figured that aerobic (oxygen-dependent) bugs were better than anaerobic bugs. Bad bugs breed where you don't get oxygen. Worms like a bit of oxygen, and they aerate the soil by poking holes in it. They drown if they don't have air.

We met our Worm Farm man at a Solar Fair at Hanging Rock. We decided to put in a worm farm-type dunny. Unlike most composting toilets these devices will chew up paper and greywater. But that was for later – we were a long way from the actual house building.

Still, we needed a dunny. Carol looked at a chemical toilet. She didn't want it in the caravan of course. But before we put a toilet somewhere, we needed an enclosure. No use having a pan in the middle of the paddock. I think we'd both prefer the snakes.

We screwed some gal onto some wood frames, made a plywood shelf, cut a squarish hole and smoothed it all down a bit, and added a door. We put the interim "thunderbox" on a mound. In a way I liked it up there and Carol put up with it for a while. We only used it for the short time we were on the block – about two weeks two years ago. We had a bucket from which to throw a scoop of lime on top and a bit of grass and silt to break it all down.

Finally the house reached a stage where a toilet was feasible – just a frame, but we knew where everything was going. So we called our Worm Farm man, very pleased with ourselves that we could finally install the system. He arrived fully loaded with everything he would need. By five the worm farm itself was in the ground with its accompanying pipes, and he had started on the trenches. The system was fully installed by nine that night and I was gingerly lowering the worms onto the pile of cardboard boxes we had thrown in.

Since then I visit daily with our kitchen scraps and the waste paper from our office. It's hard to tell at this stage if the worms are active. Whilst cleaning up the building site I find the odd fat worm and throw it in to help.

We installed a temporary flushing toilet – finally a proper loo on site! This worked well for a few weeks, flushing with a bucket – however last weekend – disaster! A pinch bar, dropped from the roof, hit three sides of the bowl without damage and went straight through the bottom. I watched this happen from the roof beams. Between bouts of guilt I wondered if we were meant to have an indoor toilet, but I haven't mentioned this to Carol. So we are now back to holding on.

We are eager to see the worm farm fully operational, but with framing not yet complete, that seems a long way off.

UPDATE

We are now in the house. The toilet has worked like a black hole into which we have poured paper, extruded solids, food scraps, pee and about two thirds of a 22500-litre tank of water since Christmas (lots of visitors).

The grass near the mega drains is very green and it's nice to know that our water is returning to the ground instead of being pumped away like the rest of town.

We are happy now – after five years – we have a flushing toilet with a door on the room (though there is a hole where the glass goes), and reading material beside the pan. I have my first dishwasher, and proper plumbing. We celebrated my (Carol) 50th birthday a few weeks ago with over 100 guests and everything coped without a hassle. We have a home with all the mod cons and no major impact on the environment (well, that will be the case when the solar panels go up anyway).

Another system has just gone in next door and after a quick inspection of ours, everything is going well. He would just like to see more composting going into it – look out thistles!

A recycled greywater loo

Recycling water from your washing machine to your toilet needn't be expensive or complicated, as Liz Ingham explains.

BY LIZ INGHAM, *YARRAVILLE, VICTORIA*

MELBOURNE'S drinking water is filtered clean by the forests of the Yarra Ranges and the Thomson River catchment. The citizens of Melbourne show their appreciation of nature's bounty in an unusual way. We pour drinking water into special porcelain containers, crap in it, then flush with more drinking water. We do this numerous times each day. We use more drinking water for crapping in than we use for drinking.

Humans are amazing. We read that water restrictions may be imposed, then we go and crap in some drinking water. A new study recommends sewage water be treated and returned to us, so we get all indignant then go and crap in some drinking water. The Premier has been poncing around asking us to save three buckets of water each day. He could start by stopping clear fell logging in water catchments. And we can start by not crapping in drinking water.

At our place, we decided to divert used clothes washing water to the toilet cistern, and began with the simple system described in Diagram 1. The beauty of this design is that the washing machine's own pump moves the used water into a holding tank, which fills the cistern by gravity. The tank is a used plastic 44-gallon pickle barrel, and cost us $10. The tank stand used timber salvaged from skips, and the filter was sewn from fly screen. You'll also need copper piping, some fittings and a length of hose.

If your washing machine is on a higher floor level to the toilet, this design could work well for you. But washing machine pumps aren't designed to raise water higher than the machine itself, so the top of the machine needs to be at least level with the top of the holding tank, which is itself higher than the cistern. We tried lowering the cistern and raising the washing machine on a platform. This worked, but I had to stand on a chair to do the washing and the pump was still being over-worked.

So we added a second pickle barrel as a "surge tank", and bought a bilge pump, as in Diagram 2, and now the system works just fine.

If you want to give it a whirl, there are some things you need to know. First, you must separate grey and fresh water with an air gap. In our case, this was done by bringing the "emergency" fresh water supply pipe into the cistern from above. We got a greenie plumber to design and install the system to make sure it was done right. You'll also need an overflow from the tank to the sewer pipe, and preferably another above the lint filter in case the filter becomes blocked. We don't have this yet, and I think we are courting disaster.

Secondly, the tanks must be easy to empty, because you are going to empty them a lot. Proper Wattworks systems flush out water held for 24 hours. We empty any unused water before each refill and clean the empty tanks about once a week. Both tanks should have an outlet underneath, and a slight tilt to make sure every drop flows to that outlet. Any old greywater left in the tank will spread

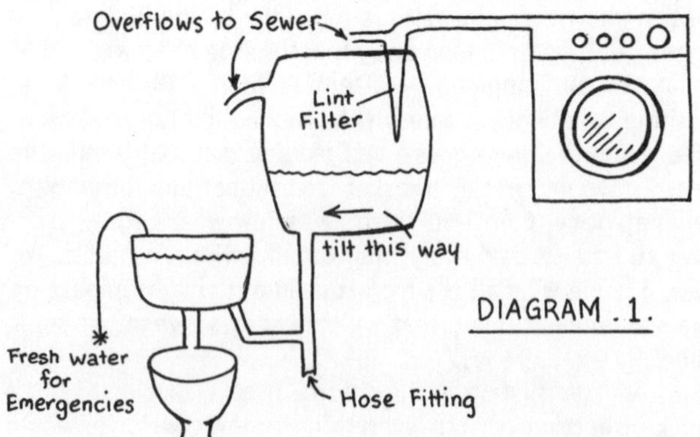

GREYWATER DUNNY

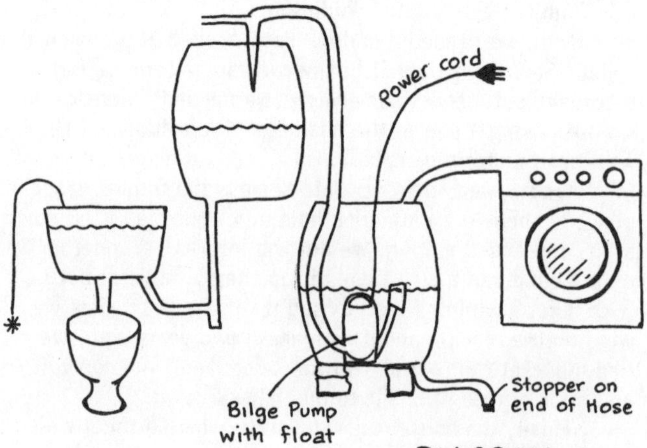

DIAGRAM.2.

The toilet has an extra pipe to separate the grey and fresh water with an air gap.

germs to the fresh greywater, and it will pong. Click a hose on the header tank outlet and water the garden with the excess. If you do this you'll need to choose your laundry soap carefully – but then again, why should you send anything down the drain you wouldn't put on your garden?

Washing machine water forms soap scum in the loo, which smells and looks yukky, so you'll need to clean it more often. It comes off easily – it's mostly soap after all. After a while the cistern might get a bit whiffy too, so you'll need to clean it from time to time. Help prevent stinky cistern syndrome by emptying it if you go away for the weekend, and use vinegar.

A year after installing the system I cottoned on to using a cup or so of cleaning vinegar in the rinse cycle of the wash. It made a huge difference. It helps rinse soap from clothes and makes greywater and containers smell fresh and clean. It even improves the pH of laundry water for garden use. Vinegar containers can be refilled at good shops, and soap for home-made washing liquid can be bought with little or no packaging, or made from scratch if you're dead keen. (Some "green" cleaners have single use packaging, and that's not good enough.)

A straw broom makes a good tank-cleaning tool – gets any skanky stuff off the sides, and it's got a nice long handle. Trigger hose nozzles deliver a strong, convenient rinsing jet to the tank and pump, and use about half a bucket of water each rinse. Cleaning takes an extra five to ten minutes each week, which isn't much, but it must be done regularly. It should be part of the routine of putting on a load of washing.

This system isn't really designed for renters, though you could try putting the hose out through a window and creating a well-braced temporary tank stand so the whole thing could be dismantled. Only a neat round hole in the top of the cistern would remain to threaten the bond refund. Watch the landlord scratch his head over that one. Traditional stand-bys like "It was like that when we got here", and "Maybe it was aliens" can be used to good effect.

Books such as *Not Just Down the Drain* by Stuart McQuire and *Create an Oasis with Greywater* by Art Ludwig give invaluable advice about design and deal with important safety issues. Greywater is a potential health hazard, so avoid splashing yourself when you flush. But anyone in the habit of splashing dunny water on themselves, recycled or otherwise, would be well advised to get a grip.

I can't believe I've just written two pages about toilets in a nationally-distributed book. How embarrassing. But at least I'm not as bad as one editor. He came over to my house to see the indigenous garden, and exclaimed "I must photograph your toilet!"

Liz and Trevor calculated that recycling their washing machine greywater makes more than 18,000 litres of water per year available to flush the loo — some gets flushed and some goes on the garden.

COSTS

Pickle barrels ($10 each)	$20
Tank stand (cement)	$10
Nails and bolts	$5
Wood: scrounged	
Washing machine hose	$15
Bilge pump (wholesale)	$300
Plumber (design, installation, copper pipe, two secondhand taps, and clamps)	$300
Total:	**$650**

Re-use/recycle products

Deks Garden Water Saver

The Deks Garden Water Saver claims to save up to 25 per cent of your water bill. The unit is simple to install. You simply unscrew the cap on your waste water pipe, insert the unit, and attach a hose to the smaller end. It redirects waste water onto your garden through your waste pipe. The unit was recommended by the Urban Water Research Association of Australia in its March 1994 report, and is available at most large hardware stores. The flexible rubber funnel is made by Ron Disney Company in Brunswick, Victoria; phone (03) 9387 1844, fax (03) 9388 1381.

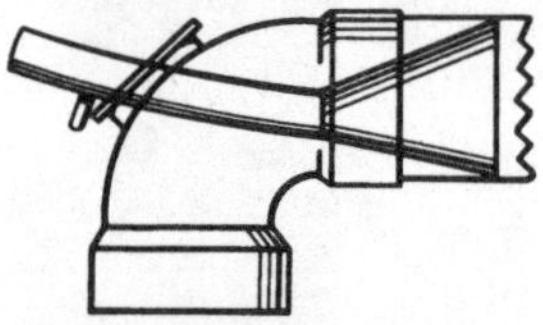

Waste Water Diverter

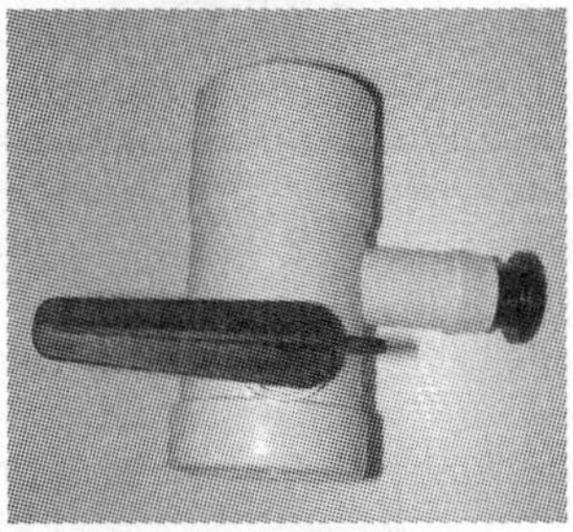

The Waste Water Diverter is a clever unit designed to intercept waste water from your kitchen or laundry sink and divert it onto your garden by attaching a 25 mm garden hose. The unit is inexpensive and available from shops like Going Solar in North Melbourne – phone (03) 9328 4123 to order – and it appears to be well made. It has a side valve to regulate the flow of the waste water. The manufacturers, GJ Products, phone/fax (03) 5282 5923, recommend that you position the unit as high as possible on the waste pipe under your sink to maximise the gravity feed through your attached garden hose.

Waterwise Recycling System

Waterwise Recycling Systems take the washing machine's waste water and use it to irrigate the garden via a gravity drip feed system. It comes as a complete package and includes an irrigation system tailored to suit each individual garden's needs. A switch fitted beside the washing machine enables the user to easily divert water to the drain during wet periods or when using an unsuitable cleaning product.

Water Savings

The system reduces garden water consumption of mains water by 50 to 100 per cent. It is classified as a simple household diversion system as set out in Victorian EPA publication 812 (confirmed in writing by EPA).
Further information: phone 1300 1333 43, web: <www.waterwisesystems.com>.

Eco-Care Grey Waste Water Diverter System

When waste water is diverted into the system, the pump is activated, pumping the water to where you need it. If the system is not used over a 24-hour period, the tank automatically dumps the waste water as per the EPA guidelines.
Features:

- Pump automatically turns off when tank empties
- Pump automatically dumps residual waste water every 24 hours
- Can be packed up and stored during wet weather
- Water can be directed back down to sewer by opening a valve.

Important points for system use:

- Always use a licensed plumber.
- Do not use with sewage (black water) and kitchen sink outlets.
- Avoid using greywater during wet weather. Wet weather increases the chance of run-off to neighbouring properties.
- Periodically drain and clean out the tank and all components in contact with greywater. This will reduce the risk of water-borne bacteria developing in the unit.
- Fully clean and store empty and dry during extended periods without use.
- Cap branches from vertical waste pipe with push fit caps supplied.
- Air borne-type sprinklers are not recommended as per EPA guidelines.

For further information ph: (03) 9836 0415, web: <www.waterworksirrigation.com.au> and <www.epa.vic.gov.au>.

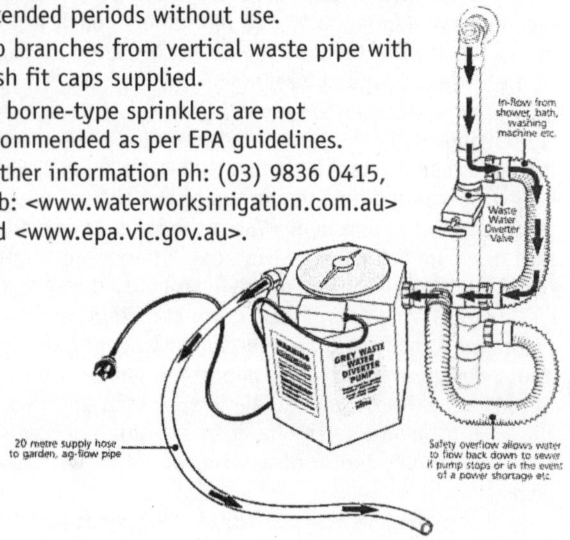

5
Water
Saving
Tips

Water-Saving Tips

FROM READERS OF *EARTH GARDEN* MAGAZINE

The following water-saving tips have been submitted by people living in the suburbs and on the land — people who've already reaped the benefits of water conservation, and who know how to help other Australians conserve our precious water resources.

CHECK FOR LEAKS

A leaking tap can waste 120 litres of water a day. To check the toilet, add a little biodegradable food dye to the toilet tank. If the dye runs into the bowl (without pressing the flush button) the cistern needs repairing. And check for leaking pipes by reading your meter last thing at night, then compare with the reading first thing in the morning.

To stop leaking taps, check and replace:

- worn or broken washers;
- damage to the washer seat (inside the tap body);
- worn or broken "O" rings (on the tap spindle); and
- check hot water systems for obvious external leaks.

Wash your car using a bucket and sponge. Hose only for a quick final rinse. By washing the car on the lawn, your grass gets some water as well.

On a recent trip to the Great Victoria Desert, the following practice saved litres of water every day. We adopted a "dry clean" method for dishes. After use each plate, cup or saucepan was wiped clear of all visible foodstuffs with kitchen paper. We have also used newsprint, paperbark and a soft rubber spatula, all with good effect. The paper was composted or used to light our next fire.

The visibly clean dishes were then hygienically washed with much less than one litre of very hot water. Sun drying enhanced the cleaning process as you don't wish to risk tummy bugs out there. On trips like these water is saved for drinking only; however, we use the dish "dry clean" method routinely at home too. The small amount of dirty dishwater produced is well suited for other cleaning jobs that don't demand a high level of hygiene.
—C. Reiher, Warners Bay, NSW.

SAVING THOUSANDS OF LITRES

We have a low-flush toilet and if it's only urine, we let it go "mellow yellow" and flushing only occurs when paper use by the female members makes it necessary to avoid any sewerage blockages. This vastly reduces the number of flushes, especially with three male family members (no paper use). With our toilet this saves us at least 7,300 litres a year (very conservatively).

The rinse water from the washing machine is pumped into the tub and buckets and is reused for the next clothes wash. This saves 75 to 80 litres a wash (large machine) which at four washes a week works out to a saving of 300 litres a week and 15,600 litres a year. Pretty good eh? The time and effort to empty the buckets and tub of water back into the machine is minimal. It only adds an extra three to five minutes to your chore.

Pure soap powder or non-phosphorous washing powder is used and the suds water is pumped out onto the lawn and sometimes the vegie garden or fruit trees. I purchased some black poly pipe to attach to the outlet hose of the washing machine. As the two pipes did not make a snug fit I cut off a thicker, stiffer piece of strong garden hose and joined it to the poly pipe using standard poly pipe joiners to prevent water leakage. To the end of the short piece of garden hose I added another joiner which gave added thickness and stiffness so it can fit snugly inside the outlet hose. You just push the hose in and pull it out when finished — easy.

During winter, the cold used water from hot water bottles is emptied into the washing machine before refilling with hot water. With four hotties used this saves 45 litres a week in cold weather.

Garden beds are mulched and in summer I hammer in some tall tomato stakes and throw over a piece of shade cloth to reduce evaporation and transpiration of the vegetables.

The fruit trees on a slope are planted in swales (hollows) so the rain water doesn't just run down the slope, past the trees and into the bush. The swales trap the water so it soaks into the soil.

This summer I altered the plumbing to divert all bath, shower and basin water down the slope to the fruit trees. As the house is on piers access was not difficult and as a DIY job, it cost less than $200.

Water-saving devices are used on the kitchen tap and shower heads. On our fairly low pressure pump, the shower heads use two litres less a minute than the conventional shower head. With five people having a seven-minute shower each day, this saves us 490 litres a week or 24,920 litres a year.
—Tara Hoy, Kundabung, NSW.

DON'T RINSE BEFORE DISHWASHING

If you have a dishwasher, don't rinse dishes before loading them. Some super-efficient dishwashing machines use less than 20 litres of water, but most machines use more than 50 – that's a lot of water to get the plates clean! If you're hand washing, don't rinse under running water – if you don't have a second sink, give the stacked dish rack the once over with a cheap spray unit.

I have been reading *Earth Garden* and I'd like to offer some ideas of mine to help save water. Having lived in Kalgoorlie for over 13 years I did learn how to save and harvest water well.

I put a plastic basin in my kitchen sink and so whenever I use the water I collect it. I wash my hands, rinse a cup, a pot, etc. and, when the basin is full, I decant it into a plastic sprinkling pot, then use it in the garden. I also put a large plastic basin in my shower and do the same. A big loss of water occurs when people turn on a tap and let the water run until the water is hot, or cooler.

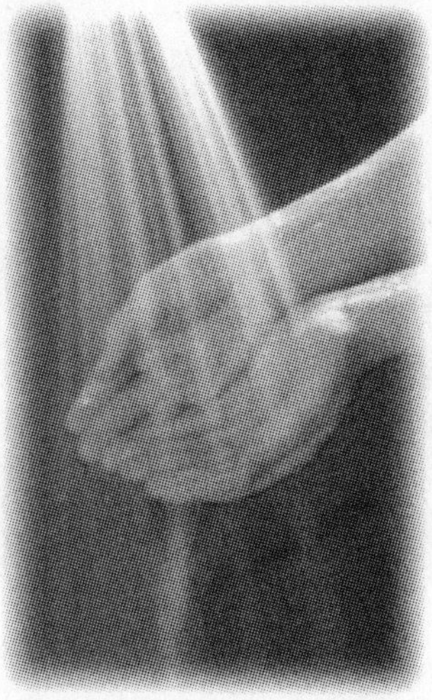

To save water when watering the garden by hand, which is often when water restrictions are in force, put the hose end in a bucket, then walk around the garden and give each plant the same amount. No water is wasted going from plant to plant; it goes only on the plant surrounds.

For many years I have used grey water, and because I am mostly a vegetarian, I do not have any real fat or grease problems. I let it run on the trees from the kitchen, using a valve in line with the drain. This has the advantage of diverting water to either the drain or the garden, depending on the nature of the waste water. Ideally this tap ought to be in the kitchen, and of course there should be one in the laundry and bathroom.

For several years I had a 20-litre plastic container wedged into the toilet, and I urinated in it, then poured in about 1.2 litres of water. I thus did not waste water flushing needlessly, and each morning I had several litres of genuine Aussie 4:1 liquid fertiliser, which I used on trees and shrubs. My neighbours never mentioned a word, so it must have been OK.

Of course, it ought to be Australian law that all houses have water tanks to help maintain our scarcest resource. I have written to politicians to get a tax refund or incentive, but no luck so far. Think of all the work it would create if tanks were required – fabrication, transport, selling, installing, testing, plumbing and so on.

Oh well, perhaps, as Bill Mollison says, when the world becomes a desert, then will they begin to listen.

—Robert Millet, Coffs Harbour, NSW.

TIPS FROM GERMANY

It might sound strange at first to read about water conservation from Germany. After growing up in the western Wimmera area of Victoria and having lived in Germany for the past three years, I can assure you that water conservation is not even an issue here. Water is simply plentiful!

But I often recall when my parents moved to their current block of land near Kaniva, Victoria, in 1989. It was mid-summer and the water system for the house was not yet complete! Mum would hand us a towel and a bar of soap, then send us off down to the dam for a bath. This procedure lasted only a couple of weeks, but even during subsequent summers we were always limited to quite short showers "because there's only a week's water left if it doesn't rain soon".

Here in Germany, Anne and I just do simple things to conserve water in our second-storey rented flat – out of principle I guess. In the morning we wash our fruit-for-the-day under the hot tap until the warm water comes through. If we are quick there's enough time to sprinkle the sprouts as well. Then we fill the electric kettle with hot water, saving electricity at the same time. Water used to boil eggs has become affectionately known as the "eier wasser" (egg water). This is fed to our various pot plants, as is the water used in the evenings to wash vegetables. The latter is collected simply by sitting a plastic bowl in the sink during the washing process.

If you have a tiny garden or even just a few herbs growing in pots, why not use the following idea to keep water use down and the plants happy? Just keep a large, sealable glass bottle always next to the sink with a normal kitchen funnel handy to fill it. Water used to rinse out fruit juice bottles, to wash vegetables etc, all gets collected and tipped in here for your mini, self-contained, kitchen greywater system!

These are all just really simple ideas that anyone can employ in their kitchen, wherever they live. Perhaps some of these ideas could be put to use in Australian homes, particularly in suburban areas where greywater systems are often not an option. Every little bit of water saved helps.

While dual-flush toilets have now become commonplace in many Australian homes, most German loos allow you to finish the flushing procedure at any moment! With a little intelligence from the user, still more water can be saved than with a dual-flush system. Unfortunately our old WC didn't have this feature but that was soon remedied with a slight modification to the internal mechanism!

I'm sure that many older Aussie dunnies could be modified to function in a similar way. All that is necessary is some sort of spring to hold the valve shut any time the button isn't being held down. This way the water will stop as soon as you release the button, not when the tank is empty. Warning: children may need a little training in this procedure!

And so it can be seen that, with a little care and planning of water usage, anyone can do their bit to save water (for longer showers perhaps?!) Maybe a modified toilet will save even more. Happy water saving!
— Andrew Champness, Essen, Germany.

FAMILY-SIZED WATER SAVINGS

Tea and coffee slops, juice drained from various things and cooking water can go into the compost bucket to keep the compost moist. You can also save cooking water for the very few pot plants – they are water-consuming.

The bits and pieces of water can go on cuttings and seedlings. Use a microwave to cook – it uses less water and energy.

We keep a bucket (a colour-coordinated plastic bucket looks best) in the shower and catch the water that runs while we are waiting for the hot water or for the temperature to be right. We easily fill a ten-litre bucket each day (with clean water) which waters the pot plants, garden or fills the bird baths.

A plastic dish in the second sink (you could use it in a single sink too) catches the water from washing fruit and vegies, hands or rinsing dishes and again waters trees or the grass or whatever.

Toilet: everyone is told not to flush when they wee and the boys are encouraged to go out to the garden or compost heap. The orchard has been planted out where the water runs out of the septic tank after "processing" – it hasn't been watered in three years.

Shower: three-minute showers for all. Or shower every second or third day in winter unless doing particularly dirty jobs. Summer can be reduced to one shower to wash the sweat off – otherwise "birdie baths".

Laundry: always full loads. In a manual machine, you can skip to the second rinse. Use dishwashing detergent for washing. Things don't need so much rinsing and it is biodegradable and cheaper. The water is recycled out to the garden via a hose attached to the machine and then out through the floor of the laundry – it is moved around so that the same part doesn't get all laundry water.

Only wash when necessary. For example, bed linen once a fortnight in winter. When tanks overflow (twice in three years) go mad with the washing and wash everything in sight!
—Judith, Jeff, Angie, Zoe & Hugh McKenzie, Macquarie, ACT.

SAVE MORE THAN 50 PER CENT OUTSIDE

Use a broom to clean paths and driveways. Ten minutes spent hosing pavements uses 200 litres of water. I plan to use a specially-designated stormwater run-off pipe from the septic tank system to enhance the growth of some cotton palms that I have been nurturing. Once the pipe work is blocked by the roots of the palms, the nutrient run-off will have done its job and the palms will be ready for transplantation.
—John O'Connor, Mangalore, Vic.

PLANTING TIP

Here is a water-saving tip for planting in heavy clay soils. Dig a hole when planting a fruit tree to say 80 cm then use a small auger for another 50 cm. Back fill 30 cm with mulch and sand, then insert an agricultural pipe (drainage type) to 50 cm above ground level. Back fill the hole with mulch or manure (as well as the tree of course) and then fill the pipe with water until it overflows. After this first planting I only fill the pipe once a month until the plant is established. Mulch is put on once a year to the drip line and water is only given to the tree in dry conditions and then only once a month. I have cut my water usage by 90 per cent.
—Hugh Suttor, Ningi, Queensland.

MARY'S SOAKER TIP

I have dug two ponds to take rain run-off and planted water-loving plants – that gives me flowers without watering and I now have lots of frogs all of whom chat away all night. Ponds also provide cooling for the house in summer.

I have a tank to catch run-off from the chook run and shed – this gives water to the chooks and gravity-fed watering or hand watering to the garden.

When changing the chook water, the old water feeds the climbers in the chook run.

Garden: use drought-tolerant plants such as natives, roses, grasses and bulbs. A soil wetting agent goes on in late spring by the gallon. Mulch, mulch and more mulch.

Use soaker hoses everywhere – I use the ones made from recycled tyres. On the whole the garden is only watered once every one to two weeks. It is still establishing so needs water.

The grass is never cut too short, but around the house is kept green for bushfire protection – the rest dies but comes back next year. Use lots of ground covering plants.

Vegie garden: use soaker hoses and mulch. I have set mine up on no-dig principles which I find retains moisture the best.
— Mary Smith, Newham, Vic.

The Australian Water Association

Whether you are an organisation or an individual, joining the AWA is the best way to remain informed and connected with water industry developments. Operating since 1962, the Australian Water Association is Australia's largest and most influential water industry association with 4,000 members of which 750 are corporate members. Membership is broad-based and multi-disciplinary. This membership diversity ensures a robust and highly credible vehicle for representing the water industry in the broadest context both at the national and international level.

Members have access to the latest technical and industry trends, information networks and ongoing professional development. There is a strong network of branches in each state and territory that covers regional trends, government policy and local issues. For membership enquiries please contact Michael Seller, phone (02) 9495 9901 or email mseller@awa.asn.au.

ACT

ACTEW Corporation www.actew.com.au
ActewAGL Distribution www.actewagl.com.au
Aqua Safe International Water Purifiers P/L www.aquasafe.com.au
Aqua-Consult Australia Pty Ltd www.aquaconsultaust.com.au
CRC for Catchment Hydrology www.catchment.crc.org.au
CRC for Freshwater Ecology www.freshwater.canberra.edu.au
CSIRO Black Mountain Library www.clw.csiro.au
Department of Agriculture Fisheries and Forestry www.daff.gov.au
Department of the Environment and Heritage www.deh.gov.au
ECOWISE Environmental www.ecowise.com.au
Queanbeyan City Council Water Directorate www.waterdirectorate.asn.au
Water Recycle Group Australia Pty Ltd www.waterrecycle.com.au

New South Wales

Australia - Instrumentation www.abb.com
Accurate Detection Pty Ltd www.accuratedetection.com
Aco Polycrete Pty Ltd www.acoaus.com.au
ADS Environmental Services www.adsenv.com
Advantica Pty Ltd www.Advantica.biz
AGAL - Aust Govt Analytical Laboratories www.agal.gov.au
Agility Management Pty Ltd www.teamagility.com
Air and Hydraulic Systems Pty Limited www.ahs.com.au
AIRVAC-RSM Pty Limited www.airvac.com.au
AJM Environmental Services Pty Ltd www.ajmenviro.com.au
Albury City Council
Alfa Laval Australia Pty Ltd www.alfalaval.com
Allens Arthur Robinson www.aar.com.au
Aqua-Audit
Aquagenics Pty Ltd www.aquagenics.com.au
Aqualab Scientific Pty Ltd www.aqualab.com.au
Aquatic Engineering Australia Pty Limited www.aquatic-engineering.com
Arrow Scientific Pty Ltd www.arrowscientific.com.au
ASpect Process Services www.ASpectPS.com.au
Atech Group Pty Ltd www.atechgroup.com.au
Australian Consumer & Specialty Products Assoc
Australian Inland Energy and Water www.aienergy.com.au
Australian Laboratory Services www.alsenviro.com
Australian Scientific Pty Ltd
Australian Water Technologies Pty Ltd www.awtpl.com.au
BA Technologies
Babcock and Brown www.babcockbrown.com.au
Baldwin Industrial Systems www.baldwinis.com.au
Baramy Engineering Pty Ltd www.baramy.com.au
Barclay Mowlem Construction Limited www.bmcl.com.au
Baulderstone Hornibrook www.bh.com.au
Berrigan Shire Council www.berriganshire.nsw.gov.au
Bio-Recycle Australia Pty Ltd www.biorecycleaustralia.com
Bioteq Limited www.bioteq.net
Blobel Environmental Engineering www.blobel.de
Blue Circle Southern Cement Ltd www.bluecirclesoutherncement.com.au
BlueScope Steel Limited www.bluescopesteel.com
BLYSS Pty Ltd www.blyss.com.au
BOC Limited www.boc.com.au
Bonnet Equipment Pty Ltd www.bonnet.com.au
Burns and Roe Worley www.burnsandroeworley.com.au
Cabonne Shire Council
Caltex Refineries Pty Ltd (NSW) www.caltex.com.au
Canpoint International
Central Tablelands Water www.ctw.nsw.gov.au
CH2M Hill Australia Pty Ltd www.ch2m.com
Chatoyer Holdings Pty Ltd www.chatoyer.com.au
Chemical Plant & Engineering Pty Ltd www.cem-int.com
Ciba Specialty Chemicals www.cibasc.com
City Water Technology Pty Ltd www.citywater.com.au
Clayton Utz www.claytonutz.com
Clearwater Technology Pty Ltd www.clearwatertechnology.com.au
Clexan-Peak Personnel www.clexanpeak.com.au
CMG Pty Ltd www.cmggroup.com.au
Commodity Resources Pty Limited www.comres.com.au
ConSep Pty Ltd www.consep.com.au
Contra-Shear Separation Technologies Ltd www.contra-shear.co.nz
Contra-Shear Technology www.cstechnology.com.au
Control Automation Pty Ltd
Control Components Pty Ltd www.controlcomponents.com.au
Corowa Shire Council
CRS Industrial Water Treatment Systems www.watertreatment.net.au
Deacons www.deacons.com.au
Decanter Pty Ltd www.decanter.com.au
Department of Energy, Utilities and Sustainability www.energy.nsw.gov.au
Department of Environment and Conservation www.epa.nsw.gov.au
Dioxide Pacific Pty Ltd www.dioxide.com
Dit Engineering Pty Ltd
Dubbo City Council www.dubbo.nsw.gov.au
Economy Concrete Tanks www.economytanks.com.au
Ecoseal www.ecoseal.com
Ecotox Services Australasia Pty Ltd www.ecotox.com.au
Electropure Industrial Australia Pty Ltd www.electropure.com.au
Endress + Hauser Australia Pty Ltd www.endress.com.au
Environmental & Earth Sciences Pty Ltd www.groundscience.com
Environmental Group Limited www.environmental.com.au
Environmental Resources Management www.erm.com
Environmental Warehouse www.envirowarehouse.com
EnvironOdour Australia Pty Ltd www.environodour.com.au
EnviroPro Waste Water Solutions Pty Ltd www.enviropro.com.au
Enware Australia Pty Ltd www.enware.com.au
Eurobodalla Shire Council www.esc.nsw.gov.au
Evans and Peck www.evanspeck.com.au
Facilities Management Australia www.f-m-a.com.au
Faculty of Engineering, UTS www.eng.uts.edu.au
Fiberglass International
Fibretank Systems Pty Ltd www.ftanks.com.au
Fieldforce Services Pty Ltd www.fieldforce.net.au
Flotech Controls Pty Ltd
Flottweg www.flottweg.com
Fulham Engineering Services Pty Ltd
GE Panametrics Pty Ltd
Geolyse Pty Ltd
George Fischer Pty Ltd www.georgefischer.com.au
GL & V Australia Pty Limited www.glv.com
Goldenfields Water County Council www.gwcc.nsw.gov.au
Gosford City Council www.gosford.nsw.gov.au
Goulburn City Council
G-Tech Separation Pty Ltd
Halgan Services Pty Ltd www.halgan.com.au
Hardman Australia Pty Ltd www.hardman.com.au
Hassall & Associates Pty Ltd www.hassall.com.au
Hastings Council www.hastings.nsw.gov.au
Henry Walker Eltin Group Ltd Simon Engineering P/L www.hwe.biz
Hornsby Shire Council www.hornsby.nsw.gov.au
Hunter- Central Rivers Catchment Management www.hcmt.org.au
Hunter Water Australia Pty Limited
Hunter Water Corporation www.hunterwater.com.au
IDEXX Laboratories www.idexx.com/water
Independent Sewer Consulting Services Pty Ltd
Institute for Sustainable Futures, UTS www.isf.uts.edu.au
Interflow Pty Limited www.interflow.com.au
Inverell Shire Council www.inverell_online.com.au
Iplex Pipelines Pty Ltd
ITT Flygt Limited
Iwaki Pumps Australia Pty Ltd
James Cumming & Sons Pty Ltd www.jamescumming.com.au
Jem Australia Pty Ltd www.jemaustralia.com.au
John Holland Water www.johnholland.com.au
John Morris Scientific Pty Limited www.johnmorris.com.au
John Young (Kelvinhaugh) Pty Ltd www.jyk.com.au
Katalyst 21 Pty Ltd www.katalyst21.com
Kelair Pumps Australia Pty Ltd
Kembla Watertech Pty Ltd www.kemblawatertech.com.au
Kempsey Shire Council www.kempsey.nsw.gov.au
Klambon Water www.klambon.com.au
Kmar Engineering Pty Ltd
Koch Membrane Systems www.kochmembranes.com
Lightnin Mixers Pty Ltd www.spxprocessequipment.com
Liquitek Pty Ltd www.liquitek.com.au
Lismore Water www.liscity.nsw.gov.au
Magytec International Pty Ltd www.magytec.com
Mainsclean www.mainsclean.com.au
Manidis Roberts Pty Ltd www.manidisroberts.com.au
Manufacturing & Engineering ESD TAFE NSW www.lg.tafensw.edu.au/1655/1903
Measuring & Control Equipment Co Pty Ltd www.macequip.com.au
Memcor Australia Pty Ltd www.memcor.com.au
Michael Graham Plumbing Pty Ltd
Mid North Coast Area Health Service
Midcoast Water
Mudgee Shire Council
Murray Irrigation Ltd www.murrayirrigation.com.au
Muswellbrook Shire Council Water & Waste
Nalco Australia Pty Ltd www.nalco.com
Nambucca Shire Council www.nambucca.nsw.gov.au
Narrandera Shire Council www.narrandera.nsw.gov.au
New Zealand Trade & Enterprise www.marketnewzealand.com
Norit Membrane Technology BV - X-Flow BV www.membranetechnology.com
North Coast Water www.ncwater.nsw.gov.au
Northside Enviromech Pty Ltd www.northsidefabrications.com
NSW Agriculture (Richmond)
NSW Department of Commerce www.commerce.nsw.gov.au
Odour Control Systems (Aust) Pty Ltd www.odours.com.au
Omron Electronics Pty Ltd www.omron.com.au
Open Spatial Technologies Pty Ltd www.openspatial.com.au
Orange City Council www.orange.nsw.gov.au
Outokumpu Technology Pty Ltd www.outokumpu.com.au
Pacific Dynamics Pty Ltd www.pacificdynamics.com.au
Palintest Australia www.palintest.com.au
Parsons Brinckerhoff www.pb.com.au or www.pbworld.com
Patrick Charles Pty Ltd www.patrickcharles.com
Patterson Britton & Partners Pty Ltd www.patbrit.com.au
Penrith Lakes Development Corp
Permastore Tanks & Silos (Australasia) www.permastore.com.au
PH Scientific Pty Ltd www.phscientific.com.au
Philips Lighting
Phillips Group www.phillipsgroup.com.au
Pipe Lining and Coating Pty Ltd www.pipelining.com.au
Port Marine Pty Ltd
Process Control Services Pty Ltd www.pcspl.com.au
Process Engineering Technologies www.processengtech.com.au
ProMinent Fluid Controls Pty Ltd www.prominentfluid.com.au
Pumpability Pty Ltd www.pumpability.com
Rad-Tel Systems Pty Ltd
Rainmaster Technologies Pty Ltd www.rainmaster.com.au
Rainsaver Pty Limited www.rainsaver.com.au
Reed Construction Australia www.reedgroup.com.au
REHAU Pty Ltd
Reliance Worldwide www.rmc.com.au
Riverina Water County Council www.rwcc.com.au
Rocla Pipeline Products www.waterquality.rocla.com.au
Rootzone Australia www.rootzone.com.au
RPC Technologies Pty Ltd www.rpctechnologies.com
SAI Global Limited www.sai-global.com.au
Sensor Technologies Pty Ltd www.sensor-tech.com.au
Sepa Waste Water Treatment Pty Ltd www.sepa.com.au
Serck Controls Pty Ltd
Sewer Equipment Company (Aust) www.seca.com.au
Shelston IP www.ShelstonIP.com
Shoalhaven Water Division www.shoalwater.nsw.gov.au
Shorco Sykes Hire www.shorcosykes.com.au
Singleton Council
Snowy Hydro Limited
Snowy River Shire Council www.snowyriver.nsw.gov.au
Southern Cross Laboratories www.southerncrosslaboratories.com.au
State Water www.statewater.nsw.gov.au
Storm Consulting Pty Ltd www.stormconsulting.com.au
Suez Environment www.australianwaterservices.com.au
Sydney Catchment Authority www.sca.nsw.gov.au
Sydney Olympic Park Authority www.sopa.com.au
Sydney Water Corporation www.sydneywater.com.au
Sydney Water Corporation Library 2nd Floor
Syskill International Pty Ltd www.syskill.com.au
Tamworth City Council www.tamworth.nsw.gov.au
Tema Multotec Pty Ltd www.temamultotec.com.au
Thiess Pty Ltd www.thiess.com.au
Transpacific Industrial Solutions P/L
Tumut Shire Council
Tweed Shire Council www.tweed.nsw.gov.au
Tyco Flow Control Pacific www.tycoflowcontrol.com.au
Tyco Water www.tycowater.com.au
Ultra Aquatic Technology Pty Ltd www.uat.com.au
United KG www.unitedgroup.com.au
URS Australia Pty Ltd www.urs.com.au
Vega Australia Pty Ltd
Veolia Water Systems (Australia) Pty Ltd www.veoliaiwater.com.au
Vinidex Pty Ltd
VoR Environmental Australia Pty Ltd www.vor-env.com
Wagga Wagga City Council www.wagga.nsw.gov.au
Wallace & Tiernan Pty Ltd www.wandt.com.au
Wallingford Software Pty Ltd www.wallingfordsoftware.com
Walter Construction Group Ltd www.walter.net.au
Waste Management and Environment Media Pty Ltd www.wme.com.au
Waste Service NSW www.wasteservice.nsw.gov.au
Water Efficiency Pty Limited
Water Research Laboratory www.wrl.unsw.edu.au
Water Treatment Australia Pty Ltd
Webb McKeown & Associates Pty Ltd www.webbmckeown.com.au
Wedeco AVP Pty Ltd www.wedeco.com.au
Weir Warman Ltd. www.weirwarman.com
Wellington Council
Westin Engineering Pty Ltd www.westinengineering.com.au
Wingecarribee Shire Council
Wyong Shire Council www.wyongsc.nsw.gov.au
Xypex Australia www.xypex.com.au
Young Shire Council www.young.nsw.gov.au

Queensland

Abigroup Contractors Pty Ltd www.abigroup.com.au
Action Instrumentation & Controls www.action-inst.com.au
Advanced Eco Products Wyemere P/L www.advancedecoproducts.com.au
Aeration Treatment Systems www.atsystems.com.au
Alldos Oceania Pty Ltd www.alldos.com.au
Ant Distribution
App-Tek Safety Pty Ltd www.apptek.com.au
Aquacure Water Treatment Pty Ltd www.aquacure.com.au
Aquatec-Maxcon Pty Ltd www.aquatecmaxcon.com.au
Australian Pipe Relining Pty Ltd www.relining.com.au
Australian Water Filter www.australianwaterfilter.com
Bacter-Basics www.bacter-basics.com.au
Beaudesert Shire Council
Biolytix Technologies Pty Ltd www.biolytix.com
BMD Consulting Pty Ltd www.bmd.com.au
Brisbane City Council (through Brisbane Water) www.brisbane.qld.gov.au
Bundaberg City Council www.bundabergcity.qld.gov.au
Burnett Water Pty Ltd www.burnettwater.com.au
Burns Bridge Transactions www.burnsbridge.com.au
Bushman Industrial www.bushmantanks.com
Caboolture Shire Council
Cairns Water www.cairns.qld.gov.au
CalAqua

Calliope Shire Council www.calliope.qld.gov.au
Caloundra City Council- Governance and Strategy
www.caloundra.qld.gov.au
Cardno MBK www.cardno.com.au
Citiwater Townsville
Clayton Engineering Pty Ltd
www.claytonengineering.com.au
Clearflow/IPP www.clearflow.com
Clearmake Environmental Equipment
www.clearmake.com.au
Condamine Electric Company Pty Ltd
www.cecpl.net
Dalby Town Council
DCM Process Control Pty Ltd
www.dcmprocesscontrol.com
Department of Natural Resources and Mines
www.nrm.qld.gov.au
Department of the Premier and Cabinet
www.sd.qld.gov.au
DHI Water and Environment Pty Ltd
www.dhiwae.com
ECE Fast www.ecefast.com.au
Ecoscope Environmental Pty Ltd
Ecosol Pty Ltd www.ecosol.com.au
Emsby Pty Ltd www.emsby.com
Enviroflow Water Technologies
www.enviroflow.com.au
Environment One Corp www.eone.com/au
Environmental and Energy Technologies Pty Ltd
www.mixaerator.com
Environmental Data Services
www.e-d-s.com.au
Environmental Protection Agency (QLD)
www.epa.qld.gov.au
Epco Australia www.epco.com.au
Everhard Industries Pty Ltd
www.everhard.com.au
Fitzroy River Water www.frw.com.au
FLUIDFLO Pty Ltd www.fluidflo.com.au
Gladstone Area Water Board
www.gawb.qld.gov.au
Gladstone City Council
Gold Coast City Council
www.goldcoast.qld.gov.au/gcwater.html
Golder Associates Pty Ltd www.golder.com
Greenspan Technology Pty Ltd
www.greenspan.com.au
Hinchinbrook Shire Council
Homa Pump Technology Australia P/L
www.homa.com.au
Humes www.humes.com.au
Integrated Chemical & Environmental Systems Pty Lt www.icespl.com
Ionics Australasia Pty Ltd www.ionics.com
Ipswich Water www.ipswichwater.com.au
John Wilson & Partners Pty Ltd
www.jwp.com.au
Johnson Screens (Australia) Pty Ltd
www.johnsonscreens.com
Kingaroy Shire Council
Laidley Shire Council
Lawson & Treloar Pty Ltd www.lat.com.au
Lloyd Consulting
Logan Water www.loganwater.com.au
Ludowici Environmental Pty Ltd
www.ludoenviron.com
Mackay Water
Maroochy Water Services
www.maroochy.qld.gov.au
Maryborough City Council
Maunsell Australia Pty Ltd www.maunsell com.
McArthur Management Services
www.mcarthur.com.au
Mount Isa Mines Ltd
MOX Products www.moxproducts.com
MultiTrode Pty Ltd www.multitrode.com.au
NanoChem Holdings Pty Ltd
National Research Centre for Environmental Toxicol www.uq.edu.au/nrcet/
Noosa Shire Council
NQ Water www.nqwater.com.au
Odour Technologies
Open Learning Institute of TAFE
Pacific Controls Pty Ltd www.paccon.com.au
Pine Water water.prsc.qld.gov.au
Pipeline Network Analysis
Port of Townsville www.townsville-port.com.au
PricewaterhouseCoopers www.pwc.com
QANTEC McWILLIAM Consulting Engineers
www.qmcw.com.au
Queensland Health Scientific Services
Rain Water Harvesting & Waste Water Systems P/L
www.rainharvesting.com.au
Redcliffe City Council
Redland Water & Waste
www.redland.qld.gov.au/redland_water.cfm
Reef HQ www.reefhq.org.au
River Sands Pty Ltd
Simmonds & Bristow Pty Ltd
www.simmondsbristow.com.au
South East Queensland Water Corporation Ltd
www.seqwater.com.au
Southern Pacific Sands
Stanthorpe Shire Council
Style Industries
www.styleindustries.com.au
Suncoast Waste Water Management
www.ozzikleen.com
SunWater www.sunwater.com.au
Thiess Services Pty Ltd www.thiess-services.com.au
Thuringowa Water
www.thuringowa.qld.gov.au
Tyco/Eurapipe www.eurapipe.com.au
University of Queensland
www.uq.edu.au
Vermeer Sales and Service (QLD) P/L
www.vermeeraustralia.com.au
Virotec International Ltd www.virotec.com
Walter Construction Group www.walter.net.au
WaterGates SP www.watermanau.com
Waters Marine Pty Ltd
Wetworld
Wide Bay Water Corporation
www.widebaywater.com.au
WJP Environmental Services

South Australia

Grundfos Pumps Pty Ltdwww.grundfos.com
CRC for Water Quality & Treatment
www.waterquality.crc.org.au
Tonkin Consulting www.tonkin.com.au
Incitec Pivot Limited
www.incitecpivot.com.au
United Utilities Australia Pty Ltd
Emflow Valves www.emflow.com
AMEC Engineering Pty Ltd www.amec.com
Aeroflo Pty Ltd www.aeroflo.com.au
Ultraviolet Technology of Australasia
www.uvta.com.au
FactorUTB www.factorutb.com.au
Environment Protection Authority (SA)
www.environment.sa.gov.au
Holden
CSIRO Land and Water www.csiro.au
Dept of Water, Land and Biodiversity Conservation www.dwr.sa.gov.au
Measurement engineering Aust P/L
www.mea.com.au
Hardy Wine Company www.brlhardy.com.au
Osmoflo Pty Ltd www.osmoflo.com.au
South Australian Catchment Water Management Boards www.catchments.net
Arup Water (Ove Arup & Partners)
www.arup.com.au
United Water International Pty Ltd
www.uwi.com.au
Wind-Water Pty Ltd
O'Donnell Griffin Water Technology
www.odg.com.au
Actaris Pty Ltd
Water Data Services Pty Ltd
www.waterdata.com.au
Baleen Filters Pty Limited
www.baleenfilters.com
Hydrosmart International Pty Ltd
www.hydrosmart.com.au
AVK Australia Pty Ltd www.avkvalves.com.au
Centre for Groundwater Studies
www.groundwater.com.au
Optimatics www.optimatics.com
Environment Protecton Authority
SA Water Corporation www.sawater.com.au
Philmac Pty Ltd www.philmac.com.au
Australian Water Quality Centre
www.awqc.com.au
Hydramet Pty Ltd (SA)
Food Processing Equipment www.fpe.net.au
Wonder Treat Australia Pty Ltd.

Tasmania

Cradle Coast Water www.ccwater.com.au
Dept of Primary Industries, Water and Environment
Devonport City Council www.dcc.tas.gov.au
Esk Water
Glamorgan/ Spring Bay Council
www.gsbc.tas.gov.au
Glenorchy City Council www.gcc.tas.gov.au
Hobart City Council www.hobartcity.com.au
Hobart Water
www.hobartwater.com.au
JR Stephenson www.jrs.com.au
Kentish Council
Launceston City Council
www.launceston.tas.gov.au
Pitt and Sherry www.pittsh.com.au
Rivers and Water Supply Commission

Victoria

Abbott, Stillman and Wilson www.asw.net.au
Abigroup Asset Services
Acromet (Australia) Pty Ltd
www.acromet.com.au
Activated Carbon Technologies Pty Ltd
www.activatedcarbon.com.au
Airepure Australia Pty Ltd www.purafil.com
Aluminates (Morwell) Pty Ltd
www.aluminates.net
Amiad Australia Pty Ltd www.amiad.com.au
Andritz Pty Ltd www.andritz.com
Australian Pollution Engineering Pty Ltd
Australian Ultra Violet Services (Operations) P/L
www.austuv.com.au
Australian Valve & Filter Industries Pty Ltd
AWMA Pty Ltd www.awma.au.com
Axial Filter Systems (Div Tylac Trading P/L)
Barwon Region Water Authority
www.barwonwater.vic.gov.au
Beca Pty Ltd www.beca.com.au
Bermad Water Technology
Blake Dawson Waldron www.bdw.com.au
Blue H20 Filtration Pty Ltd
www.blueh2ofiltration.com.au
BlueScope Steel Limited
Boddingtons Australia Pty Ltd
www.boddingtons_ltd.com
By- Jas Engineering Pty Ltd www.byjas.com.au
C - Tech Services Pty Ltd
www.c-techservices.com.au
C E Bartlett Pty Ltd www.bartlett.net.au
Cardinia Puraflo Technologies Pty Ltd
www.ecscpt.com
CDS Technologies www.cdstech.com.au
Central Highlands Water www.chw.net.au
City West Water Pty Ltd
www.citywestwater.com.au
Clean TeQ Pty Ltd www.cleanteq.com
CMW-Bua Valves www.cmwvalves.com.au
Coffey Geosciences Pty Ltd
www.coffeygeosciences.com.au
Coliban Water www.coliban.com.au
Conhur Pty Ltd www.conhur.com
Connell Wagner Pty Ltd www.conwag.com
Connolly Environmental
Coomes Consulting Group Pty Ltd
www.coomes.com.au
Corrosion Technology Australia Pty Ltd
www.ctapl.com.au
Corrs Chambers Westgarth
www.corrs.com.au
Danfoss (Australia) Pty Ltd
www.danfoss.com.au
Datataker Pty Ltd www.datataker.com
Davey Products Pty Ltd www.davey.com.au
Department of Human Services (VIC)
www.dhs.vic.gov.au
Dept Sustainability & environment, Catchment & Wat
Earth Systems Pty Ltd
www.earthsystems.com.au
Earth Tech Engineering Pty Ltd
www.earthtech.com
East Gippsland Region Water Authority
Economy Concrete Tanks
Ecotech Pty Ltd www.ecotech.com.au
Elster Metering Pty Ltd www.elstermetering.com
Environmental Systems & Services Pty Ltd
www.esands.com
Environmental Technologies (Division of Biolab)
www.biolabgroup.com/aus
Envirorent Pty Ltd www.envirorent.com.au
equipsuper www.equipsuper.com.au
Freehills www.freehills.com
FSA Environment www.fsaconsulting.net
GE Energy (Australia) Pty Ltd
www.gepower.com\Hydro
Gippsland Water www.gippswater.com.au
Glenelg Hopkins Catchment Management Authority www.glenelg-hopkins.vic.gov.au
Glenelg Region Water Authority
www.grwa.com.au
Goulburn Valley Region Water Authority
www.gvwater.vic.gov.au
Goulburn-Murray Rural Water Authority
www.g-mwater.com.au
Grampians Region Water Authority
www.grampianswater.org.au
Halcrow Pacific Pty Ltd www.halcrow.com
Hallmark Pty.Ltd
Hanna Instruments Pty Ltd
www.hannainst.com.au
Hatlar Environmental
Heraeus AMBA Australia Pty Ltd
www.heraeus-amba.com.au
Huntsman Composites
Hydro-Chem www.hydrochem.com.au
ICLEI www.iclei.org/anz/water/water.htm
Irrigation Design Consultants
JJC Engineering Pty Ltd
K2 Corporation Pty Ltd www.k2corp.com.au
Kellogg Brown & Root Pty Ltd
Kenelec Scientific Pty ltd
www.kenelec.com.au
Kingfisher Telemetry - by RTUnet Australia Pty Ltd
www.rtunet.com
KSB Ajax Pumps Pty Ltd www.ksbajax.com.au
Landers & Rogers www.landers.com.au
Leeder Consulting Pty Ltd
www.leederconsulting.com
Lormar Pacific Pty Ltd
www.lormarpacific.com.au
Lower Murray Water www.lmrwa.vic.gov.au
McConnell Dowell P/L
Melbourne Water
www.melbournewater.com.au
Merck Pty Ltd www.merck.com.au
MGT Environmental Consulting Pty Ltd
www.mgtenv.com.au
Microns to Measure
www.micron2measure.com.au
Mono Pumps (Australia) Pty Ltd
www.mono-pumps.com
Murrindindi Shire Council
MWH Australia Pty Ltd www.mwhglobal.com
North East Water www.nerwa.vic.gov.au
Omega Chemicals www.omegachem.com.au
Onga Pty Ltd www.onga.com.au
ORICA Watercare www.orica-chloralkali.com
Pacific Composites www.pacomp.com.au
Parchem Construction Products Pty Ltd
PBJ & Associates www.pbj.com.au
Peerless Industrial Systems Pty Ltd
www.epigen.com.au
Phillips Fox www.phillipsfox.com
Piping & Automation Systems
Portland Coast Region Water Authority
Pratt Water Pty Ltd www.visy.com.au
Principal Consulting Group Pty Ltd
www.principalconsulting.com.au
Pro-Bac Industries Pty Ltd
www.pro-bac.com.au
Pryde Measurement Pty Ltd www.pryde.com.au
Regent Pumps Pty Ltd
www.regentpumps.com.au
RM Consulting Group
Rubicon Systems Australia Pty Ltd
www.rubicon.com.au
Schneider Electric (Australia) Pty. Limited
www.schneider-electric.com.au
Serco Australia P/L www.serco.com
Siemens Limited www.siemens.com
Sinclair Knight Merz www.skmconsulting.com
SNF (Australia) Pty Ltd www.floerger.com
South East Water Limited
www.southeastwater.com.au
South Gippsland Region Water Authority
South West Water Authority
www.southwestwater.com.au
Spatial Vision
www.spatialvision.com.au
Stornoway Environmental Pty Ltd
www.stornoway.com.au
Strategic Change Consultant Pty Ltd
Sustainable Energy Authority
www.seav.vic.gov.au
Tech-Rentals Pty Ltd www.techrentals.com.au
Techsys Corporation www.techsys-corp.com
Tenix Alliance Pty Ltd www.tenix.com
Testech Engineering Pty Ltd
www.te-group.net
The Exel Group P/L (t/a Hepworth Australia)
www.exelgroup.com.au
Thompsons Kelly & Lewis Pty Ltd
www.tkl.com.au
Transfield Services Limited
www.transfieldservices.com.
Triangle Filtration www.filtomat.com.au
Tuthill Australia Pty Ltd www.tuthill.com
Unimin Australia Limited
Unit Process Consulting
www.unitprocessgroup.com
United KG Water Projects Pty Ltd
www.thameswaterprojects.com
VA TECH WABAG
Vision Fire and Security www.adpro.com.au & www.vesda.com
WATER ECOscience Pty Ltd
Water Industry Training Centre Pty Ltd
www.wtc.deakin.edu.au
West Gippsland Catchment Management Authority www.wgcma.vic.gov.au
Western Water
www.westernwater.com.au
Westernport Region Water Authority
www.westernportwater.com.au
Westfalia Separator Australia
Wimmera Catchment Management Authority
www.wcma.vic.gov.au
Wimmera Mallee Pipeline Project
WSL Consultants Pty Ltd www.wsl.com.au
Yarra Valley Water
www.yarravalleywater.com.au
Zeolite Australia Limited www.zeolite.com.au

Western Australia

AQ2 Pty Ltd www.smartaflow.com
Aqwest Bunbury Water Board
www.aqwest.wa.gov.au
Black & Veatch Australia/Beenyup Water Solutions) www.bv.com
Busselton Water Board
Central TAFE www.central.wa.edu.au
Central TAFE, AMTC-Subiaco Campus
Centre for Water Research
www.cwr.uwa.edu.au
Chadson Engineering P/L
Challenger TAFE
Cleanflow Technologies
www.cleanflowtech.com.au
Clough Engineering Limited
www.clough.com.au
CSBP Limited www.csbp.com.au
Department of Environment
www.wrc.wa.gov.au
Economic Regulation Authority - Water Divison
www.era.wa.gov.au
Environmental Health Directorate
Environmental Solutions International Ltd
www.environ.com.au
Floran Asia Pte. Ltd. www.cleanwater.com.au
Georgiou Group Pty Ltd www.georgiou.com.au
GHD Pty Ltd www.ghd.com.au
Global Water Resources Pty Ltd
www.nelsoncapital.com.au
Hamersley Iron Pty Limited
Hydramet Pty Ltd (WA - Head Office)
Leicon-Notley
Leighton Contractors Pty Ltd
www.leightoncontractors.com.au
Micro Control Engineering & RAINMAN Control System www.rainman.com.au
Novatron Australia Pty Ltd
www.novatron.net.au
Optum ES P/L
PathCentre-WA Centre for Pathology & Med. Research
www.pathcentre.health.wa.gov.au
Philcor Pty Ltd www.philcor.com.au
PICA Activated Carbon Australia Pty Ltd
www.pica.fr
Pioneer Water Tanks (Australia 94) Pty Ltd
www.pioneertanks.com.au
QED Occtech Limited www.qedocctech.com
RES Technologies Pty Ltd
www.restechno.com.au
SGS Environmental Services www.sgs.com.au
Shieldliner Co Limited www.shieldliner.com
SLS Technology Pty Ltd
SNC- Lavalin Australia Pty Ltd
www.snclavalin.com
Spirac Engineering Pty Ltd
www.spirac.com.au
Syrinx Environmental Pty Ltd
Telford Industries
The Swan Brewery Company Pty Ltdw
Water Corporation of Western Australia
www.watercorporation.com.au
Western Radiation Services
www.westernradiation.com.au
Windhill Pty Ltd

6 Water Saving Suburbs

Water saving suburbs

As governments and communities come to grips with continuing water shortages throughout Australia, innovative approaches to building design and even entire suburban developments are emerging. In this chapter we present a small sample of the sorts of inspiring water conservation techniques which could be adopted by householders, councils, and governments everywhere.

Christies Walk, Adelaide

The project consists of 14 dwellings, which includes four linked three-storey townhouses with full solar orientation, a three-storey block of six apartments with east–west orientation, four stand alone cottages and a community house.

A Christies Walk townhouse.

Stormwater

All water shed by the roofs, balconies and other impervious surfaces is collected for use on-site in two 20,000 litre underground tanks set beneath the carports. After filtering, the water is used for irrigation and toilet flushing, thus reducing total water imported to the site.

Greywater and blackwater

A grant from the Clean Seas Program of the National Heritage Trust has been approved to purchase an on-site chlorine-free sewage treatment system. Composted solids will be taken to rural sites as fertiliser every few years while the filtered effluent will be returned to the second-class water supply through the on-site stormwater system.

Hot water and fittings

All dwellings have solar hot water with electrical backup heating; gas backup was not practical for multi-storey use. The apartments have a shared system with banked solar panels and a single pump and backup heater. Low water use shower heads and in-line flow restrictors control the water supply. Under-bench filters provide drinking water at very low flow rates.

Landscaping

Native and indigenous species and plants with low water requirements have been used. Some exotics were used where appropriate to suit passive design considerations, the largest tree being a deciduous jacaranda. Exotics and productive food plants are supported by on-site water recycling that contributes to minimal overall water consumption.

Further information: <www.urbanecology.org.au/christiewalk>.

Eco Villages, Qld

CURRUMBIN VALLEY ECO VILLAGE

The Currumbin Valley Eco Village is on a 110-hectare site on the Gold Coast. The project development is expected to have 144 eco-homes in a variety of residential patterns and a small village centre. Its estimated completion date is late 2005. The Eco Village will feature autonomy in water, waste water and energy. The village will have environmental reserves containing native plant regeneration, edible landscapes and permaculture.

KELVIN GROVE URBAN VILLAGE

The Kelvin Grove Urban Village is the first inner-city development of its kind in Australia, where a government and a university have come together to create a new, integrated community.

The development is on a 17-hectare site five kilometres from Brisbane's city centre. The drainage system, designed by Connell Wagner, includes drainage swales with sand filters, grated trench drains (infiltration strips) that feed into planter boxes, pollution traps in gully pits and porous pavement.

Paynes Road, The Gap, Qld

This 22-allotment residential subdivision is to be built in an established area of Brisbane. It aims to demonstrate that water and energy use, waste water, solid waste and stormwater export can all be substantially reduced without loss of living standards. Water tanks and solar energy are promoted; resource use will be reduced through low embodied energy in roads, allotments and house design; recurrent energy use will be reduced and effluent recycled; and nutrient and sediment export from the site will be reduced via water-sensitive stormwater features. The developer estimates that average water demand from the development's households will be 75 per cent less than normal household requirements, and sewer demand is expected to be 66 per cent of normal requirements on average.

GreenSmart Villages

GreenSmart Villages have been built in Adelaide, Sydney and Brisbane with a focus on educating builders, designers, product manufacturers and consumers about the benefits of environmentally responsible housing. GreenSmart is an industry-driven initiative that aims to encourage a mainstream application of its principles to today's housing.

GreenSmart Village homes incorporate environmentally sustainable housing design. The main goals are:

- to improve the energy and water efficiency of the homes;
- to enable home owners to waste less and recycle more;
- to reduce the waste from the building process; and
- to improve site management during construction.

WATER EFFICIENCY MEASURES:

- Landscaping incorporates local indigenous plant species and is designed to minimise water use and encourage indigenous fauna habitation.
- AAA-rated tapware and shower heads are used throughout the homes.
- Rainwater tanks can be installed for external water usage.
- Sensored lighting and irrigation systems that can be set to minimise energy and water usage.

Ecohome, Jacksons Hill, Sunbury, Victoria

The Ecohome, designed by BP Architects, demonstrates sustainable and healthy residential construction principles with its passive solar design and active solar systems, greywater recycling, rainwater collection and animal- and bird-friendly landscaping.

CONSERVATION OF WATER RESOURCES

The garden uses greywater recycled from the washing machine. While the average family of five uses 1000 litres of water a day, this family of five uses only 520 litres.

The Aquaplate steel tank is compatible with the urban landscape; its free-standing slimline form fits under the eaves of most houses.

WATER SAVING FEATURES

- dual flush 3/6-litre toilet cistern
- cylinders in taps are adjusted to reduce water flow
- dishwasher and front-loading washing machine are water-efficient
- the garden uses drought-resistant plants and shrubs that are natural to the local environment, mulching, a mix of hard and soft paving, pebble garden beds and rockeries
- 4000 and 5000-litre rainwater tanks for the garden
- the greywater recycling system will be converted from a pump system to a gravity-fed sub-surface irrigation system for the garden beds.

Further information: Bridget Puszka, BP Architects, Studio 14, 149 Fitzroy Street, St Kilda, Vic 3182. Ph (03) 9525 3780.

Above right: the Gekko greywater system as used at the Ecohome, Jacksons Hill, Sunbury, Victoria.

Right: the slimline Aquaplate steel rainwater tank as used at the Ecohome.

Port Phillip, Victoria

Inkerman Oasis under construction.

A "Micromet" computerised irrigation system is used so that sprinklers in the parks and gardens of Melbourne's City of Port Phillip only switch on when the soil moisture drops below a certain level. Two thousand "Aqualoc" valves were installed in the taps of all town halls, council child care and community centres and libraries, which will reduce water costs by up to 45 per cent and energy costs by up to 60 per cent.

The valves replace traditional washers and last for a guaranteed five years, and, possibly, as long as ten years.

The Inkerman Oasis and 48 Ormond Road projects demonstrate water savings and sustainable living to Port Phillip residents. The Eco House, in the St Kilda Botanical Gardens runs the "sustainable living at home" program, now in its second stage. It has helped over 350 households cut down on water and energy and improve recycling habits.

The Inkerman Oasis apartment development in Melbourne's St. Kilda also incorporates stormwater reuse. First flush stormwater is treated by a large sub-surface flow wetland and sand filter. When combined with recycled domestic greywater it is used to irrigate a roof garden, other landscaping and for toilet flushing. There are 236 apartments in the development, with some reserved for community housing.

The Water Sensitive Urban Design features will include:

- Recycling of domestic greywater from approximately 50 per cent of the units in three to four buildings using an activated-sludge (aeration) tank, with secondary filtration in a 400-square-metre native wetland and sand filter area on the development site.
- Capture of first flush ground flow and roof stormwater, filtered in the wetlands and sand filter system.
- Recycling of the combined greywater and stormwater for sub-surface garden irrigation and toilet flushing across the entire development.

The incorporation of stormwater into the domestic greywater recycling system and reuse for toilet flushing has been made possible by a Commonwealth grant under the Living Cities–Urban Stormwater Initiative in 2000–2001. This grant is being matched by Inkerman Developments. The grant will be used for the provision of water balancing flow control devices in the plumbing system throughout the development. It will also fund downstream (Shakespeare Main Drain) water quality monitoring by the CRC for Catchment Hydrology. The drain runs into Port Phillip Bay near the Fairy Penguin colony at St Kilda Pier. The monitoring will involve measuring storm water quality as it leaves the site and enters the drain.

This project is the first in Australia to recycle combined domestic greywater and stormwater in a medium- to high-density residential development. Most other greywater recycling precedents are found in NSW and the ACT, although interest is emerging across Australia.

Domestic greywater

Primary treatment of domestic bathroom greywater (basins, baths and showers) from about 50 per cent of units in three buildings will use a 15,000-litre Kaboda aeration balance tank and then a 10,800-litre Kaboda membrane bio-reactor (MBR) tank. This tank is duplicated to permit maintenance on each membrane module without the system reverting to a conventional system where waste goes to the sewerage system.

Stormwater treatment

- Capture of first flush roof and ground flow stormwater from across the total site.
- Initial passage of water through a gross pollutant trap.
- Primary treatment of the water in a 400-square-metre wetland by filtration through a soil and gravel medium and absorption by wetland plants.
- Secondary treatment of the water in a 10,800-litre Kabota membrane bio-reactor (MBR) tank. This cleans the water sufficiently so that secondary treatment in the wetlands is not needed.

Reuse

The recycled greywater and stormwater is held in a 45,000-litre storage tank, then passed through an ultraviolet disinfection unit before being reticulated for its two uses:

- Underground garden irrigation across 2,500 square metres of soft landscaped areas primarily using native and indigenous plant species. Irrigation is controlled to release water to dry areas through 5,825 lineal metres of "Geoflow" slow-release dripper piping by 12 solenoids triggered by a computer and moisture sensors.
- Toilet flushing in dual flush toilets in all bathrooms. A mains-pressure-fed header tank is provided as a backup for the electrically-powered pump that distributes water through the main system.

Rouse Hill, Sydney

The Rouse Hill Development Area of more than 9400 hectares is located 30 kilometres north west of the Sydney Central Business District.

The Rouse Hill recycled water project covers parts of Rouse Hill, Parklea, Stanhope, Glenwood, Acacia Gardens, Kellyville, Kellyville Ridge and a small part of Castle Hill. The homes in the Rouse Hill Development Area have two water supplies, for drinking water and recycled water, delivered by dual reticulation. All plumbing fittings, pipe-work and taps for the recycled water supply system are coloured lilac for easy identification. The taps have removable handles and a reverse-thread hose fitting to discourage use of the same hose on both taps. These are requirements of the NSW Recycled Water Guidelines.

The aim of this project is to help protect the Hawkesbury–Nepean River. Included in the program is advanced treatment of sewage to enable recycling of waste water, and reduce pollution in the stormwater system.

Households in the project area may choose to use drinking water only, and are charged at the drinking water rate. The households using recycled water as well pay around one third the rate of drinking water for it.

EFFLUENT REUSE (2000)

Gigalitres (one gigalitre is one billion litres, the water in 1000 Olympic-sized pools)

State	Effluent	Amt reused	Reuse %
Qld	342	54	16
NSW	560	65	12
ACT	30	0.7	2
Vic	370	25	7
Tas	43	1.3	3
SA	91	15	16
WA	11.5	7.8	7
NT	21	2.4	11

Total reuse of effluent nationally (2000–01) was 10.9 per cent and is expected to rise to 14.1 per cent for 2002.

Less than 10 per cent of water used in urban areas and by industry is recycled.

Kogarah Council, Sydney

Kogarah Council, in southern Sydney, has used Water Sensitive Urban Design (WSUD) principles in its new town square development. The project, which has 220 residential apartments, 224 parking spaces, commercial retail outlets, a public library and a Town Square, uses best practice stormwater harvesting, reuse and treatment. The rainwater is collected from the soil in a series of tanks and used for toilet flushing, landscaping, car washing bays and public water sculptures, thereby reducing the demand on potable water.

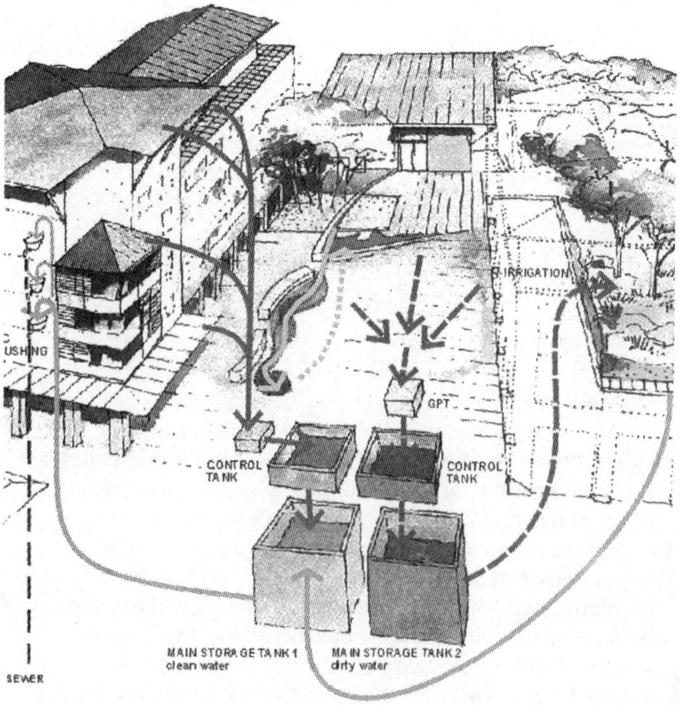

Eco-friendly commercial development:

THE 60L GREEN BUILDING

The 60L Green Building is a leading example of green commercial building in Australia. The Green Building Partnership purchased the building at 60–66 Leicester Street, Carlton, Victoria for conversion to office units for commercial and retail tenants.

The Australian Conservation Foundation (ACF) contributed to the development and implementation of the project's environmental objectives. ACF and Going Solar are two of the current tenants.

Environmental values were embodied in the construction and in the building's environmental management plan..

60L was designed around a central atrium with open stairs and landscaped features, including a roof garden, openable windows, shared facilities and meeting rooms, and bicycle parking.

The general principles on which the 60L Green Building was based were to:

- create a quality building that is commercially viable;
- minimise the consumption of materials and maximise their reuse;
- protect the natural environment by astute selection and use of materials;
- minimise energy consumption and greenhouse gas emissions;
- minimise the consumption of mains water and maximise recycling of treated waste water; and to
- adopt environmentally sound and healthy work practices, during both construction and occupancy.

The 60L Green Building is a great example of an environmentally sound commercial building. It reduced the use of new materials and the amount of materials wasted, and avoided hazardous and toxic chemicals. It is highly energy-efficient and has reduced greenhouse gas emissions. It has reduced water demand by:

Rainwater storage tanks in use at the 60L Green Building.

- rainwater collection and use;
- efficient water supply appliances;
- reduced water and sewerage infrastructure requirements;
- waterless urinals;
- on-site treatment of waste water and sewage; and
- the future recycling of treated waste water for toilet flushing and irrigation of landscape features.

The 60L Green Building has set new benchmarks for energy, greenhouse gas emissions and water efficiency in commercial buildings.

Over 500 kilolitres of rainwater is collected in an average rainfall year for use by taps and showers. Water efficient fixtures and recycling will reduce water consumption by over 60 per cent, and should produce savings in average annual mains water consumption of over 90 per cent.

Macedon Ranges, Victoria

In 2001 the Macedon Ranges Shire Council in Victoria started a program of training plumbers and sales staff for inclusion in a GreenPlumbers Directory. To date, over 1500 plumbers representing more than 700 plumbing businesses have completed one or more of the five-star GreenPlumbers training and accreditation programs. This system is now being extended to New South Wales.

The GreenPlumbers directory contains a list of plumbers that have successfully completed one or more of the training programs. The area of expertise of businesses can be easily identified by the colour and number of stars next to their details.

Your local GreenPlumber can assist householders in developing a plan for water sustainability, including:

- rainwater harvesting considerations
- size, location and use of rainwater tanks
- rainwater flushing toilet systems
- gravity feed and pump systems
- domestic greywater use (dos and don'ts)
- greywater treatment systems
- environmental and public health issues
- potential water savings planned for now or the future
- sewage treatment systems and septic tanks
- state government water rebates
- local water restrictions information

Further information: <www.greenplumbers.com.au>, Macedon Ranges Shire ph (03) 5422 0345.

Water Reclamation and Management Scheme, Olympic Park, Sydney

The Olympic Park Water Reclamation and Management Scheme (WRAMS) comprises a dual water reticulation network, a water reclamation and treatment plant and water storage.

The installation of a dual water reticulation network throughout the site, made up of separate potable and reclaimed water mains, serves all new venues and the residential suburb of Newington.

Sewage from Newington, the Novotel/Ibis and other Sydney Olympic Park venues is treated in the water reclamation plant in large concrete tanks covered with odour prevention devices. Pollutants and nutrients are removed and the liquid is disinfected by ultraviolet light and pumped to the water treatment plant for final processing.

Water from either the water reclamation plant or the Brickpit reservoir is processed by continuous micro-filtration, which can remove particles larger than 0.2 microns ensuring water parasites and bacteria are filtered out. Water can also be filtered through a reverse osmosis process to remove salts. Chlorine is used to disinfect the recycled water.

Storage is central to WRAMS as it allows for time variations between rainfall and recycled water demand.

The main stormwater storage reservoir is contained in part of a former quarry (the Brickpit). This storage reservoir has a capacity of 300 megalitres. The Brickpit also contains significant areas of viable habitat for the endangered Green and Golden Bell Frog.

The secondary collection point for stormwater and surface runoff is via a series of freshwater wetlands in the remediated Haslams Creek area. The wetlands collect stormwater from Olympic Plaza and adjacent areas, including Newington, in specially designed water storage ponds. The ponds are designed to catch the first flush of stormwater and allow the sediment to settle. Native freshwater plants absorb nutrients and lower the levels of suspended particles in the stormwater. This water is then reused in the parklands for irrigation. Drainage swales throughout the parklands control the stormwater collection and dispersion while solar-powered pumps move the water through the reticulated irrigation system.

WRAMS is designed to save more than 850 million litres of drinking water annually and was Australia's first large-scale urban water recycling scheme. In addition, the sewer mining function of WRAMS diverts a significant volume of sewage, which would have otherwise been discharged into the Pacific Ocean. The stormwater storage capacity of WRAMS further minimises stormwater pollution, assists in providing viable habitat for fauna and is used in the water recycling process.

WRAMS supplies high quality recycled water to all sporting and commercial facilities, parklands and the residential area of Newington in metropolitan Sydney. The system is used in the Sydney Olympic Park to significantly reduce the discharge of polluted water to the environment, maximise waste-water re-use, and ensure sustainability of water resources in the park. The key elements are:

- a water reclamation plant that removes water from sewage;
- water storage reservoirs;
- a water treatment plant to filter and disinfect water from the water reclamation plant and storage; and
- a separate, dedicated supply system to pipe water from the treatment plant through Sydney Olympic Park and the neighbouring suburb of Newington.

Specially designed roof rainwater collection systems have been installed within Telstra Stadium to provide water for irrigation. At the Sydney Showground and Exhibition Complex roof rainwater systems provide water for irrigation and toilet flushing.

WRAMS provides information, under real usage conditions, that demonstrates the viability of urban water recycling and encourages the improvement of water management in urban development.

Newington woodland is one of the last examples of an ecosystem once common in metropolitan Sydney. The water quality ponds in the WRAMS system also create important wetland habitats for birds and aquatic fauna, including the endangered Green and Golden Bell Frog.

Water storage ponds are designed to catch the first flush of stormwater and allow sediment to settle. Native freshwater plants absorb nutrients and lower the levels of suspended particles in the water, which is then reused in the parklands for irrigation. The Green and Golden Bell Frog, *Litoria aurea* is endangered in New South Wales. One of the few places it has been found is at Homebush where the Olympic Games were held.

Contacts and further reading

<savewater.com.au> is the first Australian web site totally dedicated to promoting, resourcing and enabling higher levels of water conservation. It is committed to providing practical, value-added information and solutions and is regularly updated. <savewater.com.au> is a comprehensive, updated information resource aimed at highlighting the significance of water conservation across all aspects of everyday life.

The aim of <savewater.com.au> is to help create a more sustainable environment by minimising water consumption and maximising water efficiency. More specifically the site aims to provide: independent expert advice, a one-stop shop for information on water conservation, access to water conserving products, real life examples of water conservation in action, and to encourage use of local knowledge, experience and products.

Most councils and water boards around the country have sites dedicated to saving water.

<www.awa.asn.au> is the website for the Australian Water Association that gives enormous amounts of information on all aspects of water production, delivery, use, saving, purification and much more. They have a Products and Services Directory that lists any organisation that has anything to do with water.

In New Zealand contact Actionline on 486 8600, web <www.nscc.gov.nz>. The North Shore City Council has plenty of comprehensive literature on all aspects of water conservation and health.

Books

Waterwise Gardening, by Kevin Walsh, Revised edition of a classic text teaches you six vital principles for saving water and having a beautiful garden. Available from The Good Life Book Club. Ph (03) 5424 1814, <goodlifebookclub.com>

Not Just Down The Drain, published by Friends Of the Earth, Melbourne. Ph (03) 9419 8700. Excellent guide for water reuse.

The Humanure Handbook. Detailed US guide to building your own composting toilet system and reusing human manure safely on the garden.

The Composting Toilet System Book. More than 50 compost toilet systems, including Australian commercial units, are detailed. Available from The Good Life Book Club. Ph (03) 5424 1814.

Creating An Oasis With Greywater. A popular, complete US guide to managing greywater in the landscape. Available from The Good Life Book Club. Ph (03) 5424 1814.

Farm Water. Loaded with valuable information for organising a good water supply for your rural property. Available from The Good Life Book Club. Ph (03) 5424 1814.

Farm Dams. Available from the CSIRO.

Australia's Drinking Water – The Coming Crisis, by John Archer. New and searching examination of our town and country water supplies, and their problems by committed water campaigner and co-founder of *Owner Builder* magazine.

The Water-Efficient Garden, by Wendy van Dok. Excellent lists of dry-tolerant plants and those to keep away from drains, in a practical guide with lots of ideas on greywater irrigation. Perfect for Australian gardeners. Available from The Good Life Book Club. Ph (03) 5424 1814.

Waterwise Gardening

Greeniology by Tanya Ha has water saving tips and ideas together with other information for a greener lifestyle. Available from The Good Life Book Club. Ph (03) 5424 1814.

Waterworks, a teacher's guide published by Melbourne Water, <www.conservewater.melbournewater.com.au> with CD-ROM. Available from The Gould League. Ph (03) 9532 0909.

Save Water, Money and Time In Your Garden. A great little free colour guide to water efficient gardening, published by Sydney Water. Email: <everydropcounts@sydneywater.com.au>, or visit web site: <www.sydneywater.com.au>.

Rain, Rain, Don't Go Away. An excellent, free water conservation kit for primary school students, published by Melbourne Water. Ph 131 722, or email <inquiry@melbournewater.com.au> to order copies.

INDEX

N

O

P

R

S

T

U

V

W

X

Y

You've Read The Book Now Try The Magazine

. . . FREE

FREE sample of Earth Garden magazine.

Fax or post a photocopy of this page, and we'll post you a free sample.

Four times a year:

- Water-saving tips, projects to build, advice for home owners and builders
- Eco-friendly owner-building: strawbale, mudbrick, stone, recycled timber.
- Solar hot water, solar electric power, wind power & micro hydros.
- Organic gardening, backyard chooks and more.

Name . . . .

Address . . . .

. . . . P/code . . . .

Where did you find *The Earth Garden Water Book*? . . . .

POST: *Earth Garden*, PO Box 2 Trentham, Victoria, 3458. **FAX:** (03) 5424 1743.

For more information about *Earth Garden*, visit our website at: www.earthgarden.com.au